Ink on cover - in general dirty

p.84 ink
153 "
223 "

PROGRESS
IN ENGLISH
Experiences in Language

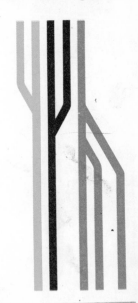

The Laidlaw Language Experiences Program

LISTENING AND TALKING *Experiences in Language*

LISTENING, READING, AND TALKING *Experiences in Language*

LISTENING, READING, TALKING, AND WRITING
Experiences in Language

ADVENTURES IN ENGLISH *Experiences in Language*

EXPLORING IN ENGLISH *Experiences in Language*

DISCOVERY IN ENGLISH *Experiences in Language*

PROGRESS IN ENGLISH *Experiences in Language*

GROWTH IN ENGLISH *Experiences in Language*

POWER IN ENGLISH *Experiences in Language*

SUCCESS IN ENGLISH *Experiences in Language*

PROGRESS
IN ENGLISH
Experiences in Language

John S. Hand
Director
Indiana Facilitator Center
Logansport Community School Corporation
Logansport, Indiana

Dr. Wayne Harsh
Associate Professor
Department of English
University of California-Davis
Davis, California

Dr. James W. Ney
Professor of English
Arizona State University
Tempe, Arizona

Dr. Harold G. Shane
University Professor of Education
School of Education
Indiana University
Bloomington, Indiana

LAIDLAW BROTHERS · PUBLISHERS
A Division of Doubleday & Company, Inc.

RIVER FOREST, ILLINOIS

Palo Alto, California   Atlanta, Georgia   Dallas, Texas
New York, New York   Toronto, Canada

Cover design by Donald C. Meighan

Chapter-opening abstracts by Donald C. Meighan

Both reality and abstraction, language is an organic whole made up of complex and intricately related parts. The chapter-opening abstracts suggest its patterns, its symmetries, and its colors.

Woodcuts by Corinne and Robert Borja

Other contributing artists:

Dev Appleyard
Auto-Write, Division of
  Boecher Studio
Shirley Blakeslee
Francis Chase
Ralph Creasman
Tom Dunnington

Stan Ekman
Jack Haesly
Paul Hazelrigg
William Heckler
Robert Johnson
Sid Jordan
Janet LaSalle

Art Lutz
Donald C. Meighan
Edward Ostendorf
John Walter
Marilou Wise

ACKNOWLEDGMENTS

"Hungry tree" by Nathan Altshuler: From MIRACLES: POEMS BY CHILDREN OF THE ENGLISH-SPEAKING WORLD by Richard Lewis. Copyright © 1966, by Richard Lewis. Reprinted by permission of Simon and Schuster, Inc./ "My Pet," from HELPING CHILDREN WRITE by Mauree Applegate: Copyright 1954 by Mauree Applegate./ "O What Is That Sound" by W. H. Auden: From COLLECTED SHORTER POEMS 1927-1957 by W. H. Auden, by permission of Random House, Inc. Copyright, 1937, by Random House, Inc. Copyright renewed, 1961, 1965, by W. H. Auden./ Excerpt from THE STORY OF SIEGFRIED by James Baldwin: Reprinted by permission of Charles Scribner's Sons from THE STORY OF SIEGFRIED by James Baldwin. Copyright 1882 Charles Scribner's Sons; renewal copyright 1910 James Baldwin./ Excerpt from "The Bestiary," from A HISTORY OF THE ENGLISH LANGUAGE by Albert C. Baugh: Copyright © 1957 by Appleton-Century-Crofts, Inc. Copyright renewed 1963 by Albert C. Baugh. By permission of Appleton-Century-Crofts, Inc./ "Thunder Dragon" by Harry Behn: From THE GOLDEN HIVE, copyright © 1962, 1966, by Harry Behn. Reprinted by permission of Harcourt Brace Jovanovich, Inc./ "Scrapyard" by Michael Benson: From MIRACLES: POEMS BY CHILDREN OF THE ENGLISH-SPEAKING WORLD by Richard Lewis. Copyright © 1966, by Richard Lewis. Reprinted by permission of Simon and Schuster, Inc./ "A diner while dining at Crewe," "There was an old man with a beard," "There was a young fellow named Hall," "There was a young fellow named Weir" from LAUGHABLE LIMERICKS by Sara and John E. Brewton. Text copyright © 1965 by Sara and John E. Brewton. Reprinted by permission of the Publishers, Thomas Y. Crowell Company, New York./ "New York in the Spring" by David Budbill: By permission of the author./ "Though it be broken" by Chūshū: From AN INTRODUCTION TO HAIKU by Harold Henderson. Copyright © 1958 by Harold Henderson. Reprinted by permission of Doubleday & Company, Inc./ Excerpt from "Abraham Lincoln" from COMPTON'S PICTURED ENCYCLOPEDIA: Reprinted with permission of the copyright owner, F. E. Compton Co., division of Encyclopaedia Britannica, Inc., Chicago, Illinois./ "Fire" by Jill Craik: From MIRACLES: POEMS BY CHILDREN OF THE ENGLISH-SPEAKING WORLD by Richard Lewis. Copyright © 1966, by Richard Lewis. Reprinted by permission of Simon and Schuster, Inc./ "November Night" by Adelaide Crapsey: Copyright 1922 by Algernon S. Crapsey. Renewed 1934 by Adelaide Crapsey. Reprinted from VERSE by Adelaide Crapsey by permission of Alfred A. Knopf, Inc./ Excerpt from THE HOUSE OF SIXTY FATHERS by Meindert DeJong: Copyright © 1956 by Meindert DeJong. Reprinted by permission

(ACKNOWLEDGMENTS continued on page 408.)

ISBN 0-8445-2426-3

5 6 7 8 9 10 11 12 13 14 15   3 2 1 0 9 8 7 6

CONTENTS

CHAPTER

8

CHAPTER

9

CHAPTER

10

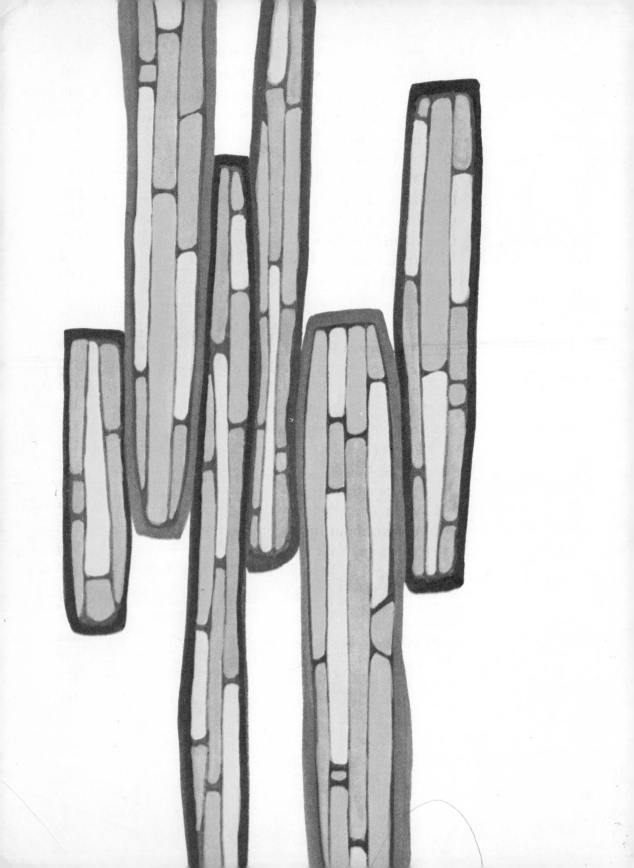

CHAPTER 1

1. English Past and Present

10TH CENTURY	Ealle mine þing sint þine.
14TH CENTURY	Alle my thingis ben thine.
16TH CENTURY	All that I have is thine.
20TH CENTURY	All that I have is yours.

10TH CENTURY	He ferde on feorlen rice.
14TH CENTURY	He wente in to a fer cuntre.
16TH CENTURY	He went into a farre countrey.
20TH CENTURY	He went to a distant country.

10TH CENTURY	Se gæst com þa þa menn slepon.
14TH CENTURY	The gast cam whanne the men slepten.
16TH CENTURY	The ghost came when the men weer asleep.
20TH CENTURY	The ghost came when the men were asleep.

All the sentences above are written in English. Compare the four sentences in each group. Notice some of the things that have happened to the English language during the past thousand years.

- What evidence can you find that there have been changes in the alphabet of English?

  Some of letters are made different

- What evidence can you find that there have been changes in English spelling?

  Some words are different

- What evidence can you find that there have been changes in the vocabulary of English?

  Some words you don't know

- What can you conclude is always happening to the English language?

  it is changing

12

For Discussion

A. In the sentence "Ealle mine þing sint þine," two words contain a letter that is no longer used. What letter combination is now used in place of that letter? How can you tell?

th because of 14th century

B. What are some earlier spellings of the following words?

1. all, *ealle, alle*
2. far, *feorlen, fer*
3. country, *countre, countrey*
4. ghost *gæst, gast*
5. came, *com, cam*
6. men, *menn*

C. What words later replaced the early English words *ferde* and *rice*?

a. wente, went   *b. countre, countrey, country*

ON YOUR OWN

The lines below are part of a poem that was written around A.D. 1250. Read the lines carefully. Then write a translation in Modern English. Here are some words that you will need: cethegrande = whale; moste = greatest; tu = you; seien = say; get = yet; gef = if; þu = you; soge = saw; flet = floats; se = sea; sond = sand.

Cethegrande is a fis,   *Whale is a fish*
þe moste þat in water is;   *The greatest that is in the water*
þat tu wuldes seien get   *That you would say yet*
gef þu it soge wan it flet,   *If you saw it when it floats*
þat it were an eilond   *That it were an*
þat sete one þe se sond.   *That set on the sea sand.*

2. Sounds and Words

Listen as you say the words in the first box. Notice that each word contains three sounds. (Do not be misled by the fact that the word *gnat* contains four letters. When you pronounce *gnat*, you use only three sounds.)

- Which sounds are the same in all three words? *at*

- Which sounds are different? *b, c, gn*

- What accounts for the difference in meaning, the sounds that are the same or those that are different? *different*

> bat
> cat
> gnat

Now listen as you say the words in the second box. Notice that all these words contain just three sounds, also.

- Which sounds are the same in all three words? *a*

- Are any of the sounds different? *no*

- What accounts for the difference in meaning? *the way they are put together*

> gnat
> tan
> ant

Think about the relationship between the sounds and the meaning of a word. Can changing one sound in a word make a difference in meaning? How? How can changing the order of the sounds in a word affect meaning?

For Discussion

A. Which word pairs below differ in meaning because they have one sound that is different? Which word pairs differ in meaning because they have the same sounds in a different order?

1. bond *different*   2. late *different*   3. mine *different*   4. felt *different*
   pond *sound*   tail *order*   might *sound*   left *order*

14

B. Which word after the colon has the same sounds as the word in italics, but in a different order? Trust your ears, not your eyes. The key is in the sounds, not the spelling.

1. *seal*: zeal, lease, tease
2. *take*: tape, Kate, cape
3. *main*: mine, Nan, name
4. *spool*: loops, spoon, moose
5. *fine*: wife, knife, fight
6. *tone*: toad, nut, note
7. *face*: safe, phase, vase
8. *vain*: main, knave, vase
9. *dock*: cod, got, cot
10. *kit*: did, tick, kid

C. Explain how you can change the order of sounds in each word below to make a word that names the object pictured.

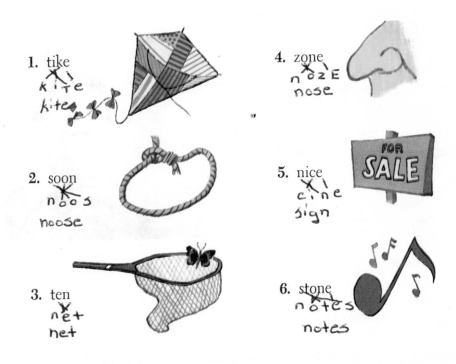

1. tike
kite
kites

2. soon
noos
noose

3. ten
net
net

4. zone
nozE
nose

5. nice
cine
sign

6. stone
notes
notes

15

3. The Production of Speech Sounds

Pronounce the first sound in each word below. As you do, be sure you are pronouncing a *sound*, not naming a *letter*.

> pat　　　fat　　　cat

■ Which sound do you make by stopping the air with your lips? *f* p

■ Which sound do you make by stopping the air with your teeth and lower lip? f

■ Which sound do you make by stopping the air with the back of your tongue and the roof of your mouth? *k*

Pronounce the first sounds in these pairs of words. As you do, place your fingers on your voice box, or "Adam's apple."

> fine　　　vine

> sip　　　zip

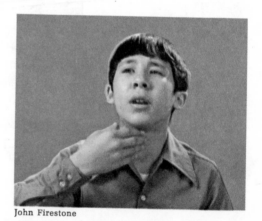

John Firestone

■ Which sound in each pair causes a vibration in your voice box? v & z

Now pronounce the first sounds in the following words. As you do, close your nostrils with your fingers.

> pat　　　bat　　　mat

■ Which of these three sounds cannot be made without letting air out through the nose?
m

Speech sounds begin with the outward flow of the air you breathe. What do you do to the flow to make different speech sounds?
stop

16

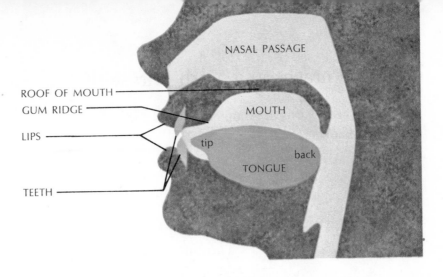

NASAL PASSAGE

ROOF OF MOUTH

GUM RIDGE

MOUTH

LIPS

tip

back

TONGUE

TEETH

For Discussion

A. What parts of the mouth are used to produce the first sound in each of the following words?

1. pat =*lips*
2. fat =*teeth & bottom lip*
3. cat =*tip*
4. bat =*lips*
5. mat =*lips*
6. tat =*tip*
7. vat=*teeth & bottom lip*
8. chat =*teeth*

B. Pronounce the first sounds in the following pairs of words. Did you use your lips and tongue and teeth in the same way for both sounds in each pair? Which sound in each pair caused a vibration in your voice box? Which sound did not cause a vibration? What makes the difference in the two sounds in each pair?

1. Sue
   zoo

2. coat
   goat

3. fail
   vale

4. tin
   din

For Practice

Oral Make new words by changing the first sound of each word below, as follows.

EXAMPLE:

sip: Make a vibration in your voice box.

sip → zip

1. pill: Make a vibration in your voice box.

2. van: Do not make a vibration in your voice box.

3. then: Stop the air with your upper and lower lips.

4. came: Make a vibration in your voice box.

5. cap: Stop the air with your tongue tip on the gum ridge behind your upper teeth.

17

4. Noun Phrases and Verb Phrases

Read the words in group A softly to yourself. Do any of the words sound like sentences?

A

your friend
my father
the carpenter
a boy in my class
Arthur

Now read the words in group B. Do any of these sound like sentences?

B

played the guitar
drove
bought his toolbox
built his own canoe
made a cucumber sandwich

Suppose you try putting words in group A before words in group B. Do the results sound like sentences?

What if you reverse the order and put words in group B before words in group A? Do the results still sound like sentences?

Sentence parts like the ones in group A above are called **noun phrases**. Sentence parts like the ones in B are called **verb phrases**. Notice that both noun phrases and verb phrases may consist of a single word or a group of words.

Think about how you combine a noun phrase and a verb phrase to make a sentence. Do you need both parts? In what order do you have to arrange the two parts?

A. What do you have to add to each example below to make a sentence, a noun phrase or a verb phrase? Explain how you decide.

1. — ran into the barn.   2. The British soldiers —.

B. What kind of sentence part is each example below? How could you use it to make a sentence?

1. needs a coat of paint   2. my sister Ethel

For Practice

Oral A. Add a noun phrase before each verb phrase to form a sentence.

1. — escaped from its cage.
2. — was swimming in the lily pond.
3. — hid under the porch.
4. — is in the oven.
5. — finally came home.
6. — sank to the ocean floor.
7. — became old and rusty.
8. — will wake the baby.
9. — sat on the windowsill.

B. Add a verb phrase after each noun phrase to form a sentence.

1. Some silvery little fish —.
2. A sticky candy cane —.
3. Some curious onlookers —.
4. Some brown sparrows —.
5. A great silver dragon —.
6. The path through the woods —.
7. A small tugboat —.
8. A stray puppy —.
9. The solitary old mansion —.

For More Practice
See Page 377

Written Make a chart like this one, with numbers extending through 10.

Noun Phrase	Verb Phrase
1.	
2.	
3.	
4.	

Put each sentence part under the proper heading in your chart. Then fill the other blanks with a noun phrase or a verb phrase.

1. my red shoes
2. gave me a kitten
3. likes science fiction
4. the doctor
5. laughed at himself
6. the basketball coach
7. a hamster
8. camped by the seashore
9. spilled on the carpet
10. the waitress

19

5. Subjects and Predicates

The following sentences are divided into two parts. Which part of each sentence is a noun phrase? Which part of each sentence is a verb phrase?

A large turtle	crossed the path.
The car	bumped along the road.
The path	was narrow and rocky.
A huge wave	overturned our boat.
Mr. Melas	is a teacher.

Think about what the noun phrase and the verb phrase do in the sentences above.

- Which part names *who* or *what* the sentence is about?

- Which part tells what someone or something *does* or *did* or *is* or *was?*

The part of a sentence that names *who* or *what* the sentence is about is called the **subject.** The part that tells what the subject *does* or *did* or *is* or *was* is called the **predicate.**

Which sentence part, a noun phrase or a verb phrase, serves as a subject? Which sentence part serves as a predicate?

For Discussion

Below are some groups of words. Which ones could be used as subjects? How can you tell? Which ones could be used as predicates? How can you tell?

1. this old wheelbarrow
2. led us back to camp
3. wrote in the sand
4. an early morning mist
5. opened the door slowly

6. cast a long shadow
7. a bumblebee
8. that streetlight
9. likes turtle soup
10. broke all previous records

For More Practice
See Page 377

Oral A. Supply a subject for each of the following predicates.

1. — made some hot chocolate.
2. — climbed the stone wall.
3. — flew over my house.
4. — paced around his cage.
5. — stayed after school.
6. — scurried across the alley.
7. — roared loudly.
8. — whistled softly.
9. — smiled.
10. — left town suddenly.

B. Supply a predicate for each of the following subjects.

1. Our neighbor's dog —.
2. The river —.
3. A freight train —.
4. The house on the corner —.
5. Grandmother's glasses —.
6. Our lazy old pony —.
7. The bacon —.
8. George's Pogo stick —.
9. Cinderella —.
10. Elmer's new kite —.

6. The mayor of the city spoke.
7. Tommy raided the refrigerator.
8. The hungry lion growled softly.
9. The clock finally struck midnight.
10. The canary escaped from its cage.

C. Change each statement below to a question beginning with *who* or *what*. Then find the subject of the statement by answering your question.

1. The shutters rattled mysteriously.
2. A mouse ran across the floor.
3. Some children played hopscotch.
4. A mole made friends with a rat.
5. The pitcher hit a home run.

Written Below is a list of noun phrases and verb phrases. Use each noun phrase as the subject in a sentence of your own. Use each verb phrase as the predicate in a sentence of your own.

1. the noon train
2. the bakery window
3. planted some zinnias
4. is calling you
5. rose above the housetops
6. the back door
7. fed the stray kitten
8. rattled mysteriously
9. the ice
10. a steam shovel

21

6. Combining Noun Phrases in the Subject

1. **A crow** sat on the wire.
2. **A cardinal** sat on the wire. } ⇒ 3. **A crow and a cardinal** sat on the wire.

Read the sentences above. Notice that sentences *1* and *2* have been combined to form sentence *3*.

- How many noun phrases does the subject of sentence *3* contain? Are they the same noun phrases that are subjects of sentences *1* and *2?*

- What connecting word is used to combine the two noun phrases in the subject of sentence *3?*

- Are the predicates of all three sentences the same or different?

Now look at the way the sentences below have been combined.

A letter came.
A package came. } ⇒ Both a letter and a package came.

Cake will be served.
Ice cream will be served. } ⇒ Cake or ice cream will be served.

Al will play shortstop.
His brother will play shortstop. } ⇒ Either Al or his brother will play shortstop.

- In each example, how were two sentences changed into a single sentence?

- What connecting words besides *and* can be used to combine noun phrases?

Read the following pairs of sentences. Decide which ones you can join by combining the noun phrases that are used as subjects. Which pair of sentences can't you join this way? Why?

1. A fire truck sped past.
   An ambulance sped past.
2. Rain fell during the night.
   Snow fell during the night.
3. My father mowed the grass.
   My sister trimmed the hedge.

For
Practice

For More Practice
See Page 378

Oral Change each pair of sentences into a single sentence by combining the noun phrases that are used as subjects. Try to use different connecting words.

1. My uncle changed the tire.
   My cousin changed the tire.
2. The pilot will land the plane.
   The copilot will land the plane.
3. My best friend visited me.
   Her mother visited me.
4. The teacher found the answer.
   The class found the answer.
5. The telephone rang.
   The doorbell rang.
6. The Ping-Pong balls were lost.
   The paddles were lost.
7. Some frogs were singing.
   Some crickets were singing.
8. The fox jumped the fence.
   The hounds jumped the fence.
9. The violin may be out of tune.
   The piano may be out of tune.

Written From each pair of sentences, make a new sentence by combining two noun phrases in the subject. Try to use different connecting words.

1. Clowns amused the children.
   Acrobats amused the children.
2. The pirate ship had been found.
   The treasure had been found.
3. The ice melted.
   The snow melted.
4. My canaries are hungry.
   My white mice are hungry.
5. My brother made the team.
   His friend made the team.
6. Shouts broke the stillness.
   Cheers broke the stillness.
7. Bob will ride the stallion.
   Peter will ride the stallion.
8. A rabbit ate the lettuce.
   A woodchuck ate the lettuce.
9. The tortoise ran a race.
   The hare ran a race.

7. Combining Verb Phrases in the Predicate

> 1. Arnie **mounted his horse.**
> 2. Arnie **rode home.** ⟹ 3. Arnie **mounted his horse and rode home.**

Read the sentences above. Notice how sentences *1* and *2* have been combined to form sentence *3.*

- How many verb phrases does the predicate of sentence *3* contain? Are they the same verb phrases that are predicates of sentences *1* and *2*?

- What connecting word is used to combine the two verb phrases in the predicate of sentence *3*?

- Are the subjects the same or different?

Now read the sentences below and answer the questions.

> We won the battle.
> We lost the war. ⟹ We won the battle but lost the war.
>
> Annette walked home.
> Annette took the bus. ⟹ Annette either walked home or took the bus.
>
> George sold his boat.
> George gave it away. ⟹ George neither sold his boat nor gave it away.

- In each example, how were the two sentences changed into a single sentence?

- What connecting words besides *and* can be used to combine verb phrases?

For Discussion

Read the following sentences. Which pairs can you join by combining the verb phrases? Which pair can't you join in this way? Why?

1. The colt leaped the fence.
   The colt trotted across the field.
2. Henry caught several fish.
   Al didn't catch any.
3. The car slid around the turn.
   The car crashed into the fence.

For Practice

For More Practice
See Page 378

Oral Change each pair of sentences into a single sentence by combining the verb phrases. Try to use different connecting words in some of your sentences.

1. Larry plunged into the pool.
   Larry rescued the child.
2. The mirror fell to the floor.
   The mirror broke.
3. Emma listened to the radio.
   Emma watched television.
4. Joe stopped a stranger.
   Joe asked directions.
5. The teacher opened the book.
   The teacher began to read aloud.
6. The water rose steadily.
   The water finally burst the dike.
7. Everyone visited Carl.
   Everyone sent him a card.
8. We hurried to the airport.
   We missed our plane.

Written From each pair of sentences, make a new sentence by combining the two verb phrases. Try to use different connecting words in some of your sentences.

1. The candles flickered.
   The candles went out.
2. The plane circled the field.
   The plane finally landed.
3. Terry swung at a wild pitch.
   Terry missed.
4. We sat on a blanket.
   We ate our picnic lunch.
5. The coin fell to the sidewalk.
   The coin rolled out of sight.
6. I heard the alarm clock.
   I went back to sleep.
7. My uncle strummed his guitar.
   My uncle sang softly.
8. They played charades.
   They sang their favorite songs.

25

8. For Review

Read and discuss the questions below.

A. Is the English language you use today just like the English spoken and written in past centuries? What evidence can you find in the following sentences to support your answer?

10TH CENTURY: Se fæder hæfde twegen suna.

14TH CENTURY: The fadir hadde twei sones.

16TH CENTURY: The father had two sonnes.

20TH CENTURY: The father had two sons.

B. What is the first sound in each word below? What part of the mouth do you use to stop the outward flow of air when you say these sounds?

1. pit   **2.** fan   **3.** tip   **4.** cut   **5.** sad

C. Which word groups below are noun phrases that can be used as the subjects of sentences? What are the other word groups called, and how are they used in sentences?

1. finished the mural   **4.** were late
2. Donna   **5.** my brother
3. hurried   **6.** the ship

D. Which of the following pairs of sentences can you combine by joining the noun phrases that are used as subjects? By joining the verb phrases that are used as predicates? How did you decide?

1. Ann played football.
Dwight played football.

2. Susan wrote.
Susan telephoned.

3. Alfred went fishing.
Martha went fishing.

4. John made a cake.
John set the table.

5. Carlos arrived on time.
Angela arrived on time.

6. We got on our bicycles.
We rode home.

Read the directions for each exercise below. Follow the directions, writing your answers on your own paper.

A. Decide which word or words in ( ) you would use to complete each statement below. Write the words on your paper.

1. The first sound in *pan* is made by stopping the air with the (lips, back of the tongue and the roof of the mouth).

2. The first sound in *cat* is made by stopping the air with the (teeth and lower lip, back of tongue and roof of mouth).

3. The first sound in *fur* is made by stopping the air with the (teeth and the lower lip, lips).

B. Write the noun phrases that are used as subjects of the sentences below.

4. Some beagles were in the window.
5. Betty won first prize.
6. Hamburgers will be served at the picnic.

C. Write the verb phrases that are used as predicates of the sentences below.

7. The lion roared.
8. Our team played well.
9. Sally will buy a sweater.

D. Write **noun phrase** for each pair of sentences that can be combined by joining two noun phrases in the subject. Write **verb phrase** for each pair that can be combined by joining two verb phrases in the predicate.

10. Kent learned to skate.
    Jeff learned to skate.

11. Mike made an outline.
    Mike wrote his report.

12. We worked all morning.
    We finished our work.

13. Bruce washed the car.
    George washed the car.

27

10. Talking about Advertisements

Look at the advertisements pictured above. Then answer these questions.

- Would the members of your family be interested in these advertisements? Why or why not?

- Do you think advertisements like these affect you and your family? If so, how?

A. Think of some advertisements you have seen for cereals, soft drinks, pet foods, cars, games, or sporting equipment.

1. Which advertisement do you like best? Why?
2. How do you explain your choice of a favorite advertisement? For example, is it colorful, or lively, or funny?

B. The pictures show some familiar means of advertising, but there are others. Did you ever see advertisements in the sky, either written in skywriting or printed in large letters on the side of a blimp? How many other means of advertising can you think of?

Activities

A. Bring to class some magazine advertisements for cars. Discuss them by answering the following questions.

1. What do you notice and like about the pictures?
2. What do you notice and like about the words?
3. Do you think the advertisements might make someone want to buy the car? Why or why not?

B. Describe an advertisement for cars that you have seen on television. Tell why you liked it or did not like it.

C. Form groups of four or five pupils to dramatize a familiar television commercial. Here are some steps to follow.

1. Decide which commercial your group will dramatize.
2. Assign parts and practice acting out the commercial. You needn't follow the real commercial word for word. Just use the general idea and make up the words and actions as you go.
3. If you wish, present your commercial to the entire class.

D. Perhaps you know a commercial that contains a song. If so, you may want to form a group with some of your classmates to sing it for the rest of the class.

11. Writing a Magazine Advertisement

Read the following magazine advertisement. Why do Crunchies sound good to eat?

At snack time serve snowy, heaping bowls of Crunchies popcorn.

Hot, buttered

Crunchies™

...a crisp, tender taste treat!

Do you have a favorite food you would like to advertise? Go back and read the advertisement for Crunchies again. Think of how you could make up an advertisement like this by answering the following questions.

■ Which words in the advertisement appeal to your senses? Which senses do they suggest—seeing, hearing, smelling, tasting, or feeling?

■ Are words like *crisp, snowy,* and *hot-buttered* better in this advertisement than words like *good, wonderful,* and *delicious*? Why?

■ Why was the product named Crunchies?

For Discussion

Suppose you wanted to write advertisements for the products pictured above. What names would you give them? What words would you use to describe them?

Activities

A. Choose a partner. Think of a favorite food and, working together, make an advertisement for it.

1. Make up a brand name.
2. Write one to three sentences describing the food. Use words that tell how it looks, sounds, feels, smells, or tastes.
3. Draw a picture to use in your advertisement.
4. If you wish, display your advertisement in your classroom.

B. Bring to class some magazine advertisements. Cut off the words. Then display the pictures where everyone can see them.

1. Choose a picture (not the one you brought) and write a short advertisement to go with it.
2. If you wish, read your advertisement to the class. The class may choose one advertisement to display with each of the magazine pictures.

12. Dramatizing a Television Commercial

Scene. <u>A close-up showing the dog, Phoebe Ann, lying under the</u>
<u>bed. Her mistress' voice can be heard from the kitchen.</u>

<u>Mistress.</u> Oh, Phoebe Ann! Here, Phoebe Ann! Supper time!

<u>Phoebe Ann</u> (<u>to the camera, in a bored voice</u>). That's just
my mistress calling. All she has is more of that same old
dry-as-dust dog food. I think I'll just lie low for a while.

<u>Mistress.</u> Phoebe Ann, where are you? Your supper's ready!

<u>Phoebe Ann.</u> Maybe if I don't come out, she'll take the hint.

<u>Mistress.</u> I certainly don't like to throw away all this
tender beef and rich brown gravy.

<u>Phoebe Ann</u> (<u>suddenly alert</u>). Tender beef? Rich brown gravy?
  (<u>Scene shifts to the kitchen.</u>)

<u>Mistress.</u> I guess I'll give it to the cat! Here, Kitty,
here, Kit...
  (<u>Phoebe Ann, running out, nearly trips her mistress.</u>)

<u>Phoebe Ann.</u> Rrruff!

<u>Mistress.</u> Oh, there you are, Phoebe Ann!
  (<u>Phoebe Ann runs to her dish and begins to gobble her</u>
  <u>supper hungrily. Then she looks at the camera.</u>)

<u>Phoebe Ann.</u> Now that's more like it. Every once in a while,
my old mistress learns a new trick.

<u>Mistress</u> (<u>to camera</u>). Want to make your dog happy? Serve
Beef-Treat tonight.

On the opposite page is a script for a television commercial. Read the script carefully. Do you think the commercial might make a dog owner want to buy Beef-Treat? Why or why not?

Suppose that you want to advertise something on television. Answer these questions to decide how you could write a script.

- How does the commercial for Beef-Treat arouse interest in the product and make it sound good?

- Does the script tell the exact words that the characters should say?

- What does the script say about the actions and voices of the characters?

For Discussion

Suppose you wanted to create your own television commercial.

1. What product would you like to advertise? A food? A game? A piece of sports equipment? A car? Why?

2. What name would you give the product? Why?

3. What words would you use in describing the product?

Activities

A. Form small groups. Each group may create some television commercials to dramatize. Here are the steps you may follow.

1. Choose a product.

2. Let each member of your group write a script. Practice acting out the scripts until they are as good as you can make them. Revise the scripts as you practice.

3. Present your commercials before the rest of the class. If you wish, use simple props and costumes.

B. Make up a product that does not exist now but might exist in the year 2000. Then write the script for a television commercial to advertise the product.

33

13. Organizing an Advertising Campaign

You have probably seen Smokey the Bear advertisements like the ones shown above. You may also have seen advertisements urging people to give up smoking, or to keep their city clean, or not to quit school. All of these are public-service advertisements.

Suppose you were concerned about a problem and thought others ought to be concerned, too. You might decide to conduct your own public-service advertising campaign. For some ideas, answer these questions about the Smokey the Bear advertisements.

- What do you like about the advertisements?

- Do the advertisements tell you something specific to do or not to do?

- How are public-service advertisements different from other advertisements?

34

Grant Heilman

For Discussion

A. What is an important problem that your school has? For example, is there litter in the hallways or school yard? Is there too much noise or crowding? Is the library misused, or not used enough?

B. Smokey the Bear helps to put across the dangers of forest fires. Can you think of a character like Smokey to help solve the problem you discussed in part A?

Activities

Plan a public-service advertising campaign about a problem in your school. Decide which of the following you will do. Make sure that everyone helps in one way or another.

1. Make posters.
2. Write articles for a class or school newspaper.
3. Plan a skit and act it out before the class.
4. Write some brief daily announcements to read before the class. These may include such things as short rhymes, riddles, or slogans.

35

14. Writing a Poem

A COMMERCIAL FOR SPRING

Tired of slush and snow and sleet?
Then try this dandy calendar treat!

You'll like the longer, king-size days;
You, too, will sing this season's praise.

It's the scientific sunshine pill
(Without that bitter winter chill).

It's naturally warmer, it's toasted through,
Exclusively mild for you and you.

It comes in the handy three-month pack:
March, April, May—or your money back.

So ask for S-P-R-I-N-
G, you'll never regret it;
Remember the name, it's headed for fame:
Be the first on your block to get it!

—Eve Merriam

Read "A Commercial for Spring." Why do you think Eve Merriam expressed her feelings about spring in a commercial?

What is your favorite season? Would you like to advertise it? Think about how you could write a poem advertising your favorite season by answering these questions.

- What lines in "A Commercial for Spring" sound like lines that you hear in real commercials?

- What are some qualities of spring that Eve Merriam likes?

For Discussion

A. What season would you choose to write a poem about? What would you say about it? What are the sights and sounds and smells of your favorite season?

B. Besides your favorite season, what is another time of year that you might want to advertise? For example, you could write a poem advertising a month or a holiday. What are some details that you could include in your poem?

Activities

A. Write a poem about your favorite season, month, or day. Call your poem "A Commercial for —." Remember that a poem doesn't always have to rhyme.

B. Paste the poem you wrote for A on a poster. The illustration on the opposite page suggests one way in which you could decorate your poster. Look through some magazines that have brightly colored pictures. Cut out some words, pictures, and parts of pictures that remind you of the time of year you wrote about in your poem. Paste them around the poem. Try to make your poster express the special feeling you have for that time of year. Display your poster in the classroom.

15. Listening to Poetry

Listen as your teacher reads the following poem to you.

CATALOGUE

Cats sleep fat and walk thin.
Cats, when they sleep, slump;
When they wake, stretch and begin
Over, pulling their ribs in.
Cats walk thin.

Cats wait in a lump,
Jump in a streak.
Cats, when they jump, are sleek
As a grape slipping its skin—
They have technique.
Oh, cats don't creak.
They sneak.

Cats sleep fat.
They spread out comfort underneath them
Like a good mat,
As if they picked the place
And then sat;
You walk around one
As if he were the City Hall
After that.

If male,
A cat is apt to sing on a major scale;
This concert is for everybody, this
Is wholesale.
For a baton, he wields a tail.
(He is also found,
When happy, to resound
With an enclosed and private sound.)

38

A cat condenses.
He pulls in his tail to go under bridges,
And himself to go under fences.
Cats fit
In any size box or kit,
And if a large pumpkin grew under one,
He would arch over it.

When everyone else is just ready to go out,
The cat is just ready to come in.
He's not where he's been.
Cats sleep fat and walk thin.

—ROSALIE MOORE

Now listen as your teacher reads the poem again. Do you think Rosalie Moore has looked closely at cats? Has she listened to them?

For Discussion

A. Find lines containing comparisons that show how a cat looks or sounds. Read them aloud and explain what the comparisons are.

B. Read lines that say something about the personality of a cat. According to the poet, what are cats like?

C. Is the poet entirely serious, or is she amused? Read lines to prove your answer.

D. Why is the poem titled "Catalogue"?

Activities

A. Practice reading "Catalogue" aloud. Let the punctuation tell you what to do with your voice.

B. Find several poems about your favorite animal. Select the one you like best and read it aloud to the class.

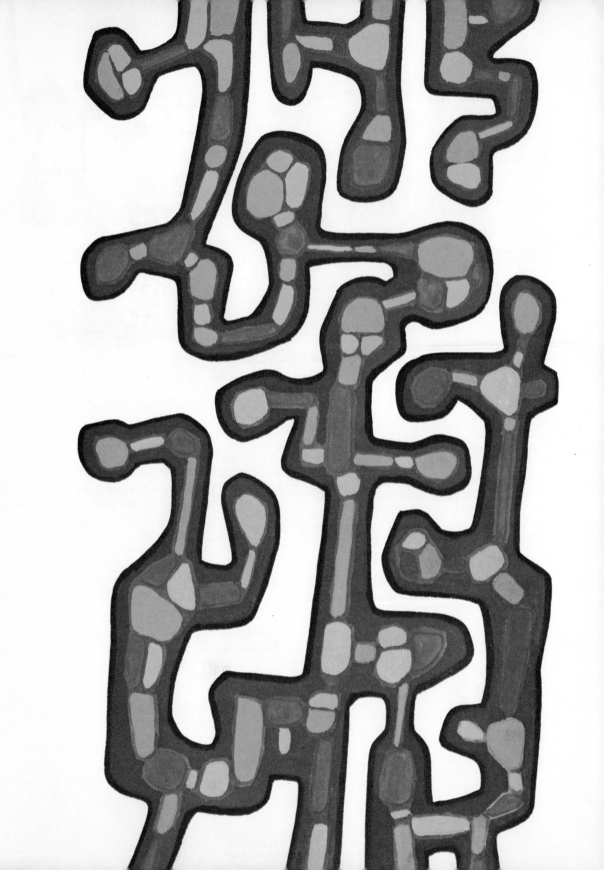

CHAPTER 2

1. Changes in the Sounds of English

Look at the animal in the picture. Pronounce its name. What are the three sounds that make up the name?

Now pronounce the same word as if it rhymed with *loose*. In the fourteenth century the word *mouse*, referring to the small rodent, sounded like the modern word *moose*.

Read aloud the words in each pair below. Now try an experiment with them. Read the words again, but this time make the second word in each pair rhyme with the first one. For example, make the first word printed in color sound like *say*.

day	soon	tour
sea	down	our
find	take	llama
joined	weak	name

No doubt the words in color sounded strange to you as you pronounced them for this experiment. But at some time in the history of English, the words were pronounced this way.

Here is another experiment for you to try. Each word below contains a "silent" letter printed in heavy type. Pronounce the words, making each letter in heavy type stand for a sound.

gnaw	shoul**d**	cas**t**le	han**d**kerchief

If you had lived many years ago, you would have pronounced these words almost as you did for this experiment.

Look again at all the words you pronounced for this lesson.

- Which ones show that vowel sounds in some English words have changed?
- Which ones show that there have been changes in consonant sounds in some English words?

For Discussion

A. How are the following words pronounced? What guesses can you make about how they were once pronounced?

1. breakfast
2. cupboard
3. sword
4. whistle
5. would
6. knit
7. gnat
8. folk
9. know

B. Many years ago an English poet might have written the following rhymed verse. Why wouldn't a poet write this verse today?

> The wind and sea
> His voice obey.

For Practice

Oral **A.** The words below contain "silent" letters. In most cases, these letters once stood for sounds. For each word listed, think of other words with the same "silent" letter. For example, the word *listen* might remind you of *fasten* and *hasten*.

1. knob
2. write
3. ghastly
4. calf
5. lamb
6. might
7. scene
8. sign

B. Discover an earlier pronunciation of each word in column *b* by making it rhyme with the modern English word or words in column *a*.

a	b
1. Ron	man
2. hay	me
3. see	I
4. toad	good
5. crooned	ground
6. feed a	ride
7. carve a	serve
8. tune	brown
9. free	by
10. line	join

43

2. Sounds and Spelling

Pronounce the following words. Look at the way the words are spelled.

> tan   bump   strand

- How many sounds does each word contain?
- What letter is used to spell each sound?
- Could you spell these words correctly if you had never seen them before? Why or why not?

Pronounce the words in the next group. Look at the way they are spelled.

> goal   mole   bowl

- What is the middle sound in each word?
- In what three ways is the middle sound spelled?
- Do you think you could spell these words correctly if you had never seen them before? Why or why not?

Now pronounce the words below and look at their spellings.

> of   eye   choir

- Could you spell these words correctly if you had never seen them before? Why or why not?

English contains many words like *tan, bump,* and *strand.* Why are such words easy to spell?

Many English words are like *goal, mole,* and *bowl.* Why are words like these harder to spell than words like *tan, bump,* and *strand?*

Only a handful of English words are like *eye, of,* and *choir.* Why is memorizing the spelling of such words the only way to learn to spell them correctly?

A	B	C
iron	fan	coast
trough	print	breeze
myrrh	melt	tame

1. Which group contains the words that are easiest to spell? What makes the spelling of these words so easy?
2. Which group contains words that are not quite so easy but follow common English spelling patterns?
3. Which group contains the words that are hardest to spell? What makes the spelling of these words so hard?

For
Practice

Written Write the following words as your teacher dictates them. Check your spellings. Decide which words were the hardest to spell and why.

A
1. lamp
2. trend
3. din
4. brand

B
5. train
6. thief
7. beaver
8. friend

C
9. business
10. debris
11. colonel
12. asthma

ON YOUR OWN

Make up a name for the imaginary animal in the picture. Write the name you made up. Try to spell it so that when others hear it, they will spell it the same way. Say the word aloud to the class while they write it down. See how many others spelled the word the same way you did.

3. Special Symbols for Sounds

Read the following poem softly to yourself.

O-U-G-H

This letter combination makes it tough
for people learning English. Who can bluff
his way, pronouncing though, bough, cough, and sough
as if, when he has finished, that's enough?

It isn't. He'll find out he's not quite through.
I'm glad we just spell do the way we do.
It might be dough. Why shouldn't cough be coo?
Sough's suff, but also sow. Bough might be boo.

—DAVID MCCORD

Now pronounce just the *ough* words in the poem. Does the spelling of a word always tell you how to pronounce it? Do the same letters always stand for the same sounds?

Linguists are men who study the science of language. Because they are scientists, linguists need an accurate way to talk and write about speech sounds. For this purpose they have created special alphabets. Each symbol in a linguist's special alphabet stands for one and only one sound, and each sound is spelled with one and only one symbol.

You are already familiar with some other special symbols used to represent speech sounds. These are the symbols used by **lexicographers,** men who make dictionaries. Like linguistic symbols, each dictionary symbol stands for only one sound. Each sound is spelled with only one symbol.

Examine the chart on the next page. In the first box are symbols from two special alphabets that linguists use. In the second box are symbols from three dictionaries. Which symbols are the same as letters in the regular alphabet?

Think about the symbols that linguists and lexicographers use. What purpose do all these special symbols have in common?

COMMON SPELLINGS	LINGUISTIC SYMBOLS		DICTIONARY SYMBOLS		
Some Vowel Sounds	**I**	**II**	**III**	**IV**	**V**
father, dock	ɑ	a	ä	ä	ä
now, **out**	ɑu	aw	ou	au̇	ou
saw, all	ɔ	ɔ	ô	ȯ	ô
so, **own**, gr**oa**n	o	ow	ō	ō	ō
p**oo**l, y**ou**th	u	uw	ü	ü	ōo
but, son	ʌ	ə	u	ə	ŭ
Some Consonant Sounds					
ban, ri**bb**on	b	b	b	b	b
chur**ch**, wi**tch**	tʃ	č	ch	ch	ch
five, cu**ff**	f	f	f	f	f
care, **k**in, ba**ck**	k	k	k	k	k
then	ð	ð	~~TH~~	<u>th</u>	t̶h̶
thin	θ	θ	th	th	th

For Discussion

Here are some *ough* words written in the special symbols on the chart.

though	ðo	ðow	~~TH~~ō	<u>th</u>ō	t̶h̶ō
cough	kɔf	kɔf	kôf	kȯf	kôf

How might special symbols like these help a reader who came across the word *calliope* for the first time? How might they help a French boy studying English who forgot how to pronounce *though* and *cough?* How might they help a linguist studying words with different pronunciations, such as *creek?*

ON YOUR OWN

Here are some proverbs written in symbols from the alphabet labeled *II* on the chart. See if you can figure out what they say.

1. tuw meni kuks spoil ðə brɔθ
2. ə rowliŋ stown gæðərz now mɔs

47

4. The Noun Phrase

A	B
The otter swam.	The otters swam.
That child played happily.	Children played happily.
An acorn fell.	Acorns fell.

Read the sentences above. The parts that are in color are noun phrases used as subjects.

■ Which words in the noun phrases have different forms in the singular and the plural?

Words like *otter*, *child*, and *acorn* that have different forms in the singular and the plural are **nouns.**

■ What other words do some of the noun phrases contain besides nouns?

■ Do these words come before or after the nouns?

Words like *the*, *that*, and *an* are **noun determiners.** A determiner is a signal that a noun is coming.

Think about the words in a noun phrase. What two kinds of words may make up a noun phrase? Which one of these has different forms in the singular and plural?

A. What kinds of words are contained in these noun phrases? Give examples to show how you could use each noun phrase as the subject of a sentence.

1. picnics   2. some picnics   3. tools   4. this tool

B. What test can you use to tell whether the following words are nouns?

1. boy   3. child   5. daisy
2. fox   4. woman   6. wife

For Practice

For More Practice
See Page 379

Oral A. In the box below is a list of determiners.

a	one	few
an	two	many
the	three	several
any	this	
every	that	
each	these	
some	those	

Make eight noun phrases by placing a determiner before each noun below. Then make eight more noun phrases by placing a determiner before the plural form of each noun.

1. grape   5. man
2. tooth   6. church
3. country   7. wolf
4. hamster   8. mouse

B. Form a sentence from each of the following verb phrases. Add a noun phrase made with a determiner and a noun.

1. — stood outside.
2. — wrote an exciting story.
3. — slept soundly.
4. — grew in the parkway.
5. — were in the box.
6. — escaped from the cage.
7. — suddenly disappeared.
8. — turned sharply to the left.
9. — stopped our car.
10. — darkened the sky.

Written Add a determiner to each of these nouns to make a new noun phrase. Then write sentences using each new noun phrase as a subject.

1. bells   6. seacoast
2. chapter   7. song
3. tea   8. silence
4. window   9. crows
5. fog   10. sheep

49

5. The Noun Phrase with Proper Nouns

A	B
The city is a seaport.	New Haven is a seaport.
That man is fishing.	Uncle Henry is fishing.
The country is mountainous.	Switzerland is mountainous.
The judge sat down.	Judge Parker sat down.
The lake was calm.	Lake Superior was calm.

Study the sentences above by answering these questions.

- What noun phrases serve as subjects in group A? In group B?

- What is special about the meaning of each noun in B? In other words, how does a noun like *New Haven* differ from a noun like *city*?

Nouns that name particular persons, places, or things, such as *New Haven*, are called **proper nouns.** All other nouns, such as *city*, are **common nouns.**

- In writing, what signals that a noun is a proper noun?

Think about noun phrases that are made with nouns. What special kind of noun can be used in a noun phrase? Does this kind of noun usually appear with a determiner or without a determiner?

For Discussion

A. Which nouns below are proper nouns? Which nouns are common nouns? Since none of the nouns are spelled with capital letters, how do you know which ones are proper nouns?

1. man
2. peter
3. mountain
4. mount washington
5. city
6. houston

B. A noun phrase can include either a common noun or a proper noun. What difference is there in the way these two kinds of nouns are written?

For More Practice
See Page 379

For Practice

Oral Make two sentences from each verb phrase below. First use a common noun in the subject noun phrase. Then use a proper noun.

1. — will answer the door.
2. — was near our campsite.
3. — can keep a secret.
4. — was covered with snow.
5. — is a democracy.
6. — gave us directions.
7. — is a good place to fish.
8. — led the parade.
9. — is on the coast.
10. — crossed the prairie.

Written Rewrite the sentences below. For each noun phrase in italics, substitute a noun phrase made with a proper noun.

1. *That girl* is lying on the rug.
2. *My aunt* plays the organ.
3. *The city* was covered with snow.
4. *That store* sells candied apples.
5. *The lake* was calm and clear.
6. *An astronaut* spoke to the crowd.
7. *The king* ruled for many years.
8. *The museum* opens at ten o'clock.
9. *The senator* was reelected.
10. *The holiday* came at last.

51

6. The Noun Phrase with Pronouns

A	B
Bert spoke quietly.	He spoke quietly.
My sister was singing.	She was singing.
The mouse was hiding.	It was hiding.
Those boys will win.	They will win.

Read the sentences above. The words in color are noun phrases serving as subjects.

- What kinds of words make up the noun phrases in group A?

- Which word in group B is a substitute word for *Bert?* For *my sister?* For *the mouse?* For *those boys?*

The words *he, she, it,* and *they* are **personal pronouns.** Other personal pronouns that can serve as noun phrases in the subject are *I, we,* and *you.*

Now look at the words on the right. Make new words by combining a word from A with a word from B. Then use each new word in the test sentence below to see whether it can be a noun phrase.

A	B
every	one
any	body
some	thing
no	

— pleases John.

- How many new words were you able to make?

- How many of these words could you fit into the space in the test sentence?

The new words you formed are called **indefinite pronouns.** How are indefinite pronouns different from personal pronouns? How are the two kinds of pronouns alike in the work they can do in sentences?

A. What is the difference in the noun phrases in italics in these sentences?

1. *He* applauded the acrobat.
2. *Everybody* applauded the acrobat.

B. Describe how the indefinite pronouns are formed.

For Practice

For More Practice
See Page 379

Oral Complete each sentence by filling the space with a personal pronoun. Then do the same using an indefinite pronoun.

1. — taught Rover a new trick.
2. — fed the squirrels peanuts.
3. — smells spicy.
4. — missed the last train.
5. — wrote a poem.
6. — said the house was haunted.
7. — is under the bed.
8. — will search the attic.
9. — lived across the alley.

Written A. Add an indefinite pronoun to each of the following verb phrases to form a sentence.

1. — could solve the riddle.
2. — ought to read this book.
3. — liked to skate on the pond.
4. — came in this morning's mail.
5. — called the dog and the cat.
6. — liked to walk in the rain.
7. — will slay the dragon.
8. — walked in without knocking.
9. — missed the train.

B. Add a personal pronoun to each verb phrase to form a sentence. Try to use each of the personal pronouns that can be subjects.

1. — gathered at the piano.
2. — wanted to go home.
3. — was on the roof.
4. — tasted good to her.
5. — ate all the watermelon.
6. — swam to the pier.
7. — depended on John.
8. — would enjoy this book.
9. — forgot his coat.

7. Finding Words in a Dictionary

Study the words below. Then answer the questions that follow.

> nebula   Niagara   nuclear   gnome

- What sound do all the words begin with?
- What two spellings of that sound are shown in these four words?
- If you had never seen the words before, which one would be the hardest to find in a dictionary? Why?

To find a word in a dictionary, you need to know what letters it begins with. Suppose you had never seen the word *gnome* before. What letters and letter combinations are used to spell the sound that *gnome* begins with? Study these words.

> **kn**ife   **gn**aw   **pn**eumonia

- Which word has a spelling that could help you find *gnome?* How?

Now think about what you can do to find an unfamiliar word in the dictionary. What letter should you look under first? What can you do if the word is not listed under that letter?

For Discussion

A. Some dictionaries have a guide to the common spellings of English. For example, here are the common spellings for the first sound of *say* when it appears at the beginning of a word.

> **c**ent   **ps**alm   **s**ay   **sc**ent

Check your dictionary to see whether it has a spelling guide. When would such a guide be useful to you?

B. Look at the cartoons above. How could you answer the question the boy in the second cartoon is asking?

For Practice

Written   A. The words below show four common spellings of the first sound in *kind*. Use these to help you complete the words that follow. Write the completed words on your paper. Use your dictionary if necessary.

coat	chemist	kind	quick

1. -alcium
2. -itchen
3. -uotation
4. -asm
5. -ernel
6. -olonel
7. -orus
8. -ueen

B. Each of the following sentences contains a word written as it might be spelled by someone who had never seen it in writing. Rewrite each word, spelling it correctly. Use your dictionary whenever you need to.

1. The tree is twisted and narled.
2. We hung a reeth on the door.
3. We thought we had seen a gost.
4. Ed's favorite subject is sience.
5. We played basketball in the jim.
6. When Aladdin rubbed the magic lamp, a jeany appeared.
7. George has a nack for getting himself into trouble.
8. A drugstore is also called a farmacy.
9. Tailand was once known as Siam.
10. Alexandra sings in the corus.

8. Dictionaries and Meaning

Read the following sentence.

The young prince pretended to his father's throne.

Suppose you had never seen *pretended* used in this way before. Would you understand the example sentence?

Webster's New Practical School Dictionary defines *pretend* in the following entry.

> **pre·tend** \pri-ˈtend\ *v.* **1** To make believe; to sham. Let's *pretend* we're pirates. **2** To represent falsely; to put forward as true something that is not true; as, to *pretend* friendship. **3** To lay claim, as to a throne or to a title.*

- How many separate meanings are listed?

- Which meaning is used in the example sentence?

- Which meaning is used in this sentence? "Agnes pretended to be sick."

- Which meaning is used in this sentence? "The children pretended to be cowboys."

Think about how you can use a dictionary to find the meaning of a word. Why must you see the sentence in which a word is used before a dictionary can help you understand its meaning?

For Discussion

Here is the entry for *pretend* as it appears in the *Thorndike Barnhart Advanced Junior Dictionary*. How is it like the entry from the Webster dictionary? How is it different?

> **pre tend** (pri tend′), **1.** make believe. **2.** claim falsely: *She pretends to like you, but talks about you behind your back.* **3.** claim falsely to have: *She pretended illness.* **4.** claim: *I don't pretend to be a musician.* **5.** lay claim: *James Stuart pretended to the English throne.* **6.** venture; attempt; presume: *I cannot pretend to judge between them.* **7.** pretended; make-believe. 1-6 *v.*, 7 *adj.*†

56

* By permission: From Webster's New Practical School Dictionary, © 1969 by G. & C. Merriam Co., Publishers of the Merriam-Webster Dictionaries.

† From THORNDIKE-BARNHART ADVANCED JUNIOR DICTIONARY by E. L. Thorndike and Clarence L. Barnhart. Copyright © 1968 by Scott, Foresman and Company.

Oral **A.** Look up the following words in a dictionary. Find the definition that fits the word as it is used in each sentence. Read the definition to the class.

measure

1. An inch is a *measure* of length.
2. The pianist practiced the difficult *measure* again and again.
3. The doctor took drastic *measures* to meet the emergency.

cool

4. The weather was fair and *cool*.
5. The uninvited guest received a *cool* greeting.
6. Jack was *cool* and unafraid during the tornado.

draft

7. We shivered in the *draft* from the open window.
8. Carl made corrections on the first *draft* of his letter.
9. The furnace will work better if you open the *draft*.

plain

10. It was *plain* that we would not be invited back.
11. The rug was *plain* blue.
12. The family lived in a *plain* house at the edge of town.

B. The words in italics have common meanings that you will easily think of. A less common meaning for each word is suggested below. Use your dictionary to find it. Read the definition for that meaning to the class.

1. *magazine* of a gun
2. *catch* as a kind of song
3. *cord* of wood
4. *bow* of a ship
5. *keep* of a castle

Written List two separate meanings that your dictionary gives for each of the following words. Then write sentences illustrating both meanings.

1. ruminate
2. spur
3. quarter
4. general
5. bearing
6. interest

ON YOUR OWN

Some riddles are made with words that have more than one meaning. What are the two meanings of each word in italics in the riddles below? Make up a riddle of your own with a word that has more than one meaning. Try out your riddle on your family and friends.

1. What kind of *bank* doesn't need money? (*Answer:* a river bank)
2. What stays *hot* longest in the refrigerator? (*Answer:* pepper)
3. What is the *hardest* thing about learning to skate? (*Answer:* the ice)

9. For Review

Read and discuss the questions below.

A. When these lines of poetry were written, the last words rhymed. What evidence do they provide to show that the pronunciations of some English words have changed over the centuries?

> The gaudy, blabbing, and remorseful day
> Is crept into the bosom of the sea.
>
> —WILLIAM SHAKESPEARE, 17TH CENTURY

> Full in the midst proud Fame's imperial seat,
> With jewels blaz'd, magnificently great.
>
> —ALEXANDER POPE, 18TH CENTURY

B. What are linguists? What are lexicographers? Why do they use special symbols like those below to show pronunciations?

Common Spellings	Linguistics Symbols	Dictionary Symbols
though	ðo	ŦHŌ
rough	rʌf	rəf
through	θru	thrü

C. What four different kinds of noun phrases are shown in the chart below? What other examples can you add to each column to complete the chart?

NOUN PHRASES

Common Nouns	Proper Nouns	Personal Pronouns	Indefinite Pronouns
1. the boy	1. John Burns	1. it	1. anyone
2. two girls	2. Texas	2.	2.
3.	3.	3.	3.
4.	4.	4.	4.

D. Why do dictionaries list several meanings for many words? Use the sentences below in explaining your answer.

1. The bank is steep here.   **2.** The bank is open today.

Read the directions for each exercise below. Follow the directions, writing your answers on your own paper.

A. Decide which words in ( ) you would use to complete each statement below. Write the words on your paper.

1. Linguists are (people who make dictionaries, people who study the science of language).
2. Lexicographers are (people who know and use several languages, people who make dictionaries).
3. Special symbols are needed to stand for sounds because (letters of the alphabet do not always stand for the same sounds, there are many different sounds in English).

B. For each term in column A below, find and write the word or words in column B that you could use to illustrate its meaning.

A	B
4. common noun	a. the
5. proper noun	b. Ethel Lang
6. determiner	c. boxes
7. personal pronoun	d. someone
8. indefinite pronoun	e. they

C. The noun phrase that serves as the subject of each sentence below is in italics. Read each noun phrase. Then answer the questions that follow the sentences.

a. *They* have arrived.
b. *Mary Ann* is late.
c. *Blueberries* are delicious.
d. *The fog* was very thick.

9. Which sentence has a noun phrase made with a determiner and a common noun?
10. Which sentence has a noun phrase made with a common noun?
11. Which sentence has a noun phrase made with a proper noun?
12. Which sentence has a noun phrase made with a personal pronoun?

59

11. Talking about Hobbies

What do you like to do in your spare time? The boys and girls pictured on the opposite page are working at their hobbies.

- Does any one of the activities shown remind you of your hobby? If so, how?

- Which of the hobbies would you like to take up? Why?

- Why do you think the people pictured enjoy their hobbies?

For Discussion

A. What is your hobby? What skills and equipment does it require? Why do you enjoy it?

B. What new hobby would you like to take up? When and how did you become interested in it?

C. What is an unusual hobby that you have heard about? Explain why someone would like such a hobby.

Activities

Go to your school library or public library and find some books about hobbies. Then do one of the following.

1. Read about your hobby. In a class discussion, share at least one new idea that you found in your reading.

2. Read about a new hobby that is related to one of your interests. For example, someone interested in nature could read about mounting moths and butterflies. Someone interested in art could read about Japanese paper folding. Someone interested in handicrafts could read about how to make a birdhouse, or how to make interesting objects from nutshells. In a class discussion, describe briefly the hobby you read about.

Zentrale Farbbild Agentur

De Wys, Inc.

Dwight Ellefsen

Dwight Ellefsen

A. Devaney, Inc.

61

12. Writing a Friendly Letter

1714 Lynndale Road
Madison, Wisconsin 53711
June 28, 197—

Dear Steve,

    How are you spending your vacation in Oklahoma? Our family is staying home this summer, but I'm having a good time anyway. I'm doing a lot with my hobby, handicrafts. Dad is fixing up my room, and I'm making some things to go in it.

    First I made a wastebasket from a large ice-cream container. It's painted blue, with white waves and white flying sea gulls. Around the top is a piece of white rope tied in a square knot. I also made some bookends out of heavy white rope and pine boards. For the design I tied the rope in a large bowline knot. My next two projects will be a lamp and some bookshelves.

    Let me know when you and your family will be home. Dad says I can invite you to go fishing with us some Saturday.

Your friend,
Al

A good friendly letter is like a visit from its writer. It sounds personal and natural, like the writer talking. And it usually deals with the same commonplace topics that the writer would talk about if he visited his friend in person. Why does a hobby make a good topic for a friendly letter?

Read the letter on the opposite page. Answer these questions to decide how you could write a letter like Al's.

- What details did Al include in order to picture exactly what he had been doing?

- What sentences make the letter sound warm and personal?

- What five parts does the letter have?

- Where did Al use capital letters? What punctuation did he use?

For Discussion

A. Suppose you received the following letter from Al. Why is Al's other letter more interesting than this one?

1714 Lynndale Road
Madison, Wisconsin 53711
June 28, 197–

Dear —,

I'm finally getting around to writing the letter I promised you. This vacation has been fun. Dad and I are fixing up my room. What have you been doing? Write and let me know.

Your friend,
Al

63

B. Think about what you would write in a letter to a friend.

1. What are your hobbies? Which one would you like to write about in a letter to your friend?

2. What are some details that you would include? Would you tell about something you did recently with your hobby? Would you tell how you first became interested in your hobby? Would you tell the reasons why you enjoy it?

Activities

A. Write a letter about your hobby to a friend or relative. Follow the correct letter form. Use the letter at the beginning of this lesson as a model.

B. If you wish, prepare a copy of your letter to mail to your friend or relative. Be sure to let your teacher check the envelope and the final copy of your letter. The envelope should look like the example below.

Sender's Address

Albert Bartram
1714 Lynndale Road
Madison, Wisconsin 53711

Receiver's Address

Steven Stryker
239 S. Main Street
Stillwater, Oklahoma 74074

13. Writing about Hobbies

Study the pictures on this page and the next. They show the steps you could follow to spatter print some stationery. Do the pictures explain the process clearly? What titles might you place under the pictures?

Here is a written explanation of the process. Read it carefully. Notice what the writer did to make the process clear.

Make Your Own Stationery

Spatter printing is a good way to make your own stationery. You can use the various leaf designs of the trees that grow around you.

The materials for spatter printing are easy to find. You will need leaves, plain paper, an old toothbrush, a small square of screening, and some poster paint. You will want some water to thin the paint and to clean the toothbrush. It's a good idea to spread some old newspapers on the table where you plan to work.

The first step in making your stationery is to lay the leaf in the upper left corner of a sheet of paper. Dip the brush into the paint and shake off the extra. Then rub the brush lightly across the screening while you hold it over the leaf. Soon the leaf and the paper around it will be covered with tiny drops of paint. Let the paint dry. When you remove the leaf, you will have a colorful leaf design on your paper.

Now answer the following questions to find out how you could write an explanation like this one.

- Which paragraph gives just about the same information as picture *1?*

- Which paragraph gives just about the same information as pictures *2, 3,* and *4?*

- In what order did the writer give the steps in his explanation? Why?

For Discussion

A. What skills or processes are part of your hobby? Remember that many kinds of activities can be hobbies, including sports, music, cooking, sewing, and even making home repairs.

B. What are some skills or processes that are part of some other hobbies that interest you?

C. What special skills have you learned at school? For example, in art you may have learned how to do clay sculpture. In science you may have learned how to mount insects.

Activities

A. Write an explanation of a simple skill or process connected with a hobby. You may choose either your own hobby or some other hobby that interests you.

B. Separate into groups of three or four pupils each. Let each pupil read his explanation aloud. The others in the group should listen and decide whether they would be able to follow the process from the explanation given in the paper. If not, they should help the writer decide how to make his explanation clearer.

C. Draw a picture or a series of pictures to go with your explanation. If possible, make your pictures so clear that someone could follow them without reading your explanation.

14. Ordering Hobby Materials

Taylor Models, Inc.

3025 N. Clark Street, Chicago, Illinois 60657

Please send me __1__ Model Boat Kit(s), Catalog No. 415, at $2.95 each. I understand that this price includes the costs of postage and handling. I am enclosing ☐ cash, ☐ check, or ☑ money order.

Name __Myron Decker__

Address __1526 Hooli Circle__

City __Pearl City__ State __Hawaii__ Zip Code __96782__

Heading

> 1526 Hooli Circle
> Pearl City, Hawaii 96782
> June 30, 197—

Inside Address

> Taylor Models, Inc.
> 3025 N. Clark Street
> Chicago, Illinois 60657

Greeting

> Gentlemen:

Body

> Please send me one Model Boat Kit, Catalog No. 415, as advertised in the March, 197—, issue of _Hobby World_. I am enclosing a money order in the amount of $2.95.

Closing

Signature

> Sincerely yours,
> Myron Decker

You have probably ordered something by filling in the blanks of a coupon. This kind of coupon is somewhat like a business letter. Compare the coupon and the letter on the opposite page.

Suppose you wanted to order some hobby materials you saw advertised, and no coupon was provided. Answer the following questions to decide how you could write a good business letter.

- What information is in Myron's letter? Is it the same as the information in the coupon?
- What are the six parts of a business letter?
- Where did Myron use capital letters? Where did he use commas? Where did he use a colon?

For Discussion

A. What are some materials that you use in your own hobby? Which of these can be ordered through the mail?

B. What advice would you give the pupil who wrote a business letter with this as the body?

Please send me the model boat kit that you advertised. Making model boats is a favorite hobby of mine.

Activities

A. Follow these steps to write a business letter ordering hobby materials.

1. Each member of the class may make up an advertisement for some hobby materials. Print the advertisement neatly as it might appear in a hobby magazine.
2. Collect the advertisements in a box. Each pupil may draw one from the box and write a business letter answering it.

B. Each pupil may read the letter that answers the advertisement he wrote. Then he may suggest ways the writer could improve his business letter.

15. Listening to Poetry

In the poem below, a husband and wife are speaking. The wife speaks first, asking a question. Follow their conversation as your teacher reads the poem aloud to you.

O WHAT IS THAT SOUND

O what is that sound which so thrills the ear
   Down in the valley drumming, drumming?
Only the scarlet soldiers, dear,
   The soldiers coming.

O what is that light I see flashing so clear
   Over the distance brightly, brightly?
Only the sun on their weapons, dear,
   As they step lightly.

O what are they doing with all that gear,
   What are they doing this morning, this morning?
Only their usual manoeuvres, dear,
   Or perhaps a warning.

O why have they left the road down there,
   Why are they suddenly wheeling, wheeling?
Perhaps a change in their orders, dear.
   Why are you kneeling?

O haven't they stopped for the doctor's care,
   Haven't they reined their horses, their horses?
Why, they are none of them wounded, dear,
   None of these forces.

O is it the parson they want, with white hair,
   Is it the parson, is it, is it?
No, they are passing his gateway, dear,
   Without a visit.

O it must be the farmer who lives so near.
 It must be the farmer, so cunning, so cunning?
They have passed the farmyard already, dear,
 And now they are running.

O where are you going? Stay with me here!
 Were the vows you swore me deceiving, deceiving?
No, I promised to love you, dear,
 But I must be leaving.

O it's broken the lock and splintered the door,
 O it's the gate where they're turning, turning;
Their boots are heavy on the floor
 And their eyes are burning.

—W. H. AUDEN

Listen as your teacher reads the poem again.

- What are the husband and wife seeing as they speak?
- What happens at the end of the poem?

For Discussion

A. In each stanza except the last one, which lines are spoken by the wife? Which lines are spoken by the husband? Who do you think is speaking in the last stanza? How can you tell?

B. What mysteries are never solved in the poem?

Activities

Follow these steps in reading the poem aloud together.

1. Read the poem in unison. Your teacher will lead you.
2. Divide the class into two groups, one group for each speaker in the poem. You may want to let the girls read the wife's lines and the boys read the husband's lines.

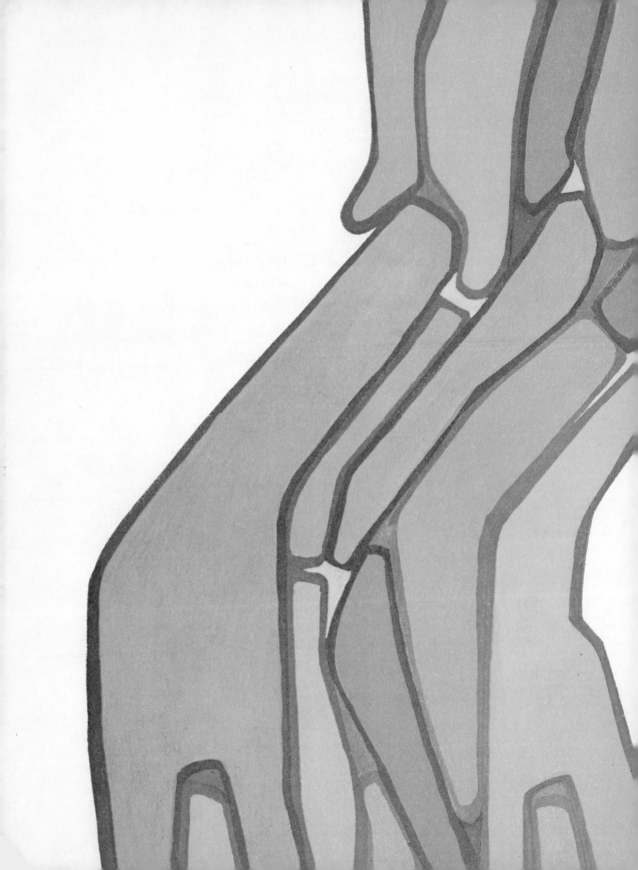

1. Losses in the Vocabulary of English

Look at the objects pictured below and at the words that name them. All these words were once part of the vocabulary of speakers of English. Are any of these words in common use today?

rebec

rockaway

seax

tungol

There are two main reasons why certain words are no longer in common use. First, the object that a word names goes out of use and is forgotten, and as a result the word too is forgotten. This is what happened to the word *rebec* when the object itself went out of date.

■ What other word under one of the pictures do you think dropped out of common use for this reason?

The second reason that certain words drop out of use is more complicated. The English language often contains two or more words that name the same object, like *car* and *automobile*. Sometimes—for what reason no one really knows—one of the words becomes more popular than the other, and gradually the other is forgotten. This is what happened to the words *seax* and *tungol*. They dropped out of the language when two other common words naming the same objects, *cnif* and *steorra*, became more popular.

■ What modern words did *cnif* and *steorra* develop into?

When words are no longer needed, they are likely to drop out of the language. What are two reasons why some words that were once common are seldom or never used today?

For Discussion

A. Each of the words that name the objects in the following pictures dropped out of common use many years ago. Give the reason that explains why words like these are almost never used today.

peruke

halberd

warming pan

brigantine

gig

75

B. English once contained two common words for each object pictured below. Tell which words are still used today and how they are spelled. Then give the reason that explains why the other words have long since dropped out of the language.

hran, hwæl   arwe, flan   cnapa, cild

gescy, scoh   mece, sweord   clud, genip

ON YOUR OWN

The words in italics were once common. Today they are seldom or never used. Which ones do you recognize from your reading? Use a large dictionary to find any words you do not know.

1. We passed a young man *bedight* in hunting clothes.
2. The mailman will be coming *anon.*
3. The new baby boy was *yclept* Steven Michael.
4. "The time has come," *quoth* he.
5. This man is telling the truth, I *wot.*
6. *Prithee,* sit here awhile and rest.
7. The *kine* were grazing in the meadow.

2. Stress

Listen as you say the following words aloud. See if you can tell how many syllables each word contains.

to   are   you   Boston   driving

- Which words have just one syllable?
- Which words have more than one syllable?
- Which syllable in each of the two-syllable words did you pronounce with greater force?

The same words can be arranged to form the sentence below. Listen as you say the sentence aloud.

Are you driving to Boston?

- How many syllables are there in the entire sentence?
- Did you pronounce one syllable with greater force than any other syllable in the sentence? If so, which one?

The degree of force that you use in pronouncing a syllable is called **stress.** In a word of two or more syllables, there is one syllable that receives heavier stress than any other. Also, in a simple sentence like the one you read aloud, there is usually one syllable that receives the heaviest stress in the entire sentence.

Now listen as you say each of the following sentences aloud. Use the heaviest stress on the syllable that is printed in capital letters.

They are RACing horses.

They are racing HORSes.

- Do both of the sentences you read have the same meaning?

- Which one means, "Those are racing horses, not workhorses"?

- What does the other sentence mean?

Next, listen as you say each of these sentences. Use the heaviest stress on the syllable that is printed in capital letters.

Are YOU driving to Boston?

Are you DRIVing to Boston?

Are you driving to BOSton?

- What difference in meaning does each change in stress make?

Think about what you have learned. What is stress? How is stress sometimes used to show differences in meaning?

For Discussion

A. Read these pairs of sentences aloud. In each pair, what is the difference in stress in the italicized words? What is the difference in meaning?

1. It was a *dark room*.
   It was a *darkroom*.

2. We saw a *blue bird*.
   We saw a *bluebird*.

B. Read the following questions aloud. Use the heaviest stress on the syllables printed in capital letters. Then match the questions with the appropriate answers.

Questions	Answers
1. Did SAM lend you this bike?	1. No, he gave it to me.
2. Did Sam LEND you this bike?	2. No, that one.
3. Did Sam lend you THIS bike?	3. No, Paul did.

For Practice

Oral **A.** The following sentences have two possible meanings, depending on which syllable you stress in the last two words. Read each sentence aloud so that it has the meaning given in parentheses.

1. They are stewing chickens. (chickens for stewing, not for frying)

2. Look at the spinning wheel. (the wheel that is spinning)

3. Get the street cleaner. (the man who cleans the streets)

B. The following sentences can mean two or more different things, depending on which syllable receives the greatest stress. Read each sentence aloud so that it has the meaning given in parentheses.

1. Ann voted for Pete. (I thought she would vote against him.)

2. Ted lost the money. (He didn't spend it.)

3. Joe told me where to find you. (It was Joe, not Art, who told me.)

ON YOUR OWN

You can make jokes by reading the following sentences aloud. Stress the italicized words to make the sentences fit the pictures. Then see if you can make up similar jokes of your own.

Did you ever see a *drinking glass?*

Did you ever see a *fishing worm?*

79

3. Pitch

Listen as you say the following sentences aloud. Notice how your voice rises and falls.

1. It's raining.
2. Do you have an umbrella?
3. Where's my raincoat?

The rising and falling of your voice as you speak is called **pitch.** Think about what you do with the pitch of your voice as you read the sentences above.

- Find the sentence that is a statement. At the end of the statement, is the pitch of your voice rising, or is it falling?

- Find the question that asks for a *yes* or *no* answer. Did you end this question with rising pitch, or with falling pitch?

- Find the question that asks for a statement as the answer. Did you end this question with rising pitch, or with falling pitch?

Now look at the sentences below. One sentence is a statement, and the other is a question that asks for a *yes* or *no* answer. There is no punctuation to tell you which is which, but you should be able to decide when you read them with the rising and falling pitch indicated by the type. Try it.

It's snowing

It's snowing

Look at the pair of sentences on the next page. Both are questions, but one requires a *yes* or *no* answer, and the other requires the answer to be either "I want milk" or "I want coffee." You

80

should be able to decide which is which when you read them with the rising and falling pitch indicated by the type.

Would you like m i l^k or c^o^{f}^{f}$_e$$_e$

Would you like m i l^k or c o f f e^e

Think about what you have learned. What is pitch? How can pitch sometimes make a difference in meaning?

For Discussion

Say these sentences aloud. Tell whether the pitch pattern at the end of each sentence is a rising or a falling pattern. Tell how the different pitch patterns affect meaning.

1. Al fed the h^a^{m}^{s} t$_e$$_r$

Al fed the h$_a$^{m}^{s}^{t}^{e}^{r}

2. Does Fido want f o^o^{d} or w^a t$_e$$_r$

Does Fido want f o^o^{d} or w$_a$^{t}^{e}^{r}

For Practice

Oral Read the following sentences aloud so that they have the meanings given in parentheses.

1. We're ready to leave?
(Are we ready to leave?)

We're ready to leave.
(I think we're ready to leave.)

2. Did you buy ice cream or cake?
(Which of the two did you buy?)

Did you buy ice cream or cake?
(Did you buy either of them?)

3. "Ann has a new friend." "Who?"
(Who is Ann's new friend?)

"Ann has a new friend." "Who?"
(Who has a new friend?)

4. Was that a good book?
(Did you think it was good?)

Was that a good book!
(It was really a good book.)

81

4. The Base Form and the s Form of the Verb

Look at the following sentences. Notice that the noun phrase used as the subject of each sentence is in color. What is the verb phrase in each sentence?

1. The drum sounds loud now.
2. My brother feels good now.
3. The boy has the book now.
4. The girl looks worried now.

Suppose you make the noun in each subject plural, as in the sentences below. What change do you also have to make in the first word in each verb phrase?

5. The drums — loud now.
6. My brothers — good now.
7. The boys — the book now.
8. The girls — worried now.

The word in the verb phrase that changes form when the noun in the subject becomes plural is called the **verb.** The form of the verb without the –s is called the **base form.** The form with the –s is called the **s form.**

All verb phrases contain a word called a verb, and all verbs have a base form and an s form. Think about how the base forms and the s forms are used in the sentences above. Which form is used with singular subjects like *the drum?* Which form is used with plural subjects like *the drums?*

A. Which form of the verb *taste*, the base form or the *s* form, could you use to complete each sentence below? Why?

1. The soup — too salty.
2. A ripe plum — sweet.
3. The lemon — bitter.
4. This — spicy.
5. One of the apples — sour.

B. Suppose you wanted to use the base form of the verb *taste* in each sentence in part A. How would you have to change each subject?

**For
Practice**

For More Practice
See Page 380

Oral **A.** Complete each sentence below with either the *s* form or the base form of a verb.

1. The owl — at night.
2. The clock on the mantel — the correct time.
3. My sister — the answer to the riddle.
4. The janitor — a key to the storage room.
5. That little boy — down the street every morning.
6. A boy scout — how to build a campfire.
7. My uncle — that farm.
8. Our host — some funny stories.
9. The bus — past my house.
10. The mailman sometimes — the pigeons.

B. Change each subject in part A from singular to plural. Then complete the sentence with the *s* form or the base form of a verb.

Written Rewrite the sentences below. Change each subject to make it singular. Then use the form of the verb that follows a singular subject.

1. Cobwebs hang from the ceiling.
2. Those birds fly south in winter.
3. These glass slippers hurt.
4. They eat at six o'clock.
5. The seals swim around the tank.
6. My sisters make good spaghetti.
7. The sopranos sing off key.
8. Sea gulls dive for fish.
9. Our cats sleep in the garage.
10. Some mice live in the attic.

83

5. The *ed* Form of the Verb

Read the sentences below and answer the questions that follow.

1. The sky looks stormy.
2. Peter wants that book.
3. My cousin plays the flute.

- What is the verb phrase in each sentence?
- What verb form, the base form or the *s* form, does each verb phrase contain?

Suppose you add the word *yesterday* to each sentence, as in the examples below. What change do you have to make in each verb so that the sentence will sound natural?

4. The sky — stormy yesterday.
5. Peter — that book yesterday.
6. My cousin — the flute yesterday.

The form of the verbs you used in the second group of sentences is called the **ed form.** Why is it a good name for this form?

Now study the sentences below. Complete the sentences in group *B* with the form of the verb that sounds natural.

A	B
He sees a comet now.	He — a comet yesterday.
The pond feels cold now.	The pond — cold yesterday.
That dog eats heartily now.	That dog — heartily yesterday.

All verbs have an *ed* form. How do you make the *ed* form of most verbs, such as *look*, *want*, and *play*? What is different about the *ed* forms of certain other verbs, such as *see*, *feel*, and *eat*? Why, do you suppose, are these forms called *ed* forms even though they do not end in *–ed?*

A. What are the verbs in the sentences below? What happens to the form of each verb when you add the word *yesterday* to each sentence? What is the name of each new verb form?

1. Weatherby travels to Washington.
2. Gene rides the bus to school.
3. The children look tired.

B. Use the following examples to show the two different ways that verbs make their *ed* forms.

1	2
walk	break
smile	swim
ask	stand

For More Practice
See Page 380

Oral A. Change each verb from an *s* form or a base form to an *ed* form.

1. Arlene smells something burning.
2. The bicycle tires need more air.
3. I hear jet planes overhead.
4. That dog wants to come inside.
5. Sam likes to play dominoes.
6. That box contains a surprise.
7. The students sound angry.
8. Dennis knows a funny joke.

B. Complete each sentence below with the *ed* form of a verb.

1. The baby — across the room.
2. This morning I — until ten.
3. Arthur — in the creek.
4. A moth — toward the light.
5. A racing car — around the bend.
6. The workers — at noon.
7. The gardener — his pumpkins.
8. That runner — his first race.

Written Copy the following chart on your paper. Complete the chart by filling in the base form, the *s* form, and the *ed* form of each verb.

Base Form	s Form	ed Form
1.	sails	
2. plan		
3.		escaped
4.	shouts	
5. try		
6. think		
7.	writes	
8. begin		
9.	bites	
10.		took

85

6. Tense

Compare the sentences in each matching pair. Then answer the questions that follow.

A	**B**
1. The sky looks gloomy	The sky looked gloomy.
2. The sun rises in the east.	The sun rose in the east.
3. Our guests leave tomorrow.	Our guests left yesterday.

- What verb forms do the sentences in group A contain?

- How was the form of each verb changed in group B to give a different idea of time?

The change you make in the form of a verb to express a different idea of time is called **tense.** English verbs have just two basic tense forms, **present** and **past.** The base form and the s form are both present tense forms. The *ed* form is the only past tense form.

Now read the two groups of sentences again. Decide what idea of time each verb form gives to each sentence.

- What idea of time do all the past tense verb forms in group B express?

- In group A, which present tense verb form expresses the idea of time in the present?

- Which present tense verb form expresses the idea that something is true at all times—past, present, and future?

- Which present tense verb form expresses the idea of time in the future?

Think about what you have learned. Which verb forms are present tense forms? Which verb form is a past tense form? What are some ideas of time that the different tense forms can express?

Answer these questions about each sentence in the box.

a. What is the verb phrase? What is the verb?
b. What is the form of the verb—the base form, the *s* form, or the *ed* form?
c. What is the tense of the verb, present or past?
d. What idea of time does the sentence express?

> 1. This chair feels lumpy.
> 2. The swallows come back every summer.
> 3. George turns twenty-one next October.
> 4. We celebrated Jo's birthday.

For Practice

For More Practice
See Page 381

Oral **A.** The verbs below are in the present tense. Tell what idea of time each verb expresses—present, future, or all times.

1. Joyce likes her new poodle.
2. I have a piano lesson tomorrow.
3. That tree blossoms each spring.
4. The wrens always wake up early.
5. The sea looks calm today.

B. Complete the sentences below with a verb in the past tense.

1. The colt — along the fence.
2. Mr. Arivett — to Atlanta.
3. My little brother — a snake.
4. I — my dinner that night.
5. The old hound — slowly.

Written Change the tense of each of the following verbs from present to past or from past to present. Write the new sentences on your paper.

1. Snails crawled around the tank.
2. That clock strikes the hour.
3. A rabbit hopped over the log.
4. Rover followed his master.
5. The early bird got the worm.
6. We often collected seashells.
7. Smoke darkens the sky.
8. The new store opens this week.

7. The Special Verb *Be*

As you read the sentences below, complete them with a present tense form of the verb *feel*.

I — happy now.   She — happy now.
We — happy now.   They — happy now.
You — happy now.   The boy — happy now.
He — happy now.   The boys — happy now.

Read the sentences again. This time use a present tense form of the verb *be*.

- How many present tense forms of *feel* did you use? What were they?

- How many present tense forms of *be* did you use? What were they?

Now complete these sentences with past tense forms. First read the sentences using the past tense forms of the verb *feel*.

I — happy yesterday.   She — happy yesterday.
We — happy yesterday.   They — happy yesterday.
You — happy yesterday.   The boy —happy yesterday.
He — happy yesterday.   The boys — happy yesterday.

Now read the sentences with a past tense form of the verb *be*.

- How many past tense forms of *feel* did you use? What were they?

- How many past tense forms of *be* did you use? What were they?

The sentences above show that *be* is a special verb. Most verbs, like *feel*, have two present tense forms and one past tense form. How many present tense forms does *be* have? How many past tense forms? In all, how many forms of *be* did you use in the sentences? Are the forms of *be* similar to one another in sound and spelling, as the three forms of *feel* are similar?

A. Read the sentence below. What would you have to do to change the verb to past tense? If you made the subject plural, what would happen to the verb?

The dolphin is hungry.

B. If you are a native speaker of English, you have used the special verb *be* all your life. It is easy and natural for you to select one of its various forms. Suppose that you were a foreign student just learning English as a second language. What are some reasons why you might find the verb *be* harder to learn than other English verbs?

For Practice

For More Practice
See Page 381

Oral Complete the sentences below with the form of the verb *be* that sounds natural to you.

1. The actors — backstage now.
2. I — hungry for lunch now.
3. Our phone — out of order now.
4. The grass — brown and dry now.
5. She — in the hospital now.
6. You — not in school yesterday.
7. The wren — on the sill yesterday.
8. It — cold and stormy yesterday.
9. The buses — late yesterday.
10. We — in your city yesterday.

Written For the verb in each of the following sentences, substitute a form of the verb *be*. Do not change the tense. Write your new sentences on your paper.

1. That pie smells delicious.
2. I feel more comfortable now.
3. Our players remain in first place.
4. This watermelon tastes sweet.
5. They look friendly.
6. We grew thirsty.
7. She sounded happy about the trip.
8. You seemed confident of success.
9. The trail became rocky.
10. I remained uncertain about it.

89

8. For Review

Read and discuss the questions below.

A. The words that name the objects below were once common, but they are seldom or never used today. What are two reasons why words like these sometimes drop out of common use?

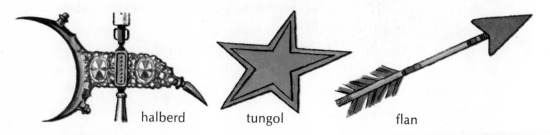

halberd   tungol   flan

B. What is stress? What is pitch? Which sentences below have different meanings because of a change in stress? Because of a change in pitch pattern at the end? How can you tell?

1. Did you GIVE it to her?
Did you give it to HER?

2. John left early.
John left early?

C. Answer the following questions about the verb in each of the sentences in the box.

1. Is the verb a present tense form or a past tense form? How can you tell?

2. What idea of time does each verb express?

> **a.** Edgar comes tomorrow.
> **b.** Sue came late Friday.
> **c.** Max ate a tortilla.
> **d.** Ann always eats something good for lunch.

D. How does the special verb *be* differ from other verbs? Use the sentences below in explaining your answers.

Present Tense Forms	**Past Tense Forms**
I *am* here today.	I *was* late yesterday.
He *is* here today.	He *was* late yesterday.
They *are* here today.	They *were* late yesterday.

Read the directions for each exercise below. Follow the directions, writing your answers on your own paper.

A. Decide which of the words in ( ) you would use to complete each statement below.

1. The rising and falling of your voice as you speak is called (stress, pitch).
2. The degree of force that you use in pronouncing a syllable is called (stress, pitch).
3. Verbs like *look* and *see* have (one, two, three) present tense forms and (one, two, three) past tense forms.
4. The special verb *be* has (one, two, three) present tense forms and (one, two, three) past tense forms.
5. Present tense verb forms (sometimes, always) express the idea of present time; past tense verb forms (sometimes, always) express the idea of past time.

B. For each italicized verb below, write **present tense** or **past tense** to show the tense of that verb. Also write **present, past, future,** or **all times** to tell what idea of time is shown by the italicized verb.

6. He always *plays* fair.
7. Thanksgiving *comes* soon.
8. They *ordered* ravioli.
9. Ben *was* at the game.
10. The sky *looks* clear now.
11. Rose *wrote* a letter.

C. Write each sentence below, completing it with the verb form in ( ). Be sure to use the verb forms that go with the subjects.

12. The sky (past tense form of *look*) cloudy yesterday.
13. The oranges (present tense form of *appear*) ripe.
14. They (past tense form of *be*) at the game.
15. Melissa (past tense form of *find*) her notebook.
16. She always (present tense form of *like*) candy.

91

10. Talking about Poems

The poems on these pages were written by boys and girls about your age. Listen as your teacher reads them to you.

When spring comes
I feel like a
Daisy just opening up into a new life.
I feel like running twenty miles
And taking off my heavy coat
And putting on a pair of sneakers.
I feel like I started a new life
And everything is better
Than it was before.
I get faster
In running and I can go swimming outdoors.
It feels like the smell of new flowers
And the animals
Coming up from their holes,
The birds coming back from their vacations.
I love spring.

—MICHAEL PATRICK, Age 10

SCRAPYARD

Old, old cars, rusting away,
Some cars whole—in these we play.
Now I am swerving round a corner,
Streaking round a bend,
Zooming past the finishing line
To the checkered flag—
Finishing a perfect first,
Ready for the autograph hunters.

—MICHAEL BENSON, Age 11

SLAVE OF THE MOON

The sea rushes up
To eat the muddy shore,
Slips back into the waves
To return once more.

Spluttering, foaming, frothing
Pulling at the land
Again it tries to eat
The dampened, salty sand.

But will it reach
Its destination soon?
Or must it always be
The slave of the moon?

—MARY YARMON, Age 11

Did you ever write a poem? Some people think that a poem has to rhyme, or that it has to be about a certain kind of "poetic" subject. How do the poems you just heard show that these ideas aren't always true?

For Discussion

A. Read the poem about spring. Which lines remind you of the way you sometimes feel in spring? What are some lines that you might add if you were writing this poem? Think of lines that begin with "I feel like" or "It feels like."

B. The poem "Scrapyard" is about a subject that usually isn't considered "poetic." What action in the poem really happens? What action takes place only in the boy's imagination?

C. Read "Slave of the Moon." Which lines rhyme? Which lines describe the sea as if it were a person?

93

11. Writing Haiku

The poems on this page are called **haiku.** Japanese people have been writing haiku for many centuries. Not all of these people are poets. Many write haiku just for their own pleasure and for the pleasure of their friends.

Read each haiku aloud several times. The first two were written by Japanese poets. The third one was written by an English-speaking girl.

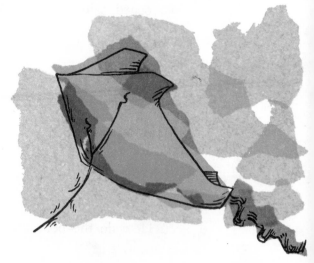

The tight string broke and
The loose kite fell fluttering,
Losing its spirit.

—KUBONTA

Though it be broken—
Broken again—still it's there:
The moon on the water.

—CHŪSHŪ

A little white mouse
Playing upon a sunbeam
Then sliding back down.

94   —MONA THOMAS, Age 11

A haiku describes a single detail, usually a detail from nature. Read all three of the haiku again. This time, notice the word picture that each haiku creates.

You may want to try writing some haiku of your own. Look at the first haiku on the opposite page to see how it is written.

- How many lines does the haiku have? Which line is the longest?

- How many syllables are in each line? How many syllables are in the complete haiku?

In the Japanese language every haiku has exactly the same number of syllables. In English it is all right to vary the number slightly. Find the haiku on the opposite page that has an extra syllable in the last line.

For Discussion

A. If your kite fell, you might say, "My kite string broke and the kite fell to the ground." Is this sentence a haiku? What did Kubonta do with this commonplace experience to make a haiku?

B. Look at the haiku about the mouse. When you write a haiku, should you use more picture words like *white, mouse,* and *playing,* or should you use more words like *a, upon,* and *then?* Explain your answer.

Activities

A. With your classmates make up some sentences that picture a single detail. Then change each sentence into a haiku.

B. Now try to write three or four haiku of your own.

C. Begin a book of poems written in your class. Illustrate the book with original drawings and paintings or with pictures cut from magazines.

12. Writing Cinquains

A poet named Adelaide Crapsey invented a new kind of poem called the **cinquain.** In some ways the cinquain is like the haiku. It creates a clear word picture of a single detail, often from nature. As you read the cinquain below, notice its form. How many lines does a cinquain have? How many syllables are in each line?

November Night

Listen . . .
With faint dry sound,
Like steps of passing ghosts,
The leaves, frost-crisped, break from the trees
And fall.

—ADELAIDE CRAPSEY

Joan Busta/Tom Stack and Associates
Zentrale Farbbild Agentur

The detail the poet noticed was a simple one—the falling of dry leaves in autumn. Read "November Night" again. Notice how the poet made a poem out of a simple, commonplace event.

- Which of your five senses does the poem appeal to—seeing, hearing, smelling, tasting, or touching?
- Which words in particular appeal to one of your senses?
- Which line contains a comparison? Do you think the comparison is a good one? Why?

Suppose you are writing a cinquain of your own. You may have difficulty getting it into the proper form the first time you try. Why will you have to choose your words carefully, then change and rearrange them?

For Discussion

What are some words you could use in a cinquain about each of the following? Think of words that appeal to your senses.

1. The sound of running water after a rainstorm
2. The way a spaceship looks during blast-off
3. The smells in an attic
4. The taste of lemonade
5. The feel of bare feet on hot sand

Activities

A. Write two or three cinquains telling how something looks, feels, sounds, tastes, or smells.

B. Read your cinquains to a partner. Share ideas about how to make your cinquains better.

C. Add the cinquains to your class poetry book. Make illustrations to go with some of the cinquains.

13. Writing Limericks

A verse to read or write just for fun is the **limerick.** Listen as your teacher reads the limericks that follow.

There was an old man with a beard,
Who said, "It's just as I feared!—
Two owls and a hen,
Four larks and a wren,
Have all built their nests in my beard!"

—EDWARD LEAR

There was a young fellow named Hall,
Who fell in the spring in the fall;
'Twould have been a sad thing
If he'd died in the spring,
But he didn't—he died in the fall.

A diner while dining at Crewe,
Found quite a large mouse in his stew.
Said the waiter, "Don't shout,
And wave it about,
Or the rest will be wanting one, too."

A scientist living at Staines
Is searching with infinite pains
For a new type of sound
Which he hopes, when it's found,
Will travel much faster than planes.

—R. J. P. HEWISON

Look at the limericks closely to find out how you could write one of your own.

- ■ How many lines does a limerick have?
- ■ Which lines rhyme?
- ■ What does the first line usually tell?
- ■ What kind of subjects are limericks about?

In the first limerick the syllables that receive heavy stress have an accent mark.

- ■ Which lines contain three syllables with heavy stress? Which lines contain two?

Now read all the limericks, listening to the patterns of rhyme and rhythm. Why, do you think, do people enjoy reading and writing limericks?

For Discussion

Read the limerick below. How is it a typical limerick in its first line, its rhyme, and its rhythm? Think of as many different last lines as you can to replace the line in parentheses.

There was a young fellow named Weir,
Who hadn't an atom of fear;
He indulged a desire
To touch a live wire;
('Most any old line will do here!)

Activities

A. Write a limerick of your own. (Or write several limericks, if you wish.) Read your limerick to the class or let someone else read it for you.

B. Add your limericks to your class poetry book.

14. Writing Free Verse

The poems in this lesson have no rhyme and no regular pattern of rhythm. They are written in **free verse.** Listen while your teacher reads them aloud to you. Notice the word picture in each poem.

Fire

Flickering flames of gold and red
Creeping forward like a cautious thief
Devouring greedily the old, dry twigs;
Wisps of light gray smoke
Floating higher and higher
In the damp air of the dawn.

—Jill Craik, Age 11

Hungry tree!
Your knife branches
Cut the pie-moon into tempting pieces.

—Nathan Altshuler, Age 13

The Garden Hose

In the gray evening
I see a long green serpent
With its tail in the dahlias.

It lies in loops across the grass
And drinks softly at the faucet.

I can hear it swallow.

—Beatrice Janosco

Trees

The trees share their shade with
all who pass by,
But their leaves whisper secrets
only to the wind.

—NELDA DISHMAN, Age 12

One way to create word pictures is by making comparisons. A comparison says that something is *like* something else. Now read the poems and notice the comparisons they contain.

- What does the first poem say that fire is like? Does the poem contain the word *like*?

- What does the third poem say that the hose is like? Does this poem contain the word *like*?

- What comparisons can you find in the two poems about trees?

Suppose you wanted to write a poem in free verse. How can comparisons help you make clear, interesting word pictures?

For Discussion

Think of comparisons to describe the following.

1. A color you like
2. A familiar sound
3. A kind of weather
4. An action or motion
5. A familiar smell
6. A facial expression

Activities

A. Write a poem in free verse. Try to use a comparison.

B. Add your free verse poems to the class poetry book. Illustrate as many of the poems as you wish to.

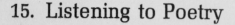

15. Listening to Poetry

Listen as your teacher reads the following poem to you.

CROWS

I like to walk
And hear the black crows talk.

I like to lie
And watch crows sail the sky.

I like the crow
That wants the wind to blow:

I like the one
That thinks the wind is fun.

I like to see
Crows spilling from a tree,

And try to find
The top crow left behind.

I like to hear
Crows caw that spring is near.

I like the great
Wild clamor of crow hate

Three farms away
When owls are out by day.

I like the slow
Tired homeward-flying crow;

I like the sight
Of crows for my good night.

—DAVID McCORD

Listen as your teacher reads the poem again.

- What does David McCord like about crows?
- Which of your five senses does the poem above appeal to?

For Discussion

A. How does the poem make you see the way crows move?

B. How does the poem make you hear the sounds that crows make?

C. What is there about crows as the poet describes them that reminds you of people?

Activities

A. Practice reading "Crows" aloud. Drop your voice at the end of a line only when a punctuation mark tells you to.

B. Try reading "Crows" in another way. Let a different student begin reading each time the poem says "I like."

C. Decide which lines you could illustrate with a drawing or painting. Make the illustration and copy the lines at the bottom. Then display all the illustrations on the bulletin board. Together they will show the poet's various ways of seeing crows.

CHAPTER 4

1. Gains in the Vocabulary of English

deer (dir), *n., pl.* deer or (*rarely*) deers. 1. a swift, graceful mammal of a group that have hoofs and chew the cud. A male deer has horns or antlers, which are shed and grow again every year. 2. any of a group of mammals including deer, elk, moose, and caribou. 3. *Obsolete.* any beast, especially a wild beast. [OE *dēor* animal]*

ee rie (ir′ē), *adj.,* -ri er, -ri est. 1. causing fear; strange; weird. 2. timid because of superstition. [ME *eri,* var. of *erg,* OE *earg* cowardly] —ee′ri ly, *adv.* —ee′ri ness, *n.* —Syn. See weird.*

ice berg (īs′bėrg′), *n.* a large mass of ice floating in the sea. [< Danish *isbjerg* or Swedish *isberg,* or Dutch *ijsberg,* literally, ice mountain]*

kin der gar ten (kin′dər gärt′n), *n.* school that educates children from 3 to 6 years old by games, toys, and pleasant occupations. [< G *Kindergarten* < *Kinder* children + *Garten* garden]*

lake (lāk), *n.* 1. a large body of water entirely or nearly surrounded by land. 2. a wide place in a river. [< L *lacus*]*

lamp (lamp), *n.* 1. thing that gives light. There are oil lamps, gas lamps, and electric lamps. 2. something that suggests the light of a lamp. 3. *Slang.* eye. [< OF < L < Gk. *lampas* < *lampein* shine]*

mus tang (mus′tang), *n.* the small, wild or half-wild horse of the American plains. [Am.E; < Sp. *mestengo* untamed]*

pap ri ka (pap rē′kə or pap′rə kə), *n.* a kind of red pepper not so strong as the ordinary kind. [< Hungarian]*

u ku le le (ü′kə lā′lē), *n.* a small guitar having four strings. [Am.E; < Hawaiian *ukulele,* originally, flea]*

When speakers of a language discover new things and ideas, they need new words. Where do these new words come from?

Look at the dictionary entries on this page. The part of each entry that is in brackets is called the **etymology.** In dictionary etymologies you can learn many things about where the words of English came from.

To understand an etymology, you need to recognize certain symbols and abbreviations. The symbol < that you see in some of the etymologies means *from* or *taken from.* The abbreviation OE stands for Old English. Now answer these questions about some other abbreviations.

- What abbreviations stand for Middle English and American English?
- What abbreviations stand for Old French, Spanish, German, Latin, and Greek?

Look at the entries once more to see what you can discover about the origins of these words.

- Which words came from earlier forms of English?
- Which words did speakers of English borrow from other languages?

* From THORNDIKE-BARNHART HIGH SCHOOL DICTIONARY by E. L. Thorndike and Clarence L. Barnhart. Copyright © 1968 by Scott, Foresman and Company.

Many English words, especially the very common ones, are like the word *deer*. That is, they have been a part of the English language from its earliest beginnings. Many words have been borrowed from other languages, especially Latin, French, and Greek. In the entries on the opposite page, what languages are listed as sources of English words?

For Discussion

Study the following etymologies from the *Thorndike-Barnhart High School Dictionary*. (The entries include abbreviations for Italian and Scandinavian.)

bamboo [< Dutch *bamboes,* probably < Malay]
below [ME *bilooghe* by low]
dander [origin uncertain]
frigate [< F < Ital. *fregata*]
silk [OE *sioloc* < Slavic < Gk. *serikos* < *Seres* the Chinese]
tornado [Am.E; alteration of Sp. *tronada* < *tronar* thunder]
window [< Scand. *vindauga* < *vindr* wind + *auga* eye]

1. Which words came from Old English or Middle English?
2. Which words were borrowed from other languages?
3. Which words mean something quite different than the words they came from?
4. What entries show that dictionary makers do not know the origin of every word?

ON YOUR OWN

Look up at least five of these words in a large dictionary to find some etymologies that paint vivid word pictures and tell interesting stories.

1. daisy
2. lumber
3. robot
4. sputnik
5. dandelion
6. tadpole
7. OK
8. atlas
9. sandwich
10. tuxedo
11. bugle
12. tantalize
13. calculate
14. handicap
15. lace

107

2. Juncture

Read these words aloud until they make sense to you.

the   boy   ate   his   lunch   was   cold

- How many sentences do the words make?
- Where does the first sentence end?
- When you say the sentences aloud, how does your voice show where the first sentence ends?

Besides dropping your voice after the word *ate*, you probably paused before you began the next sentence. A pause or interruption in a stream of speech is called **juncture.**

Now read these examples with a longer juncture at the star.

Dave let the cat out.
Dave ★ let the cat out.

- Which example means "Let the cat out, Dave"?
- What does the other example mean?

Read the examples below to see a third use of juncture. How should you read the second example to make its meaning clear?

He's a nice man.
He's an iceman.

Think about what you have learned. What is juncture? How do the examples in this lesson show that juncture is used to separate sentences, parts of sentences, and individual words?

For Discussion

A. Read these word groups aloud so that they make sense. In each one, where do you have to use the longest juncture? Why?

1. the baby drank her milk was sour
2. he waited his turn came last

108

B. The sentences below have two possible meanings. Read each sentence twice. The first time, pause at the first star; next, pause at the second star. Explain how juncture can help you to make the meanings clear in speech.

1. Firemen who fail ★ frequently ★ get fired.
2. Girls who eat sweets ★ often ★ get fat.

C. Explain how juncture is used in the advertisement below.

For Practice

Oral A. Read these examples aloud. Use a longer juncture wherever there is a star. What is the meaning of each example?

1. Can you see ★ Carlos?
   Can you see Carlos?

2. I called George an expert.
   I called George ★ an expert.

3. Alice said ★ Jim ★ it's time for lunch.
   Alice ★ said Jim ★ it's time for lunch.

B. In each example below, change the juncture of the words in italics to complete the second sentence.

1. A *nap'll* refresh you.
   Would you like — —?

2. *Might I* be able to come?
   — — has a spot on it.

3. Why do you *keep stopping*?
   She — — for the cake in the refrigerator.

4. *Keep snapping* your fingers.
   He — — during class.

109

3. Patterns of Intonation

Read the following sentences aloud, and listen. Your voice should make two different meanings clear.

1. Why don't you answer, Charles?

2. Why don't you answer Charles?

- In which sentence did you use a longer pause, or juncture, after the word *answer*?

- In which sentence did you use falling pitch at the end of the word *answer*?

- In which sentence did you use heavier stress on the word *answer*?

- What is the difference in the meanings of the two sentences?

Whenever you speak, you use pitch, stress, and juncture. Working together, these three sound effects form patterns of **intonation** in speech. Do you think intonation patterns help make meanings clear? Why?

For Discussion

The examples below are not punctuated. Read them aloud, showing the different meanings by the intonation patterns of your voice. Then tell whether you used pitch, stress, juncture, or a combination of these to make your meanings clear.

1. Warren put out the fire (spoken to Warren)
   Warren put out the fire (He did put it out.)

2. Will you call her Leslie (Will her name be Leslie?)
   Will you call her Leslie (spoken to Leslie)

3. Tanya invited Phyllis Mary Anne and Joan (four girls)
   Tanya invited Phyllis Mary Anne and Joan (three girls)

4. Let's turn right here (to the right)
   Let's turn right here (at this corner, not farther on)

5. Dinner will be at six as usual (Will it?)
   Dinner will be at six as usual (It will.)

6. Tom didn't fall off the porch (He was pushed.)
   Tom didn't fall off the porch (He fell off the roof.)

ON YOUR OWN

You may have heard jokes made by using unexpected intonation patterns. Say the sentences below in the normal way. Then say them with an extra-long juncture at the comma. What happens to the meanings? See if you can think of some similar jokes of your own.

What are we going to paint tonight, Mother?
What's this in the soup, Jean?

4. Two Kinds of Verb Phrases

A	**B**
Adrienne smiled.	Howie caught the ball.
The owl slept.	Mrs. Murphy made chowder.
Mr. Matsuda waited.	The cat chased its tail.
Carl spoke.	The boy threw the ball.

Pick out the verb phrase in each sentence above. Then answer these questions.

- Which sentences have verb phrases that are made with a verb alone?

- Which sentences have verb phrases that are made with a verb plus a noun phrase?

- Could the sentences in column *B* have ended after the verb? Why or why not?

Each verb phrase in column *A* is made with an **intransitive verb.** An intransitive verb does not need anything after it in the verb phrase.

Each verb phrase in column *B* is made with a **transitive verb.** A transitive verb needs a noun phrase after it in the verb phrase.

Now compare the sentences in each pair below. Can the same verb be transitive in one sentence and intransitive in another? How can you tell?

C	**D**
The bell rang.	The ice melted.
Mr. Mora rang the bell.	The sun melted the ice.

A verb phrase may contain either a transitive verb or an intransitive verb. Which kind of verb can appear alone in a verb phrase? Which kind must be followed by a noun phrase?

112

For More Practice
See Page 381

For Discussion

A. Below is a noun phrase. What are two kinds of verb phrases that you could add to form a sentence? Make up an example sentence with each kind of verb phrase.

The hunter —.

B. Which verb below is always transitive? Which verb is always intransitive? Which verb may be either transitive or intransitive? Make up example sentences to prove your answers.

1. disappear   2. praise   3. stop

For Practice

Oral A. With each noun phrase below, make a sentence by adding a verb phrase made with a transitive verb plus a noun phrase.

1. My science teacher —.
2. A tiny wren —.
3. Our next-door neighbors —.
4. My little sister —.
5. A brown donkey —.
6. Mr. Sitwell —.
7. A high wind —.
8. The train —.
9. The pioneer family —.
10. The gladiator —.

B. Make another sentence with each of the noun phrases in part A. This time add a verb phrase made with an intransitive verb.

Written Make two sentences with each verb below. In one sentence use

the verb as a transitive verb. Then use the same verb as an intransitive verb.

1. broke   4. blew
2. studied   5. wrote
3. played   6. sang

113

5. Noun Phrases that Follow Transitive Verbs

The verb in each sentence below is transitive. What kind of word or word group follows the verb in each sentence? Why?

1. Pirates buried the treasure.
2. A cat ate our canary.
3. They washed the car.
4. Geraldine called them.

Now study the noun phrases in each sentence.

■ Which noun phrase names the doer of the action? How is this noun phrase used?

■ Which noun phrase names the receiver of the action?

A noun phrase that comes after a transitive verb and receives its action is called the **direct object** of the verb.

Now look at the noun phrases in the example sentences above. Match each subject and direct object with one of these descriptions.

common noun
determiner plus common noun

proper noun
personal pronoun

You may have noticed that some personal pronouns have different forms in the subject and in the direct object. Complete the sentences below to discover what pronouns besides *them* are used as objects. The pronouns you use should stand for the same persons as the pronouns in color.

He treated us. Shall we treat —?
She didn't call me. Shall I call —?
We saw you there. Did you see —?
I remember you. Do you remember —?

A transitive verb is always followed by a noun phrase. What is this noun phrase called? Does it name a doer or a receiver of the action?

A. Find two noun phrases in each sentence below. Which noun phrase names the doer of the action? How is it used? Which noun phrase names the receiver of the action? How is it used?

1. The boys raided the refrigerator.
2. Cynthia made popcorn.
3. Tom's father scolded him.

B. In part A what kinds of words make up the noun phrases used as direct objects?

C. What forms of the personal pronouns will fit in the test sentence below? What forms will not fit? Why?

Everyone praised —.

**For
Practice**

For More Practice
See Page 382

Oral   A. Complete each sentence below with a noun phrase used as the direct object.

1. My cousin drives —.
2. All of us heard —.
3. The detectives searched —.
4. The tornado destroyed —.
5. The covered wagon crossed —.
6. The rabbits ate —.
7. Peter caught —.
8. Secret agents stole —.
9. The sixth graders made —.
10. One of the hikers found —.

B. From each pair of sentences, make a new sentence by combining two noun phrases in the direct object.

1. The dog followed Charlotte.
   The dog followed him.

2. The teacher welcomed her.
   The teacher welcomed me.

3. Mr. Oyama invited us.
   Mr. Oyama invited our families.

4. No one suspected them.
   No one suspected their friends.

Written   The verbs below can all be transitive verbs used with direct objects. Write sentences of your own using each verb with a noun phrase as the direct object. Try to use some noun phrases of each different kind, including pronouns.

1. painted
2. hid
3. bought
4. heard
5. moved
6. shattered
7. understood
8. washed
9. taught
10. examined

115

6. Dictionaries and Pronunciation

Here are entries for *wombat* from two different dictionaries, *Thorndike-Barnhart Advanced Junior Dictionary* and *Webster's New Practical School Dictionary*.

Thorndike Entry

wom bat (wom′bat), a burrowing Australian mammal that looks like a small bear. A female wombat has a pouch for carrying her young. *n.**

Webster Entry

wom·bat \ˈwäm-ˌbat\ *n.* A brownish gray burrowing animal of Australia, resembling a small bear in appearance, the female of which carries its young in a pouch.†

At the bottom of every page or every other page of a dictionary there is a **pronunciation key.** Here are the pronunciation keys from the dictionaries that contain the entries above. Compare the way sounds are spelled in the keys with the respellings in the entries.

Thorndike Pronunciation Key

hat, āge, cãre, fär;
let, bē, tèrm;
it, īce;
hot, gō, ôrder
oil, out;
cup, pùt, rüle, ūse;
ch, child; ng, long;
th, thin; ᴛʜ, then;
zh, measure; ə represents *a*
in about, *e* in taken, *i* in
April, *o* in lemon, *u* in circus.*

Webster Pronunciation Key

ə abut; ər burglar;
a back; ā bake; ä cot, cart;
aù out; ch chin; e less;
ē easy; g gift; i trip;
ī life; j joke; ng sing;
ō flow; ò flaw; òi coin;
th thin; t͟h this;
ü loot; ù foot;
y yet; yü few;
yù furious;
zh vision†

- How does the first entry tell you to pronounce *wombat?* How can you tell?

- Does the different respelling in the second entry mean that this dictionary is suggesting a different pronunciation? Explain.

- How do the two dictionaries show which syllable should receive heavier stress?

A dictionary can tell you how to pronounce words like *wombat* that may be unfamiliar to you. How would you explain to someone else the purpose of a pronunciation key?

* From THORNDIKE-BARNHART ADVANCED JUNIOR DICTIONARY by E. L. Thorndike and Clarence L. Barnhart. Copyright © 1968 by Scott, Foresman and Company.
† By permission. From Webster's New Practical School Dictionary. © 1969 by G. & C. Merriam Co., Publishers of the Merriam-Webster Dictionaries.

For Discussion

Find the pronunciation key in your own dictionary or in the one you use at school. Is it the same as either of those on the opposite page? If not, what are some differences?

For Practice

For More Practice
See Page 382

Oral   A. What symbols are used for these sounds in each of the pronunciation keys on the opposite page?

1. The vowel sound in *ouch, south,* and *cow.*
2. The vowel sound in *mane, rain,* and *deign.*
3. The vowel sound in *rule, blew,* and *smooth.*
4. The vowel sound in *please, be,* and *seem.*
5. The consonant sound in *thy* and *though.*

B. Use the Thorndike pronunciation key on the opposite page to help you pronounce these words.

1. cello (chel′ō)
2. chimera (kə mir′ə)
3. thesaurus (thi sô′rəs)
4. montage (mon täzh′)
5. lichen (lī′kən)
6. jocund (jok′ənd)
7. emulate (em′yə lāt)
8. infamous (in′fə məs)

C. Use the Webster pronunciation key on the opposite page to help you pronounce the next group of words.

1. abalone \ˌab-ə-'lō-nē\
2. epitome \i-'pit-ə-mē\
3. zealot \'zel-ət\
4. apropos \ˌap-rə-'pō\
5. chamois \'sham-ē\
6. leviathan \li-'vī-ə-thən\
7. heinous \'hā-nəs\
8. fruition \frù-'ish-ən\

D. Use your own dictionary or the one you use at school to answer these questions.

1. Does *scow* rhyme with *snow* or with *brow?*
2. Does *chassis* rhyme with *sassy* or with *passes?*
3. Does *indict* rhyme with *predict* or with *delight?*
4. Does *subpoena* rhyme with *Mona* or with *Lena?*
5. Does *meringue* rhyme with *fringe* or with *gang?*
6. Does *coup* rhyme with *stew* or with *soup?*
7. Does *seine* have the same sounds as *sane* or as *sign?*
8. Does the heaviest stress fall on the first syllable or on the second syllable of *affluent?*

7. More about Dictionaries and Pronunciation

Here is a simple experiment for you to try. Answer each question below.

1. Does route rhyme with *boot* or with *scout?*
2. Is the first sound in apricot the same as the vowel in *tape* or in *tap?*
3. Does the first syllable in coupon sound like *coo* or like *cue?*

Here is what the *Thorndike-Barnhart Advanced Junior Dictionary* says about the pronunciation of these words.

route (rüt or rout)

apricot (ā′prə kot or ap′rə kot)

coupon (kü′pon or kū′pon)

Now answer the following questions about each of the three words.

- Which pronunciation is listed first in the *Thorndike-Barnhart Dictionary?*
- Which pronunciation do you hear more often in your own home and community?

The pronunciation listed first is not better than the other pronunciation. It is simply the one that dictionary makers have found to be more common throughout the whole country. The second pronunciation may be more common in your community. If so, use it. The "right" pronunciation for you is the one that people use where you live.

Some people think a pronunciation is right just because it is in the dictionary. But a dictionary simply describes how a word *is* pronounced. It does not dictate how it *should be* pronounced. For many words, of course, there is only one common pronunciation. When your dictionary gives more than one, how can you decide which one to use?

A. Suppose someone in your class made this remark to you: "The new boy in our class talks funny. He says *creek* so that it rhymes with *trick*, and *route* so that it rhymes with *out*." Use your dictionary to decide how you might answer him.

B. How do you pronounce the word in italics in each sentence below? Do other people you know pronounce it the same way? What does your dictionary tell about how the word is pronounced?

1. The *tomato* was ripe.
2. Marjorie put on an *apron*.
3. She'll *measure* the distance.
4. Please answer the *inquiry*.
5. Let's go to the *rodeo*.
6. Admiral Byrd explored the *Arctic*.
7. Did you see this *advertisement*?
8. The boys swam as far as the *buoy*.
9. My *aunt* stayed for dinner.
10. My cousin is an *adult*.
11. Do you like *caramel* candy?
12. The *sloth* is a slow-moving animal.
13. The grain was stored in a *granary*.
14. Have you heard the *news*?

ON YOUR OWN

Work as a linguist works. Conduct a survey to discover how certain words are pronounced in your family, school, and community. Write the sentences in Discussion *B* on a sheet of paper. Then ask ten or fifteen people to read them aloud. Keep a record of the various ways each word is pronounced. You may want to share your findings with other members of your class.

8. For Review

Read and discuss the questions below.

A. What is meant by stress? Pitch? Juncture? Which sentences below have different meanings because of a change in stress? In pitch? In juncture?

1	2	3
I won.	Sara FELL.	I saw an arrow fly.
I won?	SARA fell.	I saw a narrow fly.

B. How do verb phrases made with transitive verbs differ from verb phrases made with intransitive verbs? Can the same verb be transitive in one sentence and intransitive in another? Use the sentences below in explaining your answers.

1	2
It rained.	I played ball.
I found a quarter.	I played.

C. Look at the noun phrases in each group below. Which noun phrases can be used both as subjects and direct objects? Which can be used only as direct objects? Explain your answers.

1. the man
Mrs. Smith
everybody

2. me
him
them

D. Discuss these questions about the dictionary entries at the right.

1. What information do the entries give about the pronunciation of each word?

2. What information do the entries give about the origin of each word?

to ma to (tə mā′tō or tə mä′tō), *n., pl.* —toes. 1. a juicy fruit used as a vegetable. Most tomatoes are red when ripe. 2. the plant it grows on. Tomatoes are spreading, strong-smelling plants that have hairy leaves and stems, and small yellow flowers. [< Sp. < Mexican *tomatl*]*

tu i tion (tü ish′ən or tū ish′ən), *n.* 1. teaching; instruction. 2. money paid for instruction. [< L *tuitio, —onis* protection < *tueri* watch over]*

Read the directions for each exercise below. Follow the directions, writing your answers on your own paper.

A. The sentences in each pair below have different meanings. Say each sentence softly. Write **stress** if the difference in meaning results from a change in stress. Write **pitch** or **juncture** if the difference results from a change in pitch or juncture.

1. We needed rain.
   We need a drain.
2. I gave the book to HIM.
   I GAVE the book to him.
3. He bought a horse?
   He bought a horse.

B. Write **transitive** for each sentence below that contains a verb phrase made with a transitive verb. Write **intransitive** for each one that has a verb phrase made with an intransitive verb.

4. Kevin lost the tickets.
5. The speaker pleased the audience.
6. The ice disappeared.
7. A cloud hid the new moon.

C. Write two sentences for each verb below. Use the verb as a transitive verb in the first sentence. Use the verb as an intransitive verb in the second sentence. After each sentence, write **transitive** or **intransitive** to show how the verb is used.

8. sang   9. studied

D. Each noun phrase in italics below is used as a subject. Write sentences using each italicized noun phrase as a direct object.

10. *Sheila* drove the car. 12. *The boys* rode bicycles.
11. *Mr. Brown* is an artist. 13. *The children* were in a hurry.

121

10. Sources of Information

The pictures on these two pages show a few of the many places you can go to find information. How many of these sources of information have you used? What others can you think of that are not pictured?

The lessons that follow will help you answer these two questions.

- How can I find the information I need?

- Once I find the information I need, how can I use it?

For Discussion

Read the assignments below. They are typical of those your teachers ask you to prepare. For each assignment, name some sources of information that you might use. The pictures on these two pages will give you some ideas. Explain why you would use each source of information you named.

1. Prepare a written report about the life of the Navaho Indians today.

Barbara Van Cleve/Van Cleve Photography   Barbara Van Cleve/Van Cleve Photography

2. Prepare a report on a city outside the United States that you would like to visit.

3. Bring to class a poem about your favorite animal.

4. Prepare an oral report on one type of folk music, such as work songs or cowboy ballads.

Activities

Visit the library you use most. Find out the answers to the questions below. Be prepared to report to the class.

1. Where is the card catalog?
2. What is the card catalog used for?
3. Where are the nonfiction books?
4. How are the nonfiction books arranged on the shelves?
5. Where are the reference books?
6. What different reference books are available?
7. Where are the magazines kept?
8. How can you locate back issues of magazines?
9. Does your library contain other sources of information, such as a record collection or a pamphlet file? If so, what are they?

123

11. Finding Information in an Encyclopedia

When you need to locate general information about a topic, you are likely to consult an encyclopedia. Below is an article about stalactites from *The World Book Encyclopedia*.

H. Armstrong Roberts

STALACTITE, *stuh LAK tite*. The beautiful stone formations that hang down from the walls and roofs of some caves are called *stalactites*. Most stalactites look somewhat like icicles. They usually form in limestone caves. They are caused when water drips through cracks in the roof of the cave and carries the mineral called *calcite* (calcium carbonate) with it. As the water evaporates, it leaves formations of the calcite hanging. Stalactites of basalt rock hang from the roofs of some lava caverns. Similar formations of ice have been found in the ice caves of Arctic regions.

Formations which build up from the floor of a cave are called *stalagmites* (see STALAGMITE). In the United States, excellent examples of stalactites and stalagmites exist in Carlsbad Caverns National Park in New Mexico, in Luray Caverns in Virginia, in Mammoth Cave in Kentucky, and also in Wyandotte Cave in southern Indiana.

ELDRED D. WILSON

See also CALCITE; CAVE.

Read the encyclopedia article about stalactites again. This time, look for answers to these two questions.

- What kinds of information about stalactites does the article contain?
- What additional articles are referred to at the end of the article? Within the article?

A listing of a related article in an encyclopedia is called a **cross-reference.**

- Why might someone want to look up one or more of the articles listed as cross-references?

Most schools and libraries have more than one set of encyclopedias. Do you think it would sometimes be a good idea to look up the same subject in more than one encyclopedia? Why?

For Discussion

If you wanted information about sleep, you would probably look for the topic "Sleep" in an encyclopedia. Why might you also be interested in the following cross-references?

Related Articles in WORLD BOOK include:

Dream	Sleeping Sickness
Hibernation	Sleepwalking
Insomnia	Snoring
Nightmare	

Activities

Look up the following topics in an encyclopedia. List the cross-references that appear with each article. Be sure to look within the article as well as at the end.

1. Cloud
2. Lightning
3. Telescope
4. Queen Victoria

12. Finding Books in the Library

One of the first things you see as you enter a library is the card catalog. This is an alphabetical file of cards listing the resources of the library. As you learn how to use a library to find information, you will discover that the card catalog of a library is something like the index of a book.

Suppose you want information about holidays, such as Christmas, Hanukkah, and New Year's Day, and how they are celebrated in other countries. What general subject would you look under in the card catalog to find the titles of some books you could use?

Here are some reference cards you might find in the card catalog under the topic "Holidays."

394.26	**HOLIDAYS**	
GAE	**Gaer, Joseph**	
	Holidays around the world	

394.26	**HOLIDAYS**	
SCH	**Schauffler, Robert Haven**	
	The days we celebrate	

394.26	**HOLIDAYS**	
MCS	**McSpadden, J. Walker**	
	The book of holidays	

394.26	**HOLIDAYS**	
SEC	**Sechrist, Elizabeth (Hough)**	
	Red letter days; a book of holiday customs	

Nonfiction books are arranged by the **call number,** which appears in the upper left corner of the reference card. Look at the picture above to see how the call number can help you find a book. The picture shows some typical shelves of nonfiction books. Compare the numbers on the cards with the numbers on the shelves.

- If you wanted the books about holidays, which shelves would you go to?

Now look at the books pictured on the right.

- What do the letters, such as GAE, stand for?
- How do the letters help you to locate a particular book on the shelves?

Another kind of card you might find in the card catalog looks like the one above.

■ How can a cross-reference card help you find the information you want about a subject?

For Discussion

Suppose you wanted information on each subject listed below. What are some subjects that you could look under in the card catalog?

1. How to build an aquarium
2. Inventors of the earliest automobiles
3. The history of football
4. The migration of the monarch butterfly
5. Types of Indian dwellings

Activities

In the card catalog of your library, look up one of the subjects suggested in For Discussion. Use the cross-reference cards if necessary. Find five books that you think might contain information on the subject you chose. Make a note for each book.

List its author, title, and call number.

13. Taking Notes

The paragraphs below are from the encyclopedia article about Abraham Lincoln that appears in *Compton's Pictured Encyclopedia*. Suppose you were looking for some information on a particular subject, Lincoln's education. You would want to remember important ideas about that particular subject. One way to remember is to write these ideas down in the form of notes.

Read the paragraphs. Decide which ideas you would write in your notes.

Sarah made Thomas send the gangling 11-year-old to school. There was no regular teacher. When some man came along who knew a little about the three R's, he might teach the boys and girls for a few weeks—usually in the winter when farm work was slack. Whenever "school kept" at Pigeon Creek, Abe hiked four miles each way, his cowhide boots sloshing in the snow. He did not mind. He was learning.

In all his life his schooling did not add up to a year, but he made up for it by reading. A cousin, Dennis Hanks, who came to live with the Lincolns, said: "I never seen Abe after he was 12 that he didn't have a book somewheres around." By the time Abe was 14 he would often read at night by the light of the log fire. His first books were the Bible, 'Aesop's Fables', and 'Robinson Crusoe'.

—Compton's Pictured
Encyclopedia

Now read the following notes. Think about your purpose in reading the article, to find some information about Lincoln's education.

Schooling

    No regular teacher

    Total schooling less than a year

Reading

    Always had a book

    Read by firelight

    First books—Bible, Aesop's Fables, Robinson Crusoe

Now read the notes again and compare them with the original paragraphs.

- Are the notes in full sentences or in parts of sentences?

- Did the writer of the notes use his own words, or did he use the words of the encyclopedia?

- Do the notes consist of the main ideas of the original paragraphs or of minor ideas?

For Discussion

At the top of the next page is a paragraph written from the notes in the lesson. How were the notes important to the writer as an aid to memory? How did taking notes help the writer to use only his own words?

Lincoln and Books

Young Abe Lincoln learned far more from reading than from formal schooling. The school he went to did not have a regular teacher, and it was often closed. He attended school less than a year in all. But he loved to read, and he read a great deal. Some of the first books he read were the Bible, *Aesop's Fables*, and *Robinson Crusoe*.

Activities

A. Here is a paragraph from another encyclopedia. Read it and then write the notes you would take if you were looking for information about Lincoln's education.

Lincoln's formal schooling totaled less than a year. Books could rarely be found on the frontier, and paper was almost as scarce. Like other boys and girls of his time, Lincoln made his own arithmetic textbook. Several pages of this book still exist. Abraham often worked his arithmetic problems on boards, then shaved the boards clean with a drawknife, and used them again and again. He would walk several miles for a book. The few that he could borrow were good ones. They included *Robinson Crusoe*, *Pilgrim's Progress*, *Aesop's Fables*, a history of the United States, and a schoolbook or two.

—THE WORLD BOOK ENCYCLOPEDIA

B. Suppose you want to find information about Abraham Lincoln's stepmother, Sarah Bush Lincoln, and the part she played in Abe's life. Find an encyclopedia article about Lincoln and take notes on this subject.

131

14. Writing from Notes

When you take notes, you usually have a purpose in mind. Here are some notes from an encyclopedia article. The writer wanted to pretend he was Marco Polo writing a letter.

Marco Polo—born in Venice
    Father was Nicolo, uncle was Maffeo
Trip to Cathay (China)
    All three Polos went
    Kublai Khan—friendly—sent Polos on missions
Return to Venice—24 years later
    Relatives scarcely knew Polos
Banquet guests doubted Polos had been to Cathay
    Polos changed robes, opened bags of jewels

Now read the letter below. Compare it with the notes. How did the writer use his notes in an imaginative way?

September 3, 1295

Dear Julio,

Our homecoming to Venice was exciting. Do you realize that it was twenty-four years ago when we left home? I guess it isn't strange that most people, even our relatives, didn't know us at first. But once we talked for a while, the family felt at ease with us. Antonio and Pietro enjoyed recalling things we did as children when we played together along the canals.

I don't think everyone believes we were really in Cathay and were friends of Kublai Khan. Maybe they will after tonight's banquet. Dad, Uncle Maffeo, and I will be wearing our colorful silk robes. In fact, we each plan to change from one set of robes to another several times during the evening. Later on we'll open the bags of jewels and spread out the rubies and emeralds for everyone to look at.

I'll see you soon, Julio. I have a lot to tell you.

Your friend,
Marco

Scala

Would you like to imagine that you are a famous person from the past? Answer these questions to find out how you could write a letter like the one you just read.

■ In which sentences did the letter writer use facts from his notes?

■ Which sentences show that the letter writer used his imagination to add interesting personal details?

For Discussion

What person from history interests you the most? What are some events in his life that you could include in a letter he might have written?

Activities

A. Read in an encyclopedia or in another book about a famous person from history. Choose some historical person who interests you. Take notes on your reading. Then use facts from your notes to write a letter that the person might have written.

B. "Mail" your letter by posting it on the bulletin board.

15. More about Writing from Notes

Sometimes you look for information on a subject in more than one book. Here are two sets of notes about seals that were taken from two different encyclopedia articles.

Notes about Seals I	**Notes about Seals II**

Live in oceans or inland seas and also on land
Spring—stay on islands
  Mate, have young
  Mother seal (cow)
    One baby (pup)
  Mother eats at sea
  Feeds pup on island
Enemies—sharks, killer whales, polar bears, man
	Food—squid, fish, shellfish
	Migration of fur seals
	  From polar regions almost to subtropics
	Uses by man
	  Hide used for boots, coats
	  Meat for food
	  Blubber—eaten for dessert
	    Burned for light and heat
	Oil

Now read the following story based on both sets of notes.

Celia Seal

My name is Celia Seal. I live in the ocean. I spend time on land, too, but I am happier in water. There I can move fast to find food or escape from an enemy.

During the warm months I stay in the northland, but every year I swim thousands of miles to the south. During the long journey I don't go ashore at all.

Now it is spring. I am living on a rocky northern island. Since I am a mother seal, or cow, I am busy feeding my pup on land and finding food for myself at sea. My favorite foods are squid, fish, and shellfish.

Large sharks and killer whales are my enemies in the water. One time, my brother was floating on an island of ice and just escaped from a polar bear. But my chief enemy is man. I hope I never become someone's fur coat or a clown balancing a ball on my nose.

Now answer the questions below to see how you could write a paper like this one.

- Who is the speaker?

- Which sentences do you think contain information from the notes?

- In which sentences does the writer imagine how a seal might feel or think if it were a person?

For Discussion

Which of the animals listed below would you like to write about? What are some things you already know about them? What other kinds of information might you find in encyclopedias?

1. giraffe
2. monarch butterfly

3. wallaby
4. housefly

5. whale
6. camel

Activities

A. Read about an animal in two different encyclopedias and take some notes. Then use your notes to write a paper like the one about Celia Seal. Let the animal tell about itself.

B. Trade reports with a partner. Read each other's reports and talk about how you could make them better.

Zentrale Farbbild Agentur

16. Writing a Summary

Read the following paragraphs carefully. Then, before you read any farther, think of a sentence or two expressing the main ideas of what you have read.

Harriet Tubman knew the meaning of freedom. All her life, from her childhood on, she had yearned for it, longed for it, dreamed of it. Finally, when she could bear her life as a slave no longer, she had run away. No one had helped her, no one had told her what to do, no one had guided her as she was to lead other runaway, escaping slaves later on. Toward the end of her journey, she met some people who aided her in her escape to the North.

But she could not enjoy her freedom for long, knowing that so many of her people were still enslaved. "I had seen their tears and sighs, and I had heard their groans, and I would give every drop of blood in my veins to free them." So Harriet became a "conductor" on the Underground Railroad. Nineteen times she went back into the South, rescuing three hundred slaves.

—ARNOLD DOLIN, *Great American Heroines*

Sometimes you want to remember the main ideas of something you have read. A statement of the main ideas is called a **summary.** Read the summary below and answer the questions that follow.

Harriet Tubman escaped slavery by running away to the North. Later she returned to the South as a "conductor" on the Underground Railroad and rescued three hundred slaves.

- What main ideas of the original paragraphs does the summary contain?
- What are some details of the original paragraphs that the summary leaves out?
- How does the length of the summary compare with the length of the original?

For Discussion

Read the following paragraph. Which ideas would you include in a summary? Which ideas would you leave out? Why?

From a distance a glacier doesn't look as if it is made of ice. It looks rather like a streak of snow, and even a few steps away you have a hard time persuading yourself that this is really ice. For it isn't glittering and polished like the ice we skate on, but rough and uneven. And the reason for the difference is this: The ice of glaciers is not made of water but of snow. Its surface often becomes matted and pockmarked by fierce winds. What is more, as a glacier moves, pressure keeps roughening and changing its top. Frequently the ice is broken up in towers, called *seracs*, some of which are high as church steeples. As the ice passes over uneven ground, crevasses open and close in it. There may be a whole network of these huge cracks, often with snow bridges over them.

—ANNE TERRY WHITE, *All about Mountains and Mountaineering*

Activities

A. Write a summary of the paragraph about glaciers. Your summary should be about two or three sentences long.

B. Read your summary to a partner. Let him judge whether your sentences express the main ideas and leave out the minor details.

17. Listening to Poetry

Listen as your teacher reads the following poem to you.

SEAL

See how he dives
From the rocks with a zoom!
See how he darts
Through his watery room
Past crabs and eels
And green seaweed,
Past fluffs of sandy
Minnow feed!
See how he swims
With a swerve and a twist,
A flip of the flipper,
A flick of the wrist!
Quicksilver-quick,
Softer than spray,
Down he plunges
And sweeps away;
Before you can think,
Before you can utter
Words like "Dill pickle"
Or "Apple butter,"
Back up he swims
Past sting-ray and shark,
Out with a zoom,
A whoop, a bark;
Before you can say
Whatever you wish,
He plops at your side
With a mouthful of fish!

—WILLIAM JAY SMITH

A book about seals would give you certain kinds of information about them.

- Is it the same kind of information a poet gives you?
- What do you think William Jay Smith wants you to know about seals?

For Discussion

A. Why do you think the poem is shaped the way it is?

B. What words in the poem suggest the way the seal moves, both in and out of water?

C. Some words, like *zoom*, sound like the sounds they describe. What other words like this can you find in "Seals"?

D. In his book *Ounce Dice Trice* Alastair Reid has lists of "light words" and "heavy words." On the list of "light words" are *ariel, willow, spinnaker, whirr, lissom, sibilant, petticoat, nimble,* and *nib*. The "heavy words" are *duffle, blunderbuss, galoshes, bowl, befuddled, mugwump, pumpkin, crumb,* and *blob*. What heading can you think of for a list of words from "Seal," such as *swerve, twist, flip, flick, quicksilver-quick, plunges,* and *sweeps*?

Activities

A. Practice reading "Seal" aloud. Listen to the sounds of the words and to the rhythm of the lines.

B. Try to create some word lists like the ones from *Ounce Dice Trice*. You may use some of the headings below, or any other headings that you think of.

Noisy Words	Rough Words	Fiery Words
Quiet Words	Smooth Words	Watery Words

CHAPTER 5

1. Extending the Meanings of Words

When the word *pipe* first came into the English language, it had only one meaning. It was the name of a long, tube-shaped musical instrument something like a flute.

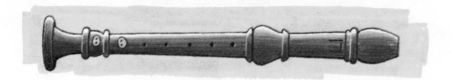

Today the word *pipe* has several meanings besides its original one. The objects below illustrate three of these meanings. What resemblances can you see in all the objects pictured on this page?

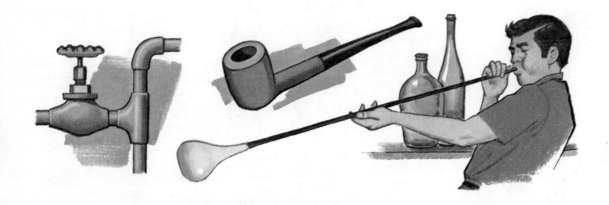

People everywhere make comparisons and notice resemblances. Often they use these resemblances to extend the meaning of a word. When people need a new word to name something, sometimes they invent a word. Sometimes they borrow one. But most of the time they extend the meaning of an existing word, like *pipe*.

How can a single word come to stand for objects as different as the ones in the pictures above?

A. Each word printed in italics has several related meanings. Which meaning does it have in each sentence? What resemblance do you think may explain why the word has both meanings?

1. His *heart* was pounding after the race.
Let's get to the *heart* of the matter.

2. Only one *leaf* still clung to the branch.
We'll put the extra *leaf* in the table.

3. Rinse the cut with a *dash* of water.
Sid ran the hundred-yard *dash*.

B. Look at the words below. How do you think each word got the meaning suggested by the picture? What are some words you could add to this group?

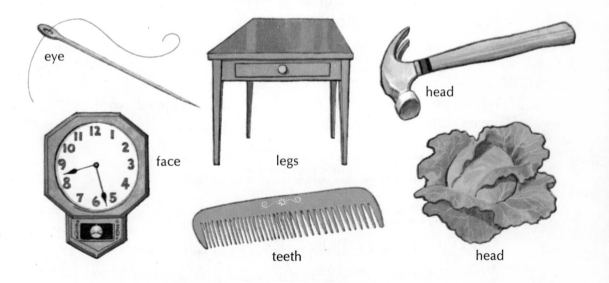

eye

face

legs

head

teeth

head

143

2. Clipped Words

The people in the cartoon above are using words that were formed in a special way.

- What words might have been used instead of the words printed in color?

- How do speakers of English create words like the ones in color?

Words like *burger*, *malt*, and *shake* are called **clipped words.** Here are dictionary entries for some other examples.

pi an o (pē an′ō), *n., pl.* -an os. a large musical instrument whose tones come from many wires. The wires are sounded by hammers that are worked by striking keys on a keyboard. [for *pianoforte*]*

van (van), *n.* 1. a covered truck or wagon for moving furniture, etc. 2. *Brit.* a railroad baggage car. [< *caravan*]*

- What long words did *piano* and *van* come from?

- What part of a dictionary entry tells you that a word is a clipped word?

Some clipped words are used only occasionally. You might say, for example, "Uncle Joe, you're my favorite *unc*." Others, like the ones you have looked at in this lesson, become permanent additions to the vocabulary of English.

144

* From THORNDIKE-BARNHART HIGH SCHOOL DICTIONARY by E. L. Thorndike and Clarence L. Barnhart. Copyright © 1968 by Scott, Foresman and Company.

How do people create a clipped word? Is *clipped word* a good name for this kind of word? Why or why not?

For More Practice
See Page 383

For Discussion

A. Explain how these clipped words were formed.

1. phone	**4.** stereo	**7.** champ	**10.** possum
2. copter	**5.** flu	**8.** sis	**11.** gas
3. fridge	**6.** ad	**9.** lab	**12.** photo

B. A few clipped words have other changes besides just the loss of a syllable or syllables. Explain how this is true of the clipped words below.

1. bike   **2.** drapes   **3.** combo   **4.** rattler

C. Some clipped words have been a part of the language for so long that the original form of the word has been all but forgotten. Such is the case with the five clipped words in the chart at the right.

Clipped Word	Original Word
wig	periwig
sport	disport
bus	omnibus
lunch	luncheon
fence	defense

1. What is the original word behind each clipped word in the chart?

2. Is the original word still in common use today? If so, does it still have the same meaning as the clipped word?

ON YOUR OWN

For a week, listen and watch for clipped words. Listen at home. Perhaps your sister refers to you as her *bro* or her *sis*. Listen at school. You are sure to hear several, including *gym* and *exam*. Watch the advertisements. You will hear about products such as *stereo* sets, electric *percs*, and *mod* clothes.

3. Blends

In Lewis Carroll's *Through the Looking Glass* there is an interesting conversation. Alice asks Humpty Dumpty to explain the poem "Jabberwocky." He agrees, and Alice recites the first verse.

> 'Twas brillig, and the slithy toves
> Did gyre and gimble in the wabe:
> All mimsy were the borogoves,
> And the mome raths outgrabe.

Read what Humpty Dumpty tells Alice about a word in the poem.

> "Well, 'slithy' means 'lithe and slimy.' 'Lithe' is the same as 'active.' You see it's like a portmanteau—there are two meanings packed up into one word."

A portmanteau is a suitcase that contains two separate compartments. Another portmanteau word that Humpty Dumpty explains is *mimsy*, which combines *flimsy* and *miserable*.

The English language contains a number of words that are just like Lewis Carroll's portmanteau words. Today these words usually are called **blends.** Here are some examples.

> smoke + fog → smog
> breakfast + lunch → brunch
> motor + hotel → motel

- How does each blend combine the sounds and spellings of two words?
- Do the blends also combine the meanings of two words?

Some blends, like *slithy* and *mimsy*, are used just for fun. They never become permanent additions to English. Others, like *smog*, are used regularly and appear in dictionaries.

What is a blend? How does the word *blend* suggest the way these words are formed?

For More Practice
See Page 384

For Discussion

A. How do you think the cities that are shown on the map got their names?

B. Two of the blends from "Jabberwocky" have been accepted and used by some speakers of English. What sort of sound do you think is a *chortle*? What sort of action do you picture in the word *galumphing*?

chuckle + snort → chortle
gallop + triumphing → galumphing

C. Linguists are not always certain about the origin of a word. Do you agree with some linguists that the words below could be blends? Why or why not?

1. splash + spatter → splatter
2. squall + squeak → squawk

3. twist + whirl → twirl
4. flutter + hurry → flurry

ON YOUR OWN

Make up some blends of your own. For example, if you sprained your ankle, you might say, "My *sprankle* hurts."

When you finish, show your blends to a friend. See if he can guess what two words you combined to make each blend.

4. *Be* Plus a Noun Phrase

The verb phrases in the sentences below are in color. Each verb phrase contains a form of the special verb *be*. Read the sentences and then answer the questions that follow.

1. The two boys were friends.
2. The building was a skyscraper.
3. That pitcher is Harry.

■ What noun phrase comes after the verb *be* in each sentence? Is the verb phrase complete without the noun phrase that follows *be*?

■ Which noun phrase after *be* consists of a common noun alone? Of a proper noun alone? Of a determiner plus a noun?

The word or word group that follows the verb *be* to complete the verb phrase is called a **completer.** What kind of word or word group serves as the completer in all the example sentences?

Now compare the two noun phrases, the subject and the completer, in each example sentence above.

■ Do the two noun phrases name the same person or thing, or does each one name a different person or thing?

The special verb *be* does not make up a verb phrase by itself. It must have a completer after it. What is one kind of completer that can follow *be* to make up a verb phrase?

For Discussion

A. Study the verb phrase in the sentence below. What is the verb? What noun phrase comes after the verb? How is this noun phrase used?

148

My father was a miner.

B. What is the completer in each sentence below? What does each completer consist of, a common noun, a proper noun, or a determiner plus a common noun?

1. The poet was Robert Frost.
2. Al and Dan are swimmers.
3. His book is an autobiography.

For More Practice
See Page 384

For Practice

Oral Complete each sentence below with a noun phrase used as a completer after a form of *be*.

1. These flowers are —.
2. I am —.
3. My favorite food is —.
4. The lost dog was —.
5. The object in the box was —.
6. That girl is —.
7. Those noisy students were —.
8. My choice for dessert is —.
9. Those trees are —.
10. Pete is —.

Written Write sentences using each noun phrase below as a completer after a form of *be*.

1. president of our club
2. English
3. my gym teacher
4. a peanut butter sandwich
5. my favorite comedian
6. a school holiday
7. Geraldine
8. a large black spider
9. a redwing blackbird
10. an interesting pet

5. *Be* Plus an Adjective

Each verb phrase in color contains a form of the special verb *be* followed by a completer. Study these sentences by answering the following questions about each verb phrase.

The mouse is small.
The hamsters were frisky.
The black swan was beautiful.

- What is the completer in each verb phrase?
- Are the completers noun phrases? How can you tell?
- Why does each verb phrase need a completer?

Noun phrases are not the only things, as you see, that can serve as completers. Words like *small, frisky,* and *beautiful* can serve as completers, too. Such words are called **adjectives.**

Here is a way of testing words to see if they are adjectives. See if *small, frisky,* and *beautiful* can fill the blanks in the test sentences below. Add an ending or a word wherever it is needed to make the sentence sound right.

1. This is very —.
2. This is — than that.
3. This is the — one of all.

- In which test sentence could you use all three adjectives without adding anything?
- Which adjectives could you use with the endings *–er* and *–est* in sentences 2 and 3?
- Which adjective did you use with the words *more* and *most* instead of the endings *–er* and *–est?*

The special verb *be* must always have a completer after it. What else besides a noun phrase can serve as a completer? What test can you use to discover whether a word is an adjective?

A. Describe the verb phrases in the sentences below. What is the verb in each verb phrase? What is the completer? Does the same kind of word or word group serve as a completer in both sentences? Explain your answer.

1. That lion is a pet.
2. That lion is hungry.

B. What are some adjectives that you can use as completers in the sentence below? How can the test sentences numbered *1* to 3 on the opposite page help you decide whether the words you use are really adjectives?

The street was —.

For Practice

For More Practice
See Page 384

Oral A. Each sentence below contains a completer in the verb phrase. Use the sentences numbered *1* to 3 on the opposite page to decide which of the completers are adjectives.

1. The candy is sweet.
2. Those children are curious.
3. This room is the kitchen.
4. The dessert is rice pudding.
5. The three little baby foxes were playful.

B. Complete each of the following sentences by adding an adjective as a completer in each verb phrase.

1. The cat was —.
2. The night is —.
3. I am —.
4. My little sisters were —.
5. The new cars are —.

Written Make a sentence by adding a verb phrase to each noun phrase below. Use verb phrases that consist of the special verb *be* plus an adjective.

1. The books —.
2. Our classroom —.
3. The deer —.
4. My bedroom window —.
5. My kid brother —.
6. That jet plane —.
7. Her hair —.
8. The sound of the drums —.
9. The smell of breakfast —.
10. The taste of peanuts —.

151

6. *Be* Plus an Adverb

Study the word in color in each sentence below.

    1. The children played **outside**.
    2. The children played **quietly**.
    3. The children played **yesterday**.

- ▪ Which word in color answers the question, "How did the children play?"

- ▪ Which word in color answers the question, "When did the children play?"

- ▪ Which word in color answers the question, "Where did the children play?"

The words in color are called **adverbs.** Adverbs that tell *where* are called **adverbs of place.** Adverbs that tell *when* are called **adverbs of time.** Adverbs that tell *how* are called **adverbs of manner.** Look at sentences *1* to *3* again. Which sentence contains an adverb of place? Time? Manner?

Now try this. Test the adverbs above to see if any of them can be used as a completer after the special verb *be* in this sentence.

152
                They are —.

■ Which one of the adverbs can fill the space? Is it an adverb of time, an adverb of place, or an adverb of manner?

The special verb *be* must always have a completer after it. The completer may be an adverb. What is an adverb? What kind of adverb can be used as a completer after the special verb *be*?

For Discussion

A. Study the adverbs in each column below. Which column contains adverbs of place? Which column contains adverbs of time? Which column contains adverbs of manner?

1	2	3
angrily	soon	here
kindly	today	upstairs
sadly	now	indoors
noisily	later	out

B. Which group in part A contains adverbs of place that can be used as completers after the special verb *be*?

For Practice

For More Practice
See Page 385

Oral Each sentence below contains an adverb of place, an adverb of time, or an adverb of manner. Pick out each adverb and decide which kind it is.

1. The goldfish ate greedily.
2. The alarm clock rang early.
3. The stranger walked in.
4. The children slept late.
5. He will know the answer soon.

Written Write sentences of your own using each adverb of place below as a completer after a form of the special verb *be*. Try to use all five forms of *be*.

1. here	6. somewhere
2. there	7. inside
3. indoors	8. upstairs
4. outdoors	9. nearby
5. everywhere	10. out

153

7. *Be* Plus a Prepositional Phrase

All the sentences below contain a form of the special verb *be*. Compare the sentences in group A with those in group B.

A	**B**
Your dog is here.	Your dog is on the porch.
The creek was nearby.	The creek was near the house.
Some mice were upstairs.	Some mice were in the attic.

- What word is the completer in each sentence in group A? What kind of word is it?

- What word group is the completer in each sentence in group B?

The completer in each sentence in group B is a **prepositional phrase.** A prepositional phrase has two parts. The first part is a **preposition** like *on, near,* or *in.* What kind of word group comes after the preposition in each prepositional phrase?

Look again at the completers in the six example sentences.

- Is the completer in each sentence in group A an adverb of place, time, or manner?

- Are the prepositional phrases in group B used as adverbs of place, time, or manner?

The special verb *be* always has a completer after it. One kind of completer is a prepositional phrase. What is a prepositional phrase? When a prepositional phrase serves as a completer, is it used as a noun phrase, an adjective, or an adverb?

For Discussion

A. Study the verb phrase in the sentence below. What is the verb? What is the completer? Which word is a preposition? What kind of word group comes after the preposition?

154

The jets were above the clouds.

B. Study the completers in the sentences below. Tell whether the completer in each sentence is a noun phrase, an adjective, a single-word adverb, or a prepositional phrase used as an adverb. How can you tell?

1. The horses were inside.
2. The horses were race horses.
3. The horses were in the barn.
4. The horses were thirsty.

For Practice

For More Practice
See Page 385

Oral Each sentence below contains an adverb of place used as the completer. For each adverb substitute a prepositional phrase.

1. Your suitcase is there.
2. Mr. Oyama is out.
3. The water was everywhere.
4. Your portable radio is outside.
5. The railroad station was nearby.
6. My house is here.
7. Dr. Winton's office is upstairs.
8. The doctor is in.
9. A narrow bridge is ahead.
10. All the children are indoors.

Written Complete each of the following sentences. Use a prepositional phrase as a completer after the form of *be* in each sentence.

1. The pond is —.
2. Your lost coat was —.
3. The twins are —.
4. I am —.
5. The black cat was —.
6. The path is —.
7. Your friends are —.
8. Our reserved seats were —.
9. An urgent message is —.
10. The bear cubs were —.

155

8. For Review

Read and discuss the questions below.

A. What are clipped words? What are blends? Use the information in the chart below in explaining your answers.

Clipped Words	**Blends**
telephone → phone	broil + roast → broast
omnibus → bus	breakfast + lunch → brunch

B. How can you test a word to see if it is an adjective? Use these test sentences and the words in the box in your answer.

Test Sentences
1. This is very —.
2. This is — than that.
3. This is the — one of all.

large	hungry	lazy
study	joyous	room
roof	bright	sing

C. What are adverbs? What are the names of three different kinds? What are prepositional phrases? How are prepositional phrases like adverbs? Use these sentences in your answers.

Adverbs	**Prepositional Phrases**
We worked *indoors*.	We worked *in the house*.
We worked *quietly*.	We worked *with speed*.
We worked *yesterday*.	We worked *during the day*.

D. What examples can you add to the chart below? What do you need to know about each kind of completer in order to do so?

Completers Used after the Verb Be

Noun Phrases	Ann *is my sister*.	Those flowers *are roses*.
Adjectives	Uncle Ed *is amusing*.	The houses *are old*.
Adverbs	The school *is nearby*.	Al *is outdoors*.
Prep. Phrases	It *is on the table*.	Sue *is at the door*.

Read the directions for each exercise below. Follow the directions, writing your answers on your own paper.

A. Answer the following questions about the words in the box at the right.

photo	smog
vanilla	ankle
brunch	lab
sounds	motel
burger	house

   1. Which three words are clipped words?
   2. Which three words are blends?

B. Each sentence in the box below contains a verb phrase made with the special verb *be* plus a completer.

> **a.** The poplar tree *was tall.*
> **b.** The mail *is on the table.*
> **c.** That animal *is a wallaby.*
> **d.** Your friend *is outside.*

   3. In which sentence is the completer a noun phrase?
   4. In which sentence is the completer an adjective?
   5. In which sentence is the completer an adverb of place?
   6. In which sentence is the completer a prepositional phrase used as an adverb?

C. Write the following sentences. Complete each one with the kind of completer named in the parentheses.

   7. Frieda's father is —. (a noun phrase)
   8. The new school is —. (a prepositional phrase used as an adverb)
   9. That movie was —. (an adjective)
   10. The boys are —. (an adverb)

157

10. Talking about Reports

One day Mr. Burton began his science class by showing this cartoon. What point is the cartoonist making?

For the rest of the period the class talked about man and his relationship to the animal kingdom. The talk centered on one question, which Mr. Burton wrote on the board.

What harm is man doing to the animals that share the earth with him?

Then Mr. Burton made an assignment. The class would prepare reports to answer the question.

How often has one of your teachers assigned a report for you to write? Do you know how to start? Do you know how to proceed? Do you know how to complete the assignment?

Writing a report requires a great deal of thinking and planning. Once you have a general subject, there are four main steps you should follow. How many of the four steps take place *before* you begin to write the report itself?

1. Focusing the subject
2. Gathering information
3. Organizing your ideas
4. Writing your report

In the next few lessons you will work step by step to prepare a report of your own. The skills you learn you can apply to other reports you write.

For Discussion

Talk about some subjects in science that your class could write about in reports. The subjects should be broad and general, like the one Mr. Burton wrote on the board. You may want to talk about a subject that you have studied in your science class recently. Or you may want to talk about subjects like the following.

1. The solar system
2. Light
3. Weather
4. Sound
5. Mars

6. Space travel
7. Migration
8. Animal communication systems
9. Digestion
10. The atom

Activities

Decide on a general subject for your report. If you wish, use one of the ideas from For Discussion. Think about some things you might like to learn about in preparing your report.

Cratie Sandlin/Van Cleve Photography

11. Focusing the Subject

Look at the chart below. How is each topic related to the subject? How are all the topics different from the subject?

Subject: What harm is man doing to the animals that share the earth with him?

Topic: Why some animals become extinct
Topic: The story of the whooping crane
Topic: The story of the Carolina parrakeet
Topic: The story of the grizzly bear
Topic: The story of the bald eagle
Topic: Effects of pollution on fish in the Great Lakes
Topic: Effects of ocean oil slicks on birds and fish

The subject above is too broad to handle in a single report. Once you have a general subject like this you need to focus it. This means you need to find a **topic.** The topic should be narrow enough and limited enough to handle in a report of two or three pages.

One way to focus a general subject is to list as many topics related to the subject as you can think of. Read over the list of topics. Then choose the topic that you find most interesting.

Look at the chart again. Are all the topics limited enough for a report of two or three pages? Which topic would you like to write about?

For Discussion

Suppose the general subject you chose for your report is weather. Which list below contains topics that are still too broad for a report of two or three pages? Which list contains suitable topics? Why are they suitable? What other topics can you think of that would be suitable?

1	2
Climates of the world	Ways of controlling weather
Weather forecasting	Early methods of forecasting weather
The seasons	Hurricanes
Kinds of weather	The uses of weather satellites

Activities

Choose a suitable topic for the science report you will write by following these directions.

1. Think about the general subject you chose for your report. Make a list of five topics that would be suitable for a report of two or three pages.

2. Read over your list of topics. Decide which topic you find most interesting. That can be the topic for your report.

3. Think about some of the things you might like to learn about the topic you chose.

12. Gathering Information

Once you have decided on a topic for a report, you are ready to gather information. Gathering information for a report includes the three steps shown on the chart below. Look at the chart. Then answer the questions at the top of the next page.

1. Find Possible Sources of Information

Books:
   Green, Ivah, *Wildlife in Danger*
   McClung, Robert M., *Lost Wild America*
Magazines:
   Hancock, David, "Can We Save the Eagles?" *Nature and Science*, March 18, 1968
   Ott, George, "Is the Bald Eagle Doomed?" *National Wildlife*, April-May 1970
Encyclopedia:
   World Book Encyclopedia, "Eagle," Vol. 6

2. Question the Topic

Topic: The story of the bald eagle

Questions to Explore:
   1. Why is the bald eagle important?
   2. Why may the bald eagle become extinct?
   3. What is being done about saving it?

3. Read and Take Notes

At one time bald eagle inhabited most of N. America

Harmful poisons (especially DDT)
   Get into eagles' water supply
   Interfere with bearing young

- What is the first step to take in gathering information for a report? Where can you find sources of information?

- What is the second step to take in gathering information for a report? How will the "Questions to Explore" serve as a guide when you read and take notes?

- What is the third step in gathering information for a report?

For Discussion

Answer these questions about the three steps you should take in gathering information for a report.

1. How will you locate sources of information for your report? What are three kinds of sources to look for? Why is it a good idea to make a list of the sources you find?

2. Why is it a good idea to write some "Questions to Explore" before you read and take notes? What questions about your topic do you want to explore?

3. Why should you keep referring to your list of "Questions to Explore" as you read and take notes?

Activities

Follow these steps to gather information for your report.

1. Locate four or five sources that contain information about your topic. If possible, find both books and magazine articles. Do not use more than two encyclopedias. Make a list of the sources you find.

2. Make a list of three or four questions about your topic that you want to explore.

3. Read the information and take notes. Be sure your notes help you answer the questions you listed.

13. Organizing Your Ideas

When you finish gathering information for a report, you will have a set of questions and a set of notes like these.

Topic: The story of the bald eagle
Questions to Explore:
1. Why is the bald eagle important?
2. Why may the bald eagle become extinct?
3. What is being done about saving it?

At one time bald eagle inhabited most of N. America

1782—became national symbol
Appears on Great Seal, dollar bills, coins, stamps, documents

Harmful poisons (especially DDT)
Get into eagles' water supply
Interfere with bearing young

Homelands destroyed by man

Nests protected in National Wildlife Refuges

Number of eagles
May be no more than 3500 left in U.S., not counting Alaska

The next step in preparing a report is to organize your ideas by making an outline. To do this, you will need both your questions and your notes. Read the outline below. Then answer the questions that follow.

Outline

I. Importance of the bald eagle to man
  A. Appreciation of strength and beauty
  B. National emblem of the United States
II. Reasons the bald eagle could become extinct
  A. Decrease in numbers
  B. Advancing civilization
  C. Hunting
  D. Poisons in waters
III. Steps being taken to prevent extinction
  A. Laws
  B. Wildlife refuges
  C. Banning of pesticides

- How do the "Questions to Explore" help to provide the main topics for the outline?
- How are the subtopics in the outline related to the main topics?
- How do the notes help to provide the subtopics?
- What parts of the outline are labeled with Roman numerals? What parts are labeled with capital letters?

Photo
Research
International

For Discussion

Writing a real report is not always as neat a process as it sounds in a textbook like this one. At any time, you may have to change your direction because something won't work. Think about whether this has been true in preparing your science report.

1. Did you have to change your topic at any point? For example, you might have found that there wasn't enough material available on your original topic. Or your reading might have caused you to find a different focus.

2. Were your original questions exactly the same as the ones you finally decided to answer in your report? Why or why not?

3. Why can you make a better outline on your topic now than you could have when you began?

4. Do you think you might still make changes in your outline while you are writing the report itself? Why or why not?

Activities

Use your questions and notes to prepare an outline for your science report. Let the outline in this lesson serve as a model.

14. Writing Your Report

Read the following report carefully. Compare it with the outline in Lesson 13.

Saving the Bald Eagle

Men have always admired the strength and beauty of the eagle. One kind of eagle, the bald eagle, is native only to North America. In 1782 this noble bird became the national symbol of the United States. He is seen on the Great Seal, on dollar bills, and on coins, stamps, and documents. But most Americans do not see him in the skies. Today he can be found in great numbers only in Florida and Alaska. In fact, unless something is done, the bald eagle may soon be extinct.

At one time there were hundreds of thousands of bald eagles. They flew over most of North America. Now there may be only 3500 to 5000 bald eagles left in the United States, not counting Alaska. What has happened?

The eagle's main problem has been the advance of civilization. Like many other wild creatures, eagles need trees for nesting and shelter. They need other animals for food and pure streams for drinking water. As men settle in a new land, they cannot avoid disturbing the animals. But men have also needlessly hunted and killed many thousands of eagles. Sometimes men have even stolen the eagles' eggs and their young.

Poisons such as DDT are another threat to the bald eagle. These poisons are used to kill insects and other small pests. Eventually they get into the streams that supply water to the eagles. The poisons interfere with the eagles' bearing of young.

William Garst/Tom Stack and Associates

Today eagles are protected from hunters by strict laws. Bald eagles now nest in National Wildlife Refuges. Private conservation groups, such as the National Audubon Society, also shelter and protect them. Some states are banning the use of DDT and other pesticides.

But the bald eagle is still in danger. More Americans need to learn about his problems. Men must provide places where the eagle can live free of danger. Once an animal has become extinct, man can never bring it back. We must give our national bird a chance for survival.

Sources

Green, Ivah, Wildlife in Danger
Hancock, David, "Can We Save the Eagles?" Nature and Science, March 18, 1968
McClung, Robert M., Lost Wild America
Ott, George, "Is the Bald Eagle Doomed?" National Wildlife, April-May 1970
World Book Encyclopedia, "Eagle," Vol. 6

See whether you can match each paragraph of the report with a topic or topics in the outline on page 165. Then answer these questions.

- Do you think the report includes all the information from the notes? Why or why not?

- What information is included in the list of sources?

For Discussion

Before your class completes the science reports, decide who will read them. Perhaps you could make a display of the reports for parents' night. Or you could make a class science magazine, including illustrations, to display in the classroom or school library. What other ideas can you think of?

Activities

A. Complete your science report by following these directions.

1. Use your notes and your outline to write your report. Prepare a rough first copy and a neat final copy.
2. Give your report a title.
3. List your sources at the end of your report.
4. If you wish, include one or more pictures or other illustrations in your report.

B. With your teacher's help, decide whether to present your report orally as well as in writing. Here is what you should do to get ready to present your report orally.

1. Think of visual aids that you might use. These can include pictures, maps, charts, diagrams, objects related to your topic, or experiments performed in front of the class.
2. Practice presenting your report from your outline. Do not read your written report to the class.

15. Listening to Poetry

Listen as your teacher reads the poem "Thunder Dragon" to you.

For Discussion

A. What is really happening at the beginning of the poem? What is really happening at the end of the poem? Read the lines that tell you.

B. Some words, such as *buzz, murmur,* and *splash,* have sounds that suggest their meanings. What words in "Thunder Dragon" are like this? Why do you think Harry Behn used several of these words?

C. Most of the lines in "Thunder Dragon" describe sounds. What lines can you pick out that describe sights?

D. The words *baleful* and *roiled* may be new to you. *Baleful* means "evil and harmful." *Roiled* means "made muddy by stirring up sediment." Were you able to make a good guess about either meaning by noticing the way the word was used in the poem? Explain.

Activities

A. Practice reading "Thunder Dragon" aloud. Let the punctuation tell you what to do with your voice.

B. Suppose you were writing a poem about fire, rain, a stream, a motorcycle, an ice skater, a busy street corner, or a city at night. Choose one of these subjects or one of your choice and list some words you might use to describe sounds. If you wish, write a few lines of free verse using some of the words you listed.

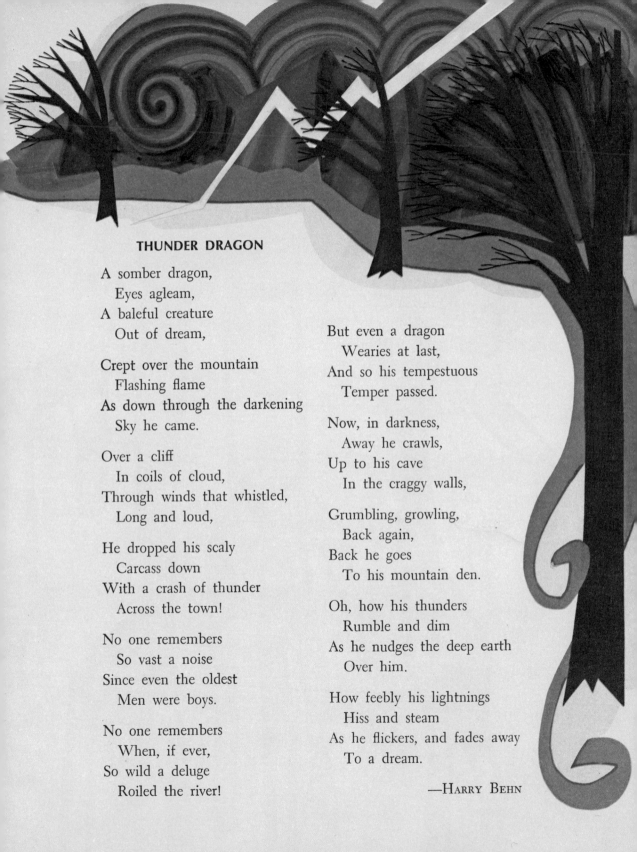

THUNDER DRAGON

A somber dragon,
  Eyes agleam,
A baleful creature
  Out of dream,

Crept over the mountain
  Flashing flame
As down through the darkening
  Sky he came.

Over a cliff
  In coils of cloud,
Through winds that whistled,
  Long and loud,

He dropped his scaly
  Carcass down
With a crash of thunder
  Across the town!

No one remembers
  So vast a noise
Since even the oldest
  Men were boys.

No one remembers
  When, if ever,
So wild a deluge
  Roiled the river!

But even a dragon
  Wearies at last,
And so his tempestuous
  Temper passed.

Now, in darkness,
  Away he crawls,
Up to his cave
  In the craggy walls,

Grumbling, growling,
  Back again,
Back he goes
  To his mountain den.

Oh, how his thunders
  Rumble and dim
As he nudges the deep earth
  Over him.

How feebly his lightnings
  Hiss and steam
As he flickers, and fades away
  To a dream.

—HARRY BEHN

CHAPTER 6

1. Changes in Word Meanings

Suppose you wanted to put a label under the picture at the top of this page. Which of these labels would you choose?

DEER   ANIMALS

A thousand years ago you could have used the word *deer* to label this picture. At that time the word *deer* referred to any animal. Over the years the meaning of *deer* changed. The word came to be used to name only one kind of animal.

Now decide which of the following labels you would put under the picture at the right.

BOY   KNIGHT

A thousand years ago you could have used the word *knight* to label this picture. At that time the word *knight* meant simply "a boy" or "a servant boy."

Some English words have different meanings today than they once had. Changes in word meanings are usually gradual. But as you have discovered, the later meaning of a word may be very different from its earlier meaning. Compare the earlier meanings of *deer* and *knight* with today's meanings.

- How is the present-day meaning of each word similar to the earlier meaning?

- How is the present-day meaning different from the earlier meaning?

For Discussion

For each word below, an earlier meaning is given. What is the meaning of each word today? Which words have meanings that seem very far from their earlier meanings? Which words have meanings that seem close to their earlier meanings?

1. *silly:* happy or blessed
2. *fond:* foolish
3. *meat:* food
4. *slay:* strike or beat
5. *angel:* messenger
6. *gossip:* a friend or comrade
7. *pretty:* crafty or sly
8. *mansion:* any dwelling place or abode
9. *counterfeiter:* anyone who imitates

ON YOUR OWN

Below are some words that refer to people. These words have different meanings today than they once had. In a large dictionary look up the etymology for each word. What do the etymologies tell you about how the meanings of these words have changed?

1. queen
2. villain
3. girl
4. clown

2. Compound Words

Study the words printed in color in the following list.

air + craft → aircraft

fare + well → farewell

over + coat → overcoat

black + berry → blackberry

apple + sauce → applesauce

The words in color are called **compound words**, or **compounds**.

- How was each compound word formed?

Here are some compounds made with the word *sun*. Answer the questions below to see how compounds are written.

sunbath	sunfast	sun parlor
sunbonnet	sunfish	sun porch
sunburn	sunflower	sunrise
sun deck	sunglasses	sunset
sundial	sun-god	sunshine
sundown	sunlight	sunup

- Which of the compounds above are written as single words?
- Which compound is written with a hyphen?
- Which compounds are written as two words?

You have seen that many compounds, but not all, are written as single words. Sometimes you may forget how to write a particular compound. If so, use your dictionary.

Creating compound words has always been a common way of adding new words to the English language. What is a compound word? What are three ways of writing compounds?

spaceflight   spacecraft   launching pad   countdown

blast-off   lift-off   space walk   moon walk   splashdown

For Discussion

In telling the story of a spaceflight, you would use a number of compound words, including the ones below the pictures. Many other new compounds have entered the language in the twentieth century as a result of modern science and technology. Some examples are *wiretap, tape recorder, fallout,* and *drip-dry.* What other examples can you think of?

For Practice

Oral A. Say each sentence below, substituting a compound word for the group of words in italics.

1. The whole city felt the *shaking of the earth.*
2. That boat belongs to an old *man who fishes.*
3. We found our way home by *the light of the moon.*
4. *Drops of rain* were falling.
5. Rex has a bad *pain in his tooth.*
6. The thieves waited for *the coming of night.*

B. Add a word in each space to make a colorful compound that means the same thing as the phrase.

1. To get a free automobile ride: hitch—
2. A person who drops rubbish in a public place: litter—
3. A person who is hard or grasping in money matters: skin—
4. A turned-up tuft of hair, usually at the forehead: cow—

5. An object designed to scare away birds that might destroy crops: scare—
6. A narrow passageway or street that hinders the progress of traffic: bottle—
7. A turned-down corner of a leaf in a book: dog—
8. A short doze: cat—
9. A leaping, plant-eating insect: grass—
10. A very tall building: sky—

Written The compound words listed below have been written as two separate words. Look up these compounds in your dictionary to find out how they should be written. Then write them on your paper.

1. milk man	7. dining room
2. garbage man	8. book store
3. work man	9. candy store
4. side walk	10. shut in
5. side street	11. build up
6. bed room	12. hang out

ON YOUR OWN

Americans have added many colorful compounds to the English language. Here are a few of them. Look up any unfamiliar ones in your dictionary. Listen for other compounds that create colorful and interesting word pictures. If you wish, make a list of some to share with the class.

1. cloud burst	6. crazy quilt
2. prairie schooner	7. eelgrass
3. bellhop	8. hot dog
4. cowcatcher	9. cowpuncher
5. beeline	10. monkey business

178

3. Acronyms

The sentences below have the same meaning. Which sentence contains a word that is a shortened name for something?

1. Carl wore a self-contained underwater breathing apparatus.
2. Carl was wearing scuba equipment.

The word *scuba* is an **acronym.** An acronym is a word that is formed by combining the first one or two letters of other words. What letters from the full name were used to form the acronym *scuba*?

Now compare the three acronyms below with the full names that they stand for. How were these acronyms formed?

NATO: North Atlantic Treaty Organization

CARE: Co-operative for American Remittances to Everywhere

laser: light amplification by stimulated emission of radiation

For Discussion

Occasionally some letters are added to initials to form an acronym. Two familiar examples are *veep* and *emcee*. What do these acronyms mean? How were they formed?

For Practice

Oral   What familiar acronym was made from each of these?

1. Zone Improvement Plan (Code)
2. absent without leave
3. Women's Army Corps
4. National Aeronautics and Space Administration
5. sound navigation ranging
6. United Nations Educational, Scientific, and Cultural Organization
7. Southeast Asia Treaty Organization
8. Congress of Racial Equality
9. radio detecting and ranging

179

4. The Auxiliary *Have*

The verb in each sentence below is in color. Compare the verb phrases in A with those in B to see how they differ.

A	B
I **drive** to school.	I have **driven** to school.
They **write** every day.	They have **written** every day.
The ducks **eat** grain.	The ducks have **eaten** grain.

- What is the verb in each verb phrase in A?
- What word comes before the verb in each verb phrase in B?
- What ending does each verb in B have?

When *have* comes before the verb in a verb phrase, it is called the **auxiliary *have*.** The form of the verb that always follows the auxiliary *have* is called the **en form.** Look back at the verbs in the sentences above. What are the *en* forms of *drive, write,* and *eat*?

Now compare the verb phrases in the next two groups of sentences. Notice that a verb like *drive* has present and past tense forms when it comes first in the verb phrase. Try to discover whether the auxiliary *have* has present and past tense forms when it comes first.

C	D
We **drive** to school.	We **have** driven to school.
He **drives** to school.	He **has** driven to school.
We **drove** to school.	We **had** driven to school.
He **drove** to school.	He **had** driven to school.

- Which verb phrases in C contain present tense forms of *drive*? Which contain past tense forms?
- Which verb phrases in D contain present tense forms of the auxiliary *have*? Which contain past tense forms?

A verb phrase may contain a form of the auxiliary *have* before the verb. If a verb has no auxiliary, the verb shows the tense. If the auxiliary *have* comes before the verb, the auxiliary shows the tense. What are the present tense forms of the auxiliary *have*? What is the past tense form? What form of a verb always follows the auxiliary *have*?

For Discussion

In the sentences below, what part of the verb phrase shows present or past tense? Is it the verb, or is it the auxiliary *have*? How can you tell?

1. The pond has frozen early this year.
2. The pond had frozen early that year.

For Practice

For More Practice
See Page 385

Oral Complete each example below in two ways. First use a present tense form of the auxiliary *have* with the verb in parentheses. Then use the past tense form of the auxiliary *have* with the verb in parentheses. Be sure to make the necessary change in the form of the verb.

1. Clouds (hide) the sun.
2. A bear (shake) the tent.
3. Jane (eat) the coconut.
4. I (forget) the story.
5. Someone (steal) our new picnic basket.
6. The sun (rise) at seven.
7. The dog never (bite) anyone.
8. Tom's injured finger (swell).
9. Our window (break) during the storm.

Written **A.** Rewrite each sentence. To each verb phrase add a form of the auxiliary *have* in the present tense. Make any other changes that are needed.

1. Andy chooses pie for dessert.
2. The children ride the pony.
3. Jess forsakes his friends.
4. The actors speak clearly.
5. Peter takes his dog with him.

B. Rewrite each sentence. To each verb phrase add the past tense form of the auxiliary *have*. Make any other changes that are needed.

1. The water froze in the glass.
2. A rabbit hid under the porch.
3. The speaker rose from his chair.
4. Snow fell all night.
5. Our team beat its opponents.

181

5. More about the *en* Form

Notice the spelling of the *en* form of the verb in each sentence below. How do you think the *en* form got its name?

> The water has risen.
>
> Jim had forgotten his lunch.
>
> I have eaten breakfast.

Not all *en* forms end with the letters *–en*, however. Try this. Find the *en* form of each verb in parentheses by deciding which form is needed to complete each sentence.

A

The hikers have (climb) the hill.

George has (study) history.

The audience had (applaud) wildly.

B

The boys had (sleep) in a tent.

The steak has (burn) to a crisp.

The trees have (bend) under the snow.

C

Mr. Kuska had (teach) the sixth grade.

Sam has (catch) the last bus.

The Rosens have (buy) a new car.

D

Karen has (do) her work.

The bell had (ring).

The visitors have (go) home.

- Do any of the *en* forms you used end in *–en?*
- What other verbs can you think of that have *en* forms like those you used in each group above?

As you have discovered, the auxiliary *have* determines that an *en* form will follow. Does the term *en form* refer to the way the verb is spelled, or is it simply the name of a verb form?

For Discussion

Which *en* form below shows how the form got its name? Does the other *en* form follow the same pattern as many other verbs in English? Explain.

1. The mouse has crawled into its hole.
2. The girls have taken the bus home.

For Practice

For More Practice
See Page 386

Oral Read each of the following sentences, using the *en* form of the verb in parentheses.

1. The fox had (jump) the fence.
2. That rabbit had (scurry) away.
3. The boys have (leave) the country for Europe.
4. Arlan had (make) a tree house.
5. Sara has (stand) on her head.
6. The hunters had (wear) coats.
7. The knight had (slay) the dragon.
8. Carla has (sing) on television.
9. The boys have (go) to the circus in town.
10. The boat had (spring) a leak.

Written Write each of the following sentences, using the *en* form of the verb in parentheses.

1. The puppies have (learn) some new tricks.
2. The rain had (put) out the fire.
3. Rodney has (drink) the cider.
4. I have (swim) across the river.
5. My sister has (go) to kindergarten all year.
6. A wren has (sit) on the wire.
7. Al had (tear) his sleeve.
8. We have (see) the parade.
9. The water has (shrink) my hat.
10. Everyone had (do) his best.

183

6. The Auxiliary *Be*

The verb in each sentence below is in color. Compare the verb phrases in A with those in B.

A	**B**
I work every day.	I am working every day.
Ruby works every day.	Ruby is working every day.
They work every day.	They are working every day.
Stanley worked yesterday.	Stanley was working yesterday.
The men worked yesterday.	The men were working yesterday.

- What is the verb in each verb phrase in A?

- What words come before the verb in the verb phrases in B?

- What ending does each verb in B have?

Am, is, are, was, and *were* are all forms of *be*. *Am, is,* and *are* are present tense forms. *Was* and *were* are past tense forms.

When *be* comes before a verb, it is called the **auxiliary *be*.** When *be* is the first word in the verb phrase, it shows tense, either present or past. The form of *work* that follows *be* in each sentence is called the ***ing* form.**

Think about what you have learned about the auxiliary *be*. What are its present tense forms? What are its past tense forms? What verb form follows this auxiliary?

For Discussion

Which sentence below contains a present tense form of the auxiliary *be*? Which contains a past tense form? How can you tell? What verb form follows the auxiliary *be* in each sentence?

1. Someone is knocking at our door.
2. Someone was knocking at our door.

For Practice

For More Practice
See Page 386

Oral Complete each example below in two ways. First use a present tense form of the auxiliary *be* with the verb in parentheses. Then use a past tense form of *be* with the verb in parentheses. Be sure to make the necessary change in the form of the verb.

1. The spider (spin) its web.
2. I (keep) a diary.
3. You (learn) something new.
4. We (make) ice cream.
5. They (walk) on thin ice.
6. He (head) for the moon.
7. Those dogs (bark) loudly.
8. I (wear) your sweater.
9. The altos (sing) off key.
10. The scouts (climb) Pikes Peak.

Written A. Rewrite the sentences below. To each verb phrase add a form of the auxiliary *be* in the present tense. Make any other changes that are needed.

1. I collect foreign stamps.
2. He tells the truth.
3. The geese fly south.
4. Those planes land in Iceland.
5. Silas hides his money.

B. Rewrite the sentences below. To each verb phrase add a form of the auxiliary *be* in the past tense. Make any other changes that are needed.

1. Some wolves searched for food.
2. I bought a microscope.
3. A wren rested on the ledge.
4. It rained last night.
5. We hid the prizes.

185

7. Verb Phrases with *Have* and *Be*

Parts of the verb phrases in the following sentences are in color. Compare the sentences. See if you can tell how the auxiliaries *have* and *be* can be used together in a verb phrase. Then answer the questions that follow.

Mr. Santo **has** painted many pictures.
Mr. Santo **is** painting now.
Mr. Santo **has been** painting all day.

- What word follows *has* in the first sentence? What form does it take?

- What word follows *is* in the second sentence? What form does it take?

- What two words are auxiliaries in the third sentence?

- What form does *be* take when it follows *have*? Why?

- What form does *paint* take in the third sentence? Why?

Now look at this pair of sentences.

Mr. Santo has been painting all day.
Mr. Santo had been painting yesterday.

- Which word in the verb phrase changes form to show past or present tense?

- Do any of the other words in the verb phrase change to show tense?

186

The auxiliaries *have* and *be* can both appear as part of the same verb phrase. When they do, which always comes first? Which word in the verb phrase shows the tense? Which word determines the form of the auxiliary *be?* Which word determines the form of the verb?

For Discussion

Complete the sentence below by changing the form of each word in parentheses. What form does *be* take when it follows the auxiliary *have?* What form does the verb take when it follows the auxiliary *be?*

Geraldine has (be) (read).

For Practice

Oral   Read each of the following sentences, providing the verb phrase described in parentheses.

1. Paula (past form of *have* + *en* form of *be* + *ing* form of *talk*).
2. That car (present form of *have* + *en* form of *win*).
3. We (present form of *be* + *ing* form of *joke*).
4. Lonnie (present form of *have* + *en* form of *be* + *ing* form of *run*).

Written   A. Make sentences from the following word groups by using forms of the words in parentheses. Make your sentences in the present tense.

1. Paula (have) (be) (make) a Halloween costume for the party.
2. I (have) (be) (try) to reach you by telephone.

For More Practice
See Page 386

3. Howard (have) (be) (wear) glasses for a year.
4. The students (have) (be) (plan) a picnic.
5. My brother (have) (be) (look) for his lost dog.

B. Make sentences from the word groups below by using forms of the words in parentheses. Make your sentences in the past tense.

1. Frank (have) (be) (rake) leaves all morning.
2. Mr. Labecki (have) (be) (wait) for an hour.
3. The actors (have) (be) (get) ready for their performance.
4. The girls (have) (be) (practice) their duet.
5. I (have) (be) (study) for a science test.

8. Writing Direct Quotations

The following sentences show different ways of writing what someone said. Which sentences tell someone's exact words?

A

1. Agnes asked what the cat's name was.
2. Agnes asked, "What is the cat's name?"
3. "What is the cat's name?" Agnes asked.

B

4. Joe said that her name was Sybil.
5. Joe said, "Her name is Sybil."
6. "Her name is Sybil," said Joe.
7. "Her name," said Joe, "is Sybil."

Sentences that tell the speaker's exact words contain **direct quotations.** Answer the questions below to discover how to write direct quotations.

- In each sentence containing a direct quotation, what part of the sentence is enclosed in quotation marks?

- Where are commas used in the sentences that contain a direct quotation?

- Does other punctuation, such as a question mark, come before the quotation marks or after them?

- Where are capital letters used in writing quotations?

188

- In number 7 why is *Her* capitalized but not *is?*

What punctuation marks would you use in writing each of these sentences? Where would you add a capital letter? Why?

1. There will be a blizzard today said Arthur
2. Marjorie asked will school be dismissed early
3. Yes, if a blizzard comes said the teacher we will go home early today

For
Practice

For More Practice
See Page 387

Written **A.** Write the following sentences on your paper. Add quotation marks wherever they are needed.

1. The farmer said, I will catch the red fox.
2. I will catch the red fox, said the farmer.
3. Will you catch the red fox? asked the farmer.
4. Do you think, asked the farmer, that you can catch the red fox?

B. Write the following sentences. Use capital letters and punctuation marks wherever they are needed.

1. Angelo said I forgot to bring my baseball mitt
2. Someone suggested let's buy a watermelon
3. Did you eat the peaches asked Mother I was saving them for lunch
4. I have to paint the fence said Rudolph before I can go fishing

189

9. Writing Dialogue

Most of the fable below is a conversation, or **dialogue.** Study the fable to find out how a dialogue should be written.

The Ant and the Grasshopper

One cold day in late autumn an ant was busily storing some kernels of wheat that he had gathered during the summer. A grasshopper, weak with hunger, came by. Noticing what the ant was doing, the grasshopper said, "Please, will you give me a morsel to save my life?"

"What were you doing all summer while I was busy harvesting this wheat?" asked the ant.

"Oh, I wasn't idle," replied the grasshopper. "All day long I sang and chirped and hopped about the meadow."

As the ant locked his granary door, he answered, "Since you sang all summer, I'm afraid you'll have to dance all winter."

■ Does the dialogue between the ant and the grasshopper consist of direct quotations?

■ How many paragraphs does the fable contain? When did the writer begin each new paragraph?

For Discussion

Suppose the fable you read included the following dialogue between the ant and the grasshopper. How many direct quotations does the dialogue contain? Where should each new paragraph begin? Why?

The grasshopper said, "Unless I have some food, I may perish from hunger." "All last summer you played and sang while I worked to prepare for winter," replied the ant. "But think about my family," the grasshopper begged. "Would you let them starve?" As the ant walked away, he said, "I too have a family. Goodbye, my friend."

For Practice

Written Rewrite the fable "The Cat and the Fox." Use as many direct quotations as possible. Begin a new paragraph each time there is a different speaker.

For More Practice
See Page 387

The Cat and the Fox

A fox once boasted to a cat about how clever he was. The fox said that he had at least a hundred ways of escaping from his enemies, the dogs. The cat replied that she had only one trick. She asked the fox to teach her some of his. The fox said that someday he would when he had nothing better to do.

Just then they heard the yelping of dogs. The cat scrambled up into a tree. She called down to the fox that this was the trick she had told him about. She said it was her only one. Then she asked the fox which trick he was going to use.

Before the fox could decide, the dogs were upon him, and that was the end of the fox.

191

Read and discuss the questions below.

A. What are compound words? What are acronyms? Use the examples below in explaining your answers.

Compound Words	Acronyms
sundial	radar
sun-god	sonar
sun porch	AWOL

B. Refer to the sentences in the box in answering the questions below.

a	b	c	d
Al *runs*.	Al *has run*.	Al *is running*.	Al *has been running*.
Al *ran*.	Al *had run*.	Al *was running*.	Al *had been running*.

1. What word in a verb phrase shows the tense when the verb phrase has no auxiliary?
2. What word shows the tense when the verb phrase begins with the auxiliary *have*? What is the name of the verb form that follows *have*?
3. What word shows the tense when the verb phrase begins with the auxiliary *be*? What is the name of the verb form that follows *be*?
4. What word shows the tense when a verb phrase contains *have* + *be*? What form of *be* follows the auxiliary *have*?

C. Where would you use quotation marks in writing each sentence below? Why? What other punctuation marks would you use?

1. Edward asked What happened after I left
2. What happened after I left asked Edward
3. What happened Edward asked after I left

Read the directions for each exercise below. Follow the directions, writing your answers on your own paper.

A. Write the word or words in the box that are examples of the terms listed below.

1. compound word
2. acronym
3. *ing* form of a verb
4. *en* form of a verb
5. present tense form of an auxiliary
6. past tense form of an auxiliary

raincoat	waiting
gone	are
written	drip-dry
has	walking
CARE	was

B. Complete the sentences below. Supply the verb phrases described in parentheses.

7. All the boys (past tense form of *have* + *en* form of *eat*).
8. Sara (past tense form of *be* + *ing* form of *read*).
9. Ronald (present tense form of *have* + *en* form of *be* + *ing* form of *try*).

C. Make sentences from the word groups below by using forms of the words in parentheses. Make your sentences in the past tense.

10. Mrs. Santo (have) (bake) some cookies.
11. Karen (be) (practice) her piano lesson.
12. It (have) (be) (rain) hard for four hours.

D. Each sentence below contains a direct quotation. Write the sentences. Use quotation marks and other marks of punctuation where they are needed.

13. I found your ticket said Terry
14. Al asked Whose book is this
15. Do you think asked Joe that we will be late

193

12. Talking about Stories

Read the following story.

A Cat Called Blackie

It was my brother's birthday party. He was twelve. I was only nine. He invited a lot of boys I did not know.

We were in the middle of a game when someone shouted out, "He's a bit young, isn't he?"

I looked towards where he was pointing; then I gasped in horror: he was pointing at me!

"Yes," shouted another, "let's get rid of him." He gave me a sharp poke in the side; my brother tried to stop him, but to no avail. Before anyone could do a thing to stop him, he had thrown me into the hall.

I walked past the sitting room into the dining room. Blackie was on the most comfortable chair as usual. I looked at him. I fell into tears. I walked forward cautiously, so as not to wake him; but he lifted up his head as if he sensed me; then dropped it again and purred. I fell beside him. As I put my head against his, I could not stop the attack of sobs that followed.

I stroked his head. He purred again. I tried to wipe the tears out of my eyes; but I could not.

I rested my head against his black furry stomach. He twitched his ears. The steady thump of his tail calmed me.

I looked at the wet on his side. The steady rhythm of his heartbeat ticked in my ears. But suddenly I could not look at him, as I remembered those boys, and how they would laugh if they saw me and my cat.

—RICHARD IRON

Richard Iron, who lives in England, wrote this story when he was about your age.

- What did Richard tell about in the first paragraph? Does this make a good beginning? Why?

- In the last sentence, what did Richard say he remembered? Does this make a good ending? Why?

A young writer sometimes thinks he has nothing to write about because nothing exciting ever happens to him. Have you ever thought this? Is Richard's story about an exciting and unusual event, or is it about a commonplace experience? Do you think everyone has the kind of experiences that make good stories?

For Discussion

A. Can you remember a time when some older children wouldn't let you play with them? Do you think this experience is one that most children have at some time?

B. Richard's story tells only one thing that happened at his brother's party. Why didn't he tell about other things, such as the food and the gifts?

13. Writing a Story

Read the story below. It was written by a boy about your age. How does the writer make his story interesting?

My Dog Pal

A friend and I were playing "Monopoly" on the floor when my dog Pal came running in. She was coming full speed and slid on the rug right into the "Monopoly" game, like a baseball player when he's sliding home. The money went flying like advertisements when the pilot drops them from an airplane.

She looked rather ridiculous, her front paws spread out straight and her back paws bent under her. She looked surprised and so did we. Her big brown eyes shone. Her ears were flopping and her tail was wagging. After her sudden stop, she just stood there and looked at us with a cocked head. Then she tried to swallow one of the dice.

It took half an hour to clean up the mess and all Pal did was to lie on the rug and grin at us as if it were a joke.

Suppose you wanted to write a story about something that happened to you. For some ideas of how to go about it, take a close look at the story "My Dog Pal."

- Where did the writer find something to write about?

- Look at the first and last sentences. Do you think the writer began and ended his story at the right places? Explain your answer.

- What are some details that make the story real and interesting?

For Discussion

Here are some story beginnings. If you were writing each story, how could you continue it? How could you end it?

1

One time at camp we scouts took a midnight walk. One of the leaders stopped along the trail to look at a strange plant. When I got to the plant, I stopped to look, too. By this time the rest of the troop had started away, but I didn't notice. When I finally looked up, I discovered that the others were gone.

2

I could hardly believe the words of the tall, grave police officer. "A dog has been run over and killed. I'm pretty sure it's yours."

3

On the first day of March a blizzard dumped two feet of snow on the city. Eric and I stood at the window and looked out. We were wondering how we could spend an entire day indoors.

I lay in bed that morning and knew I didn't want to get up. Then I remembered why. Today was moving day. Our family was leaving town to live in another state a thousand miles away.

Activities

A. Story ideas come in different ways. Use one of the following to find an idea for a story about something that happened to you.

1. The writer of "A Cat Called Blackie" felt hurt and unhappy. The writer of "My Dog Pal" was amused. You have had experiences that made you feel a certain way—happy, proud, embarrassed, disappointed, or afraid. Think of an experience that you remember well because it made you feel a strong emotion.

2. Sometimes a title may remind you of an experience you had. Could you write a story to fit one of these titles?

   Welcome Home   An Unusual Friendship

   Was It a Ghost?   Strike Three

   Late Again   The Trouble with Grown-ups

B. Write a story based on an idea you thought of for part A.

C. If you wish, draw or paint a picture to illustrate your story.

D. Begin a class storybook. Each member of your class should put at least one story into the book. A good idea is to make a blank book with an attractive cover and large sheets of paper. Prepare a neat final copy of your story. Then paste it into the book.

14. Writing from an Unusual Point of View

The paragraphs below are reprinted from the book *Ben and Me*. Read the words that appear on the cover of the book to learn the identity of the main characters.

Now read from Chapter 1, in which Amos, cold and hungry, came in and found food and then spent his first night with Ben.

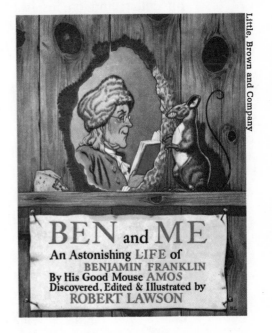

Little, Brown and Company

BEN and ME
An Astonishing LIFE of
BENJAMIN FRANKLIN
By His Good Mouse AMOS
Discovered, Edited & Illustrated by
ROBERT LAWSON

Upstairs were two rooms. One was dark, and from it came the sound of snoring; the other had a light, and the sound of sneezing. I chose the sneezy one.

In a large chair close to the fireplace sat a short, thick, round-faced man, trying to write by the light of a candle. Every few moments he would sneeze, and his square-rimmed glasses would fly off. Reaching for these he would drop his pen; by the time he found that and got settled to write, the candle would flicker from the draught; when that calmed down, the sneezing would start again, and so it went. He was not accomplishing much in the way of writing.

Of course I recognized him. Everyone in Philadelphia knew the great Doctor Benjamin. Franklin, scientist, inventor, printer, editor, author, soldier, statesman and philosopher.

He didn't look great or famous that night, though, he just looked cold—and a bit silly.

He was wrapped in a sort of dressing-gown, with a dirty fur collar; and on his head was perched an odd-looking fur cap.

The cap interested me, for I was still chilled to the bone—and this room was just as bleak as the rest of the house. It was a rather disreputable-looking affair, that cap; but in one side of it I spied a hole—just about my size.

Up the back of the chair I went, and under cover of the next fit of sneezes, in I slid. What a cozy place *that* was! Plenty of room to move about a bit; just enough air; such soft fur, and such warmth!

"Here," said I to myself, "is my home. No more cold streets, or cellars, or vestries. HERE I stay."

At the moment, of course, I never realized how true this was to prove. All I realized was that I was warm, well fed and—oh, so sleepy!

And so to bed.

—ROBERT LAWSON

200

- Who is telling the story?
- Which details could you read in any book about Benjamin Franklin? Which details would you read only in this book? Why?

Since the story is told by Ben Franklin's mouse, the people and events are seen from the mouse's **point of view.**

- Why do you think the author chose to tell the story from a mouse's point of view?

Suppose you wanted to tell about something that happened in your home or school. Could you tell the story from an unusual point of view? Who or what could you choose to tell your story?

For Discussion

What details can you think of that you might use in the following stories?

1. A fish tells about the time he almost didn't get away.
2. A kitten tells about the antics of your baby sister, which are more amusing to people than to kittens.
3. A Martian describes what he first saw as he stepped from his spaceship to Earth.
4. Your dog explains what people mean when they say, "It's a dog's life."
5. Your dog tells about something that happened on an automobile trip with his human family.

Activities

A. Write a story from an unusual point of view. Use an idea from For Discussion, or think of an idea of your own.

B. If you wish, prepare a neat final copy of your story and paste it into the class storybook.

15. Telling a Story in Dialogue

Read the story below. Notice that most of it is a dialogue.

The Picnic

Greg and his sister Julie were having a picnic in the woods near their house. Just as they finished setting the food out, a seven-foot bear stepped into the clearing.

"Don't move, Julie!" Greg whispered. "You've got to show him you're not afraid of him."

"I've got to show him *what?*" Julie whispered back. "Look at the size of him!"

"I know, I know. But my wildlife book says that if you just keep still, the bear will probably go away."

The bear walked over to the blanket, looked at the food, and sat down across from Greg and Julie. He picked up a piece of chicken and began gnawing at it.

"What now?" Julie asked.

"I don't know," said Greg. "Maybe we could offer him some salt."

The bear dropped the chicken bone and picked up a piece of watermelon.

"Hey!" Julie yelled at him. "That's our dessert."

The bear dropped the watermelon and gave Julie what she thought was a sad look.

"Oh, hey, listen, bear, I'm sorry," Julie said. But it was too late. He was already up and dragging himself back into the woods.

"Whew, that was close," Greg said.

"Oh, the poor thing," said Julie. "I think I hurt his feelings. Maybe we should find him and give him some watermelon."

"Tell you what," Greg said. "*You* find him." He was repacking the food in the picnic basket. "I just remembered I have to mow the lawn."

Now answer the following questions about "The Picnic" to see how you could write a story in dialogue.

- What kind of sentences did the writer use to make the dialogue sound like real people talking?

- What actions did you picture as you read the dialogue?

For Discussion

Sometimes a picture may suggest a story. What do you think the boy and girl in the picture might be saying? How could you tell the story in a dialogue?

Activities

A. Write a dialogue that tells a story. Use one of the ideas below, or an idea of your own.

1. Two boys try to decide what to do with a stray dog that has been following them.

2. A girl strikes up a conversation with another girl who is new in class that day.

3. Two boys, walking home late at night, discuss whether to cut through a cemetery or take the long way around.

B. If you wish, make a copy of your story for the class storybook.

16. Listening to Poetry

Listen as your teacher reads the following poem to you.

APRIL

It's lemonade, it's lemonade, it's daisy.
It's a roller-skating, scissor-grinding day;
It's gingham-waisted, chocolate flavored, lazy,
With the children flower-scattered at their play.

It's the sun like watermelon,
And the sidewalks overlaid
With a glaze of yellow yellow
Like a jar of marmalade.

It's the mower gently mowing,
And the stars like startled glass,
While the mower keeps on going
Through a waterfall of grass.

Then the rich magenta evening
Like a sauce upon the walk,
And the porches softly swinging
With a hammockful of talk.

It's the hobo at the corner
With his lilac-sniffing gait,
And the shy departing thunder
Of the fast departing skate.

It's lemonade, it's lemonade, it's April!
A water sprinkler, puddle winking time,
When a boy who peddles slowly, with a smile remote and holy,
Sells you April chocolate flavored for a dime.

—MARCIA MASTERS

To tell what April means to her, Marcia Masters lists things like roller-skating, mowing the grass, and drinking lemonade. Listen as your teacher reads the poem again. What other things does Marcia Masters list to tell what April means to her?

For Discussion

A. Pick out the lines from the poem that you like best. Read them aloud to the class. Then tell what the lines mean and why you like them.

B. The poem "April" contains many words that appeal to one or more of the five senses. Pick out lines that make you see something clearly and read them to the class. Do the same with lines that make you hear, smell, feel, and taste.

Activities

A. Read the poem "April" to yourself two or three times. Pick out one or more lines that make you think of a picture. Draw or paint the picture, and print the lines from the poem at the bottom.

B. Find other poems about the different seasons, months, or days of the year. You might want to collect the poems in a class poetry book.

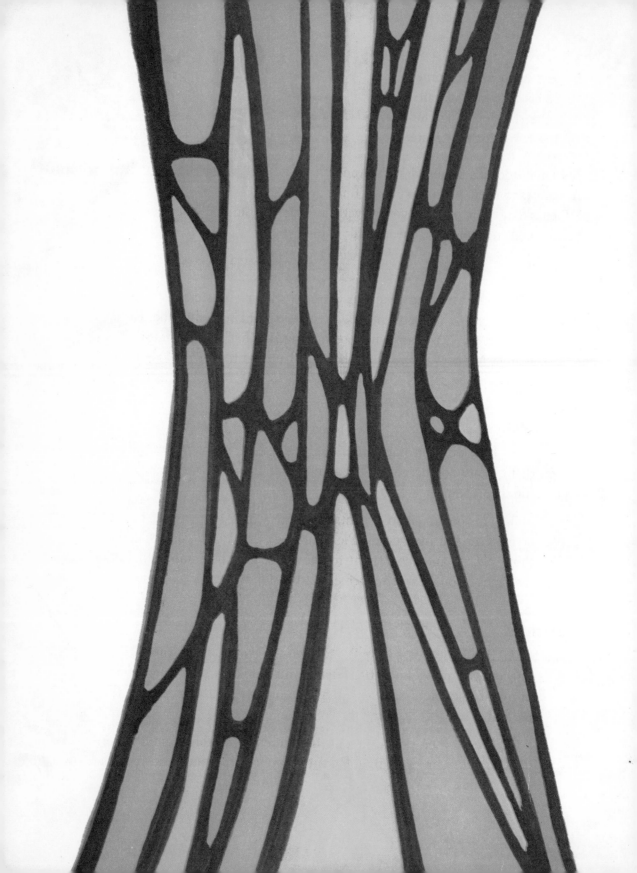

CHAPTER 7

1. English Spelling

Can you read the sign in the picture? Do any of the spellings seem more sensible to you than the real spellings of these words?

Everyone agrees that English spelling doesn't always seem to make sense. Some people have a difficult time learning to spell correctly. There are two main reasons why some English words are hard to spell. Both reasons can be found in the history of the English language.

First, speakers of English have borrowed many words from other languages. In doing so, they have often kept the original spellings, even when those spellings don't follow native English spelling patterns. Here are some words that originally came from French and Greek. The letters in heavy type stand for sounds that have more common spellings in English. How are the sounds usually spelled?

FRENCH: bur**eau**   an**tique**   **ch**ateau   debris

GREEK: **ch**orus   **ph**rase   **pn**eumonia   **rh**inoceros

There is a second important reason why English spelling is difficult. The pronunciations of English words change, but the spellings often remain the same. For example, many words have "silent" letters that once stood for sounds. How would you pronounce

208

the following words if each letter in heavy type stood for a sound, as it once did?

knee   **g**nat   com**b**   hal**f**   **w**ren

The history of the English language explains many of the spellings that today seem difficult and illogical. Why are borrowed words sometimes hard to spell? How do changes in the pronunciations of words cause spelling problems?

For Discussion

A. Below are some dictionary etymologies for words that came from Greek and French. How can you explain the unusual spellings of the English words?

chlorine   [< Gk. *chloros* green]
chauffeur [< F *chauffeur* stoker < *chauffer* to heat;
                 term from days of steam automobiles]

B. Read the etymology below. How does the Old English spelling help to explain the silent letters in *knight?*

knight [OE *cniht* boy]

For Practice

Oral   The words listed below came from French and Greek. Which letters stand for sounds that have more common spellings in English?

French	Greek
1. souvenir	**7.** prophet
2. chalet	**8.** psychology
3. porpoise	**9.** pneumatic
4. croquet	**10.** rhubarb
5. chef	**11.** scheme
6. unique	**12.** sapphire

Written   The words below are misspelled to follow more common English spelling patterns. Write the words as they are actually spelled. Use your dictionary if necessary.

1. rithum	**7.** tortus
2. anser	**8.** simfony
3. atmosfear	**9.** plack
4. picturesk	**10.** sargent
5. lewtenant	**11.** whisle
6. skedjule	**12.** strate

2. Bases, Prefixes, and Suffixes

What word parts are combined to form each word in color?

Prefix		Base		Suffix		Word
		act	+	–ive	→	active
		act	+	–or	→	actor
		act	+	–ion	→	action
re–	+	act				react
in–	+	act	+	–ive	→	inactive

Many English words are formed by adding **prefixes** and **suffixes** to **bases**. Look at the chart again.

- Which word part of each word in color carries the principal meaning, the base, the prefix, or the suffix?
- Which word part comes before the base?
- Which word part comes after the base?

Now study the chart below.

Prefix		Base		Suffix		Suffix		Word
		act	+	–ive	+	–ly	→	actively
		act	+	–ive	+	–ity	→	activity
in–	+	act	+	–ive	+	–ity	→	inactivity

- How many suffixes were added to the base to form each word?

Thousands of English words are made by combining bases, prefixes, and suffixes. Which word part does every word have? Where do the other two word parts appear in a word?

For Discussion

A. Name the parts of each of the following words: base, prefix, or suffix. Explain how you decided which part is the base.

1. freedom   **2.** miscount   **3.** outstanding   **4.** trustfully

B. The base *friend* is a part of several other words. Which of the prefixes and suffixes below can you add to *friend* to make a word that will complete each of these sentences?

be–   un–   –ship   –ly   –less

1. Tanya was a cheerful, — girl.
2. Have you read about the — between David and Jonathan?
3. I wanted to speak to the stranger, but he looked —.
4. Marlowe was in a strange city, alone and —.
5. Phil decided to — the new student.

For Practice

Oral A. Add a prefix or a suffix to each base below to make a word that will complete the sentence.

1. kind: The teacher spoke — to the visitor.
2. home: The travelers finally turned —.
3. cloud: The sky became — just before the storm.
4. color: Bleach will make that shirt —.
5. act: Jane likes stories with a lot of —.
6. amaze: The crowd gazed in — at the lion tamer.
7. humor: Everyone laughed at the — story Manuel told.
8. leisure: After supper we took a — stroll around the block.
9. safe: It is — to jaywalk.
10. fresh: A big cup of hot tea will — you.

For More Practice
See Page 388

B. Three of the words in each group below consist of a prefix and a base. Which word in each group consists of a base alone?

1. untie, uncle, unfurl, unfold
2. indoors, inside, income, indigo
3. preschool, prewar, pretzel, preview
4. beagle, belittle, behead, befriend
5. reread, rebuild, repaint, region

Written Make ten words by combining the word parts below. Use each word you make in a sentence of your own.

Prefixes	Bases	Suffixes	
over–	spell	–er	–ness
re–	wise	–ing	–ful
un–	hard	–dom	–less
mis–	joy	–ly	–ous
dis–	favor	–ship	–able
		–en	–ite

211

3. Free Bases and Bound Bases

Study the words in the two lists below.

A	B
lightly	vision
lighten	visible
enlighten	visual
relight	visibility
lightness	invisible

- What is the base of each word in group A? What is the base of each word in group B? How can you tell?

- Which base can be used as a word by itself?

- Which base cannot be used as a word? What is the meaning of this base?

A base that can be used as a word by itself is called a **free base.** A base that cannot be used as a word by itself is called a **bound base.**

Many English words are formed by adding prefixes and suffixes to bound bases that come from Latin. A few of the most common bound bases are listed below. What words can you think of that contain these bases?

Base	Meaning
aud	hear
dic, dict	say
duce, duct	lead
fract, frag, fring	break
miss, mit	send
mob, mot	move
scrib, script	write
spec, spect	see
tract	draw

212

Think about what you have discovered about bases. How do bound bases differ from free bases? What language do many bound bases come from?

For More Practice
See Page 388

For Discussion

A. What bound base appears in the words in each group below? What meaning does each bound base carry?

1. motion, motor, commotion
2. predict, dictate, diction
3. inspect, spectator, spectacle
4. fraction, fracture, fragile

B. Sometimes a familiar bound base can help you guess the meaning of an unfamiliar word. For each word in italics, what is the bound base? What meaning clue does it provide?

1. There was a penalty for any *infraction* of the rules.
2. The speaker's voice was scarcely *audible*.
3. The captain of the team was *immobilized* by a sprained ankle.

For Practice

Oral For each word below the meaning of the bound base is given. What is the meaning of the word? What is another word that contains the same bound base? Use a dictionary if you need help.

Word	Meaning of Base
1. dormitory	sleep
2. manual	hand
3. solitude	alone
4. portable	carry
5. projector	throw

Written Combine word parts from each group to form three different words. Use each word in a sentence that shows you understand its meaning.

1. tract, dis–, re–, con–, at–, de–, –ion, –ive
2. miss or mit, trans–, com–, per–, dis–, –al, –ion
3. duce or duct, re–, intro–, pro–, de–, –ion, –ive
4. scrib or script, in–, sub–, de–, –ive, –ion

213

4. Combining Sentences with Conjunctions

Notice how two sentences in A are combined to form one in B.

A	B
The bell rang. Everyone stood up. $\Rightarrow$	The bell rang, **and** everyone stood up.
Carter rarely studies. He always passes the tests. $\Rightarrow$	Carter rarely studies, **but** he always passes the tests.
The wind grew colder. I closed the window. $\Rightarrow$	The wind grew colder, **so** I closed the window.
We must leave at once. We will be late. $\Rightarrow$	We must leave at once, **or** we will be late.

■ What word was used to combine each pair of sentences in A to form each sentence in B?

■ Where does a comma appear in each sentence in B?

The sentences in B are called **compound sentences.** Words like *and, but, so,* and *or* that are used in forming compound sentences are called **conjunctions.**

Notice how different conjunctions create different meanings.

It rained, but we found shelter.
It rained, so we found shelter.

■ What two sentences were combined to form each compound sentence?

■ How do the different conjunctions make a difference in meaning?

You have discovered how to combine two sentences to form a compound sentence. How would you explain the process to a classmate? How can conjunctions help you to express exact meanings?

For Discussion

A. How can you make compound sentences from the sentence pairs below? Explain why you selected a particular conjunction in each sentence.

1. That plant must have sunlight. It will die.
2. I ordered chocolate ice cream. The waitress brought apple pie.

B. What are two conjunctions that could be used to join the sentences below? How does the conjunction you select make a difference in meaning?

Vicki will play the guitar.
Camille will play the piano.

For Practice

Oral Combine each pair of sentences with a conjunction.

1. John likes pistachio ice cream. His sister prefers maple nut.
2. Ethan washed the car. Henry waxed it.
3. I would like to go with you. I have to study for a test.
4. We must hurry. We will miss the train.
5. The earth trembled. A mountain slipped into the sea.
6. We tried to open the door. It was locked.
7. The ice was hard. We decided to go skating.

For More Practice
See Page 389

Written Combine each pair of sentences with a conjunction. Be sure to use commas where they are needed.

1. The tires squealed. The car stopped suddenly.
2. I ordered the tickets. They didn't come in time.
3. You should eat a sandwich now. You will be hungry later on.
4. The electricity went off. We lighted some candles.
5. The curtain went down. The audience applauded loudly.
6. Emily can swim well. She is afraid to dive.
7. They hurried to the store. It had already closed.

215

5. Combining Sentences with Subordinators

Read the sentences below. Notice how the sentences in *A* are combined to form the sentences in *B*.

A	B
We toasted marshmallows. The fire died down. ⟹	We toasted marshmallows **after** the fire died down.
They will fail. They try harder. ⟹	They will fail **unless** they try harder.

■ What word was used to combine each pair of sentences in A to form each sentence in B?

Words like *unless* and *after* that are used to combine sentences are **subordinators.** Study the subordinators below. Test each one in the blank in the sentence that follows.

when	whenever	if	until	where
after	since	as if	while	unless
before	as	because	just as	although

Roy got up. The alarm clock rang. ⟹	Roy got up — the alarm clock rang.

■ Which of the subordinators could you use in the blank to form a new sentence?

■ How do the different subordinators make different meanings?

You have discovered how to change two sentences into one with a subordinator. How would you explain the process to a classmate. How can subordinators help you to express exact meanings?

What subordinators could you use to combine the sentences below? What different meanings would result from selecting different subordinators?

Aunt Isabel falls asleep.

She watches the late show.

For Practice

For More Practice
See Page 389

Oral **A.** Combine each pair of sentences with a subordinator.

1. Everyone cheered.
   Mother announced dinner.
2. Dad read to the children.
   They went to sleep.
3. Bill has written us only once.
   He moved away.
4. We couldn't go skating today.
   The ice was too thin.

B. Change each sentence below. Use a different subordinator to express a different meaning.

1. The children came indoors after it got dark.
2. I won't finish this jigsaw puzzle until you help me.
3. We ate our lunch before we went swimming.
4. I will visit you next summer when I come to New York.
5. The boat began to leak as we reached the center of the lake.

Written Combine each pair of sentences with a subordinator.

1. Alice held the puppy.
   Ethel washed it.
2. You must use the stairs.
   The elevator is broken.
3. The turtle went into his shell.
   He saw us coming.
4. I'll let you read this book.
   I've finished it.
5. The animals growled hungrily.
   The keeper threw them raw meat.
6. I will wait for you.
   The two roads meet.
7. I'll lend you a quarter.
   You'll pay me back tomorrow.
8. Arthur jumped into the lake.
   He was still fully dressed.
9. We liked the house.
   It was old and rickety.
10. The sea flooded the village.
    The dike broke.

217

6. Using Conjunctions and Subordinators

Sometimes the same sentences can be combined in more than one way. Study the following examples.

A	B
	I built a fire, and Al put up the tent.
I built a fire. Al put up the tent. $\Rightarrow$	
	I built a fire while Al put up the tent.

- Which sentence in *B* was formed with a conjunction?
- Which sentence was formed with a subordinator?
- Which sentence contains a comma? Why?

Now see what happens when you rearrange the sentences in *B*.

And Al put up the tent I built a fire

While Al put up the tent, I built a fire.

- Which group of words is an acceptable sentence?

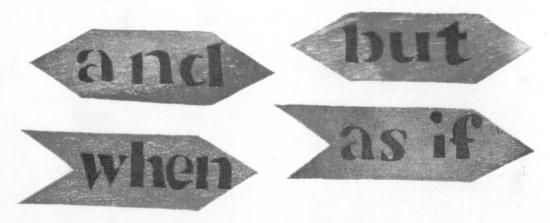

■ Which kind of sentence can be rearranged, one with a conjunction or one with a subordinator?

■ Where is a comma used in the new sentence?

You have discovered two ways of combining sentences. What are the two ways, and how do they differ?

For Discussion

How can you combine the sentences in each pair with a conjunction? How can you combine them with a subordinator?

1. The cage door opened.
   The tiger escaped.

2. George was very tired.
   He wouldn't admit it.

For Practice

Oral A. Rearrange each sentence so that it begins with a subordinator.

1. We will be late unless we hurry.
2. The seeds began to sprout as the sun warmed the soil.
3. We will eat in the backyard if it doesn't rain.
4. Perkins ordered me to sit down before I could say a word.

B. Join each pair of sentences in two ways. Tell whether you used a conjunction or a subordinator.

1. The road was steep and rough.
   We had to drive slowly.
2. The senator began to speak.
   Everyone stopped talking.
3. Mr. Tabor was angry.
   He concealed his feelings.
4. You have work to do.
   I won't disturb you.

For More Practice
See Page 390

Written Join each pair of sentences with a conjunction or a subordinator. Use commas wherever they are needed.

1. The bus reached the mountaintop.
   We got out to admire the view.
2. The weather turns cooler.
   We will cancel the picnic.
3. You must keep the cat out.
   It will eat the parrakeet.
4. I did as well as I could.
   Reginald would have done better.
5. I wouldn't buy that car.
   It has been in a wreck.
6. Alexander was just a boy.
   He wanted to travel.
7. He would not leave the sinking ship.
   Everyone else was safe.
8. We heard tornado warnings.
   We ran to the basement.

7. Using Commas

Read the following sentences silently. Notice where commas have been used.

Introductory expressions
1. Well, I think it's time to go home.
2. Yes, it's nine o'clock.

Interrupters
3. You will, of course, stay for lunch.
4. However, Carl won't wait for us.

Nouns in direct address
5. Charles, have you had lunch yet?
6. I think, Vivian, that it's your turn.

Items in a series
7. For lunch we had ham salad, cake, and milk.
8. We picked apples, raked leaves, and mowed the grass.

Now read the same sentences aloud, and listen. Notice what you do with your voice as you read.

- Where do you hear one or two slight pauses as you read each sentence?

- Are the pauses related to the commas that appear in the sentences?

Commas in writing are sometimes related to pauses in speech. However, pauses are not always a reliable guide to punctuation. Some people pause in their speech more often than others. In addition, some commas do not signal pauses in speech. Read the following sentences aloud.

Dates
9. The *Titanic* sank on the night of April 14, 1912.
10. He was born in May, 1948, in Phoenix.

Cities and states

11. His home in Springfield, Illinois, is open to the public.
12. She lived most of her life in Tacoma, Washington.

Commas are used in certain places just because it is the custom to use them there. In fact, your best guide in using commas is custom, not pauses in speech.

Read sentences *1* to *12* once more. This time pay special attention to the labels above each set of sentences. What rule can you state to explain the commas that appear in each set?

For Discussion

A. Read the following sentences aloud. Where do you pause slightly as you read each sentence? How do these sentences show one important reason why commas are used in writing?

1. I was hoping, Irene, that you would call.
2. No, I haven't met your father before.
3. It will snow, I think, before morning.

B. Listen as several members of your class read the sentence below. How does this sentence prove that commas do not always signal pauses in speech? What rule explains the comma?

Manuel moved to Grand Rapids, Michigan.

For Practice

For More Practice
See Page 390

Written Write the following sentences. Use commas wherever they are needed. Be prepared to explain why you put commas where you did.

1. Oh I hope you didn't hurt yourself.
2. The price in fact is too high.
3. Pineville Kentucky was my teacher's hometown.
4. I bought some lumber bricks and paint.
5. Melissa have you seen Frances?
6. He was born in Richmond Virginia in September 1939.
7. Kyoko jumped out of bed dressed quickly and ran downstairs.
8. The election I believe was fair.

221

8. More about Using Commas

Read the sentences below. Compare each sentence in A with the matching sentence in B.

A	**B**
1. Rex mowed the lawn and swept the sidewalk.	Rex mowed the lawn, and Darryl swept the sidewalk.
2. Max ran in the race but finished last.	Max ran in the race, but he finished last.

- Which sentences have one noun phrase in the subject but two verb phrases in the predicate?

- Which sentences are compound sentences made by combining two shorter sentences?

- Which sentences have a comma before *and* or *but*?

Now compare each sentence in C with the matching one in D.

C	**D**
3. I'll rest in the hammock while you paint the fence.	While you paint the fence, I'll rest in the hammock.
4. We'll cancel the picnic if it rains.	If it rains, we'll cancel the picnic.

Notice that all the sentences in C and D consist of two smaller sentences that are combined with a subordinator.

- How are the sentences in C different from the sentences in D?

- When should you use a comma in sentences like these?

Knowing when to use commas is important. Knowing when *not* to use them is also important. Look again at the example sentences. When should you use a comma before *and* or *but?* When shouldn't you use a comma before *and* or *but?* When should you use a comma in combining two sentences with a subordinator? When shouldn't you use a comma in combining two sentences with a subordinator?

A. Read the following sentences aloud. Did you hear a slight pause within some of the sentences? Explain. Which sentences should have a comma? Why?

1. We set up our camp when we came to the river.
2. When we came to the river we set up our camp.
3. Joe fed the canary and watered the plants.
4. Joe fed the canary and Kevin watered the plants.

B. Read the following sentence aloud. Where should it have a comma? How does the comma help to prevent misreading?

Unless you eat your dinner will get cold.

For
Practice

For More Practice
See Page 391

Written Write the following sentences on your paper. Use commas wherever they are needed. (Not all the sentences need a comma.)

1. Wentworth made a shopping list, but he left it at home.
2. Otis knew everyone in town, and everyone in town knew him.
3. Maggie entered the soap-carving contest and won first prize.
4. Jerry cut the boards, and Phil nailed them together.
5. Unless the wind dies, the forest fire will spread.
6. The dike will break, if the water rises much higher.
7. After the music stopped, we put the records away.
8. The children, should come indoors before it gets dark.

9. For Review

Read and discuss the questions below.

A. How does a prefix differ from a suffix? How does a free base differ from a bound base? Use the words below in explaining your answers.

Words with Free Bases	**Words with Bound Bases**
unsafely (un– + safe + –ly)	invisible (in– + vis + –ible)
discovery (dis– + cover + –y)	reduction (re– + duct + –ion)
inactive (in– + act + –ive)	dismissal (dis– + miss + –al)

B. Which sentences below have been joined with a conjunction? With a subordinator? Prove your answers by showing that only the sentence containing the subordinator can be rearranged so that the connecting word comes first.

1. It began to rain hard.
We stayed home. $\Rightarrow$ It began to rain hard, so we stayed home.

2. Everyone cheered.
Al announced the winner. $\Rightarrow$ Everyone cheered when Al announced the winner.

C. What rules explain the use of commas in the following sentences?

1. Sue began to knit a sweater, but she didn't finish it.

2. Before you go, please give me your telephone number.

3. No, I have never ridden a motorcycle.

4. However, the plane may be delayed.

5. It may rain, I suppose, by afternoon.

6. Brian, will you please close that door?

7. I hope, Gloria, that Judy can come too.

8. We had soup, sandwiches, and cake for lunch.

9. The date to remember is May 21, 1947.

10. They came here in April, 1965.

11. That house in Williamsburg, Virginia, isn't open today.

Read the directions for each exercise below. Follow the directions, writing your answers on your own paper.

A. Answer the following questions about the words in the box at the right.

unwisely	previewing
react	inaudible
unafraid	prediction

1. Which two words contain a prefix and a free base?
2. Which two words contain a prefix, a free base, and a suffix?
3. Which two words contain a prefix, a bound base, and a suffix?

B. Combine each pair of sentences below by using a suitable conjunction. Write the new sentences, using commas where they are necessary.

4. Uncle Dan arrived yesterday.
   We showed him our city.
5. A storm came up suddenly.
   We were delayed.

C. Choose the sentence in each pair that contains a subordinator. Write it on your paper. Then rearrange the sentence so that it begins with a subordinator. Use commas where necessary.

6. I cooked the dinner, and Tina set the table.
   I cooked the dinner while Tina set the table.
7. I was just getting up and the telephone rang.
   I was just getting up when the telephone rang.

D. Write these sentences. Use commas where necessary.

8. No Hilda I don't think I will be able to come.
9. Carol Rita and Joan are all on the committee.
10. I was born in Houston Texas on January 21 1962.

225

11. Telling Tall Tales

Imagine yourself in the bunkhouse or shanty of a North Woods logging camp. Your day's work is over, and you are relaxing with your companions, joking and swapping stories. Soon everyone stops talking and sits back to listen as an old-timer begins to tell a story. It is a tale about Paul Bunyan, the greatest lumberjack who ever lived, and Babe, his Great Blue Ox.

It is well known that the Great Blue Ox was so powerful that he could pull anything that had two ends, and so when Paul wanted a crooked logging trail straightened out, he would just hitch Babe up to one end of it, tell his pet to go ahead, and, lo and behold! the crooked trail would be pulled out perfectly straight.

226

There was one particularly bad stretch of road, about twenty or thirty miles long, that gave Babe and Paul a lot of trouble before they finally got all the crooks pulled out of it. It certainly must have been the crookedest road in the world—it twisted and turned so much that it spelled out every letter of the alphabet, some of the letters two or three times. Paul taught Babe how to read just by leading him over it a few times, and men going along it met themselves coming from the other direction so often that the whole camp was near crazy before long.

So Paul decided that the road would have to be straightened out without any further delay, and with that end in view he ordered Ole to make for him the strongest chain he knew how. The Big Swede set to work with a will, and when the chain was completed it had links four feet long and two feet across and the steel they were made of was thirteen inches thick.

The chain being ready, Paul hitched Babe up to one end of the road with it. At his master's word the Great Blue Ox began to puff and pull and strain away as he had never done before, and at last he got the end pulled out a little ways. Paul chirped to him again, and he pulled away harder than ever. With every tug he made, one of the twists in the road would straighten out, and then Babe would pull away again, hind legs straight out behind and belly to the ground. It was the hardest job Babe had ever been put up against, but he stuck to it most admirably.

When the task was finally done, the Ox was nearly fagged out, a condition that he had never known before, and that big chain had been pulled on so hard that it was pulled out into a solid steel bar. The road was straightened out, however, which was the thing Paul wanted, and he considered the time and energy expended as well worth while, since the nuisance had been transformed into something useful. He found, though, that since all the kinks and twists had been pulled out, there was now a whole lot more of the road than was needed, but—never being a person who could stand to waste anything which might be useful—he rolled up all the extra length and laid it down in a place where one might come in handy some time.

—Retold by WALLACE WADSWORTH

The stories of Paul Bunyan are **tall tales.** In a tall tale the qualities of the characters and events are greatly exaggerated. What are some of the exaggerations in the story you just read?

For Discussion

A. Paul Bunyan is the best known of several famous tall-tale heroes. Others are Pecos Bill the cowboy, Stormalong the sailor, John Henry the steel driver, Mike Fink the keelboatman, Davy Crockett the frontiersman, and Casey Jones the railroad engineer. Which of these heroes have you heard or read about? What other tall-tale heroes do you know of?

B. Imagine once again that you are listening as someone tells the tale about Paul Bunyan. He could laugh at his own story, or he could tell it deadpan, without showing any amusement. Which way do you think would be better? Why?

Activities

Find and read some tall tales, either about Paul Bunyan or about some other hero. Perhaps you know some of these stories already. Plan to spend one session of your English class swapping tall tales. You may want to sit on the floor around an imaginary campfire. Your tall tale can be short or long, but you should learn it so that you can tell it well without reading it. You may want to tell more than one tale.

12. Writing a Tall Tale

Many tall tales may be told about the same hero. One hero of American folklore is Captain Stormalong, the greatest sailor who ever sailed the seas. His adventures began while he was still a baby.

Stormy was so big that his parents had to blow a fog-horn to wake him up. His cradle was a whaleboat anchored in the bay. There he swam and wrestled with the sharks, always being careful not to hurt them.

One time when Stormy was older, he worked on a whaling ship, the *Greasy Ann*. A terrible storm came up and blew away the sails. Stormy harpooned ten whales to pull the ship while he guided it home safely. The whales started out so fast that they pulled the ship right out of her coat of paint.

Another ship, the *Silver Maid*, stopped suddenly and couldn't go on, even though the wind was filling her sails. An octopus had wrapped its tentacles around the keel. Stormy dived to the bottom of the ship and tied the tentacles into ten different sailor knots.

Stormalong grew so big that he had a special ship built for him, the *Courser*. The masts were so tall that they were equipped with hinges and folded back to let the moon go by. The tips of the masts and spars were round so they wouldn't punch holes in the rain clouds.

Suppose you wanted to make up another tall tale about Stormalong. Answer these questions to see how you might go about it.

- What people and objects in the story of Captain Stormalong are made to seem far beyond normal size?

- What events that might actually occur are greatly exaggerated?

- Why should a tall tale like this one be told seriously, as if it really happened?

A. Think of some new problems that Paul Bunyan, Stormalong, or another tall-tale hero might solve. Which problem could you use to begin a new tall tale about a familiar hero?

B. Notice the first sentence in the story about Stormalong. "Stormy was so big that his parents had to blow a foghorn to wake him up." Tall tales contain many sentences like this one. Paul Bunyan could roll a log so fast that it made foam on the water solid enough to walk on. Pecos Bill had a bowie knife so sharp that he could shave himself with its shadow.

Now you try some tall talk like this. Make up sentences about these and other familiar tall-tale heroes.

Activities

A. Make up a new tall tale about a familiar hero, such as Paul Bunyan or Captain Stormalong.

B. Draw or paint a picture to go with your tall tale.

C. Separate into groups of five or six, and read your tall tales aloud to one another.

232

13. Writing Another Tall Tale

Tall tales are not always about heroes. In fact, you probably make up a tall tale about yourself every once in a while. Suppose someone asks you how you got your black eye. You might tell him what happened—or you might make up a whopper. Whoppers, yarns, fish stories, tall tales—these are told just for fun, since the teller doesn't intend to be believed. Here are a few stories that probably began as ordinary tall talk but have since become permanent parts of American folklore.

Mosquitoes

Almost every state in the Union has bigger mosquitoes than any other state in the Union. In Mississippi four of them can hold a man down. In Florida they are so ferocious that the people have to sleep with their heads in iron kettles, and even then they can't sleep because of the noise the creatures make drilling through the iron with their stingers. In New Jersey they have hit on a way to put a stop to this kind of thing by riveting the stinger just as it comes through. People from New York say that Texas mosquitoes are as big as pelicans and just as hungry; Texans, however, say that they never get bigger than mockingbirds.

Icebergs

Once there was a man who had snow scenes and icebergs painted on his bedroom wall during a hot spell. The water froze in the water pitcher the first night, and he had to build a fire the second night and write off to Sears, Roebuck for five blankets.

They Just Go Round

Then there's that crooked stream down on the farm: so crooked that anyone who tries to jump across it lands on the same side every time! People don't try it any more. They just go round.

Here's a tall tale written by someone around your age. Read it to see how you could write a tall tale of your own.

My Father's Onions

Minnesota winters get mighty cold, and my father raises onions that are mighty hot. One day last winter when the highest temperature of the day was below zero, my father cut one of his onions in two and was working outside in his undershirt with the sweat pouring off of him. After that, we used one onion a day to heat the house.

234

- How is "My Father's Onions" similar to the tall tales that are a part of American folklore?
- What parts of the story "My Father's Onions" probably happened?
- How did the writer exaggerate what happened to make a tall tale?

For Discussion

A. Suppose you wanted to make up a tall tale about yourself. What physical or mental abilities would you like to imagine you have? What fearless or clever deeds might you do? What has happened to you that you could exaggerate to make a tall tale?

B. Suppose you wanted to make up a tall tale about a person or an animal you know. What relative has an interesting occupation that might help you think of a tall tale? How could you exaggerate something that happened to a pet or something the pet did? You might even want to imagine a pet you never had, or invent an animal that could never really exist.

Activities

A. Write a tall tale about yourself, a member of your family, or a pet.

B. Put together a book of tall tales written by the members of your class. Include at least one by each person. Illustrate as many of the tales as you wish to.

14. A Tall-tale Limerick

Read the following limericks. How are they similar to tall tales?

There once was a Rhode Island Red
That heard a clock tick in her head.
　　All the eggs she would lay
　　Were stamped with the day
That she laid 'em, or so I've heard said.

A very tall man named MacBain
Has suffered a terrible pain.
　　While walking one day,
　　I'm sorry to say,
He crashed with a low-flying plane.

A racer named Algernon Black
Could run very fast on the track.
    He left for Rangoon
    And got there so soon
He met himself on the way back.

To write a tall-tale limerick like the ones you just read, first think of an unusual animal, plant, person, or machine. Give it an exaggerated quality, such as great size, strength, or speed. What are some topics of this kind that you could write about in your own tall-tale limerick?

For Discussion

A. What are some lines you might use to complete the limericks below? Your class may be able to think of more than one way to complete each limerick.

> 1. A brave mountain climber named Dowd
>   Performed for a wondering crowd.
>   — — — — — —
>   — — — — — —
>   And now he is off on a cloud.

> 2. An evil magician did tricks
>   With anything made out of bricks.
>   Twelve buildings, I hear,
>   He made disappear
>   — — — — — — — —.

B. What are some topics that you could use in a tall-tale limerick of your own?

Activities

Write two or three tall-tale limericks. Add your limericks to your class book of tall tales.

15. Listening to Poetry

The ballad below tells the story of John Henry, the famous steel driver who helped to build the nation's railroads. With his mighty hammer, John Henry would pound a steel spike into rock in order to make holes for blasting with explosives. The ballad was first sung around a hundred years ago by workmen in southern construction gangs and work camps. Listen as your teacher reads it aloud to you.

JOHN HENRY

When John Henry was about three days old,
A-sitting on his Pappy's knee,
He gave one loud and mournful cry,
"The hammer'll be the death of me,
The hammer'll be the death of me."

John Henry had a little woman
And her name was Polly Ann;
When John Henry was sick and lay on his bed,
Polly drove steel like a man,
Polly drove steel like a man.

The captain says to John Henry one day:
"Gonna bring me a steam drill round,
Gonna take that steam drill out on the job,
Gonna whop that steel on down,
Gonna whop that steel on down."

John Henry says to the captain one day:
"Lord, a man ain't nothing but a man;
But before I'd let this old steam drill beat me down,
I'd die with my hammer in my hand,
I'd die with my hammer in my hand."

The man that invented the steam drill,
He thought he was mighty fine;
John Henry drove his fifteen feet
And the steam drill only made nine,
The steam drill only made nine.

John Henry was hammering on the mountain
And his hammer was striking fire;
He drove so hard 'til he broke his poor heart
And he laid down his hammer and he died,
He laid down his hammer and he died.

Listen as your teacher reads the ballad again.

- Who or what was John Henry's enemy?
- How is this ballad like a tall tale?

For Discussion

A. In what way did John Henry defeat his enemy? In what way was John Henry finally defeated? Find lines in the ballad that prove your answers.

B. There was probably a real person named John Henry. What details of the story told in the ballad do you think might be true? What details do you think were added by the people who told stories and sang songs about him?

Activities

A. Your class may want to sing the ballad of John Henry. If someone knows the ballad well enough, let him lead the class in singing it. There may be someone in your class who can accompany the singing on a piano or a guitar.

B. Find some other folk ballads and bring them to class. Your class may want to sing some of the familiar ones.

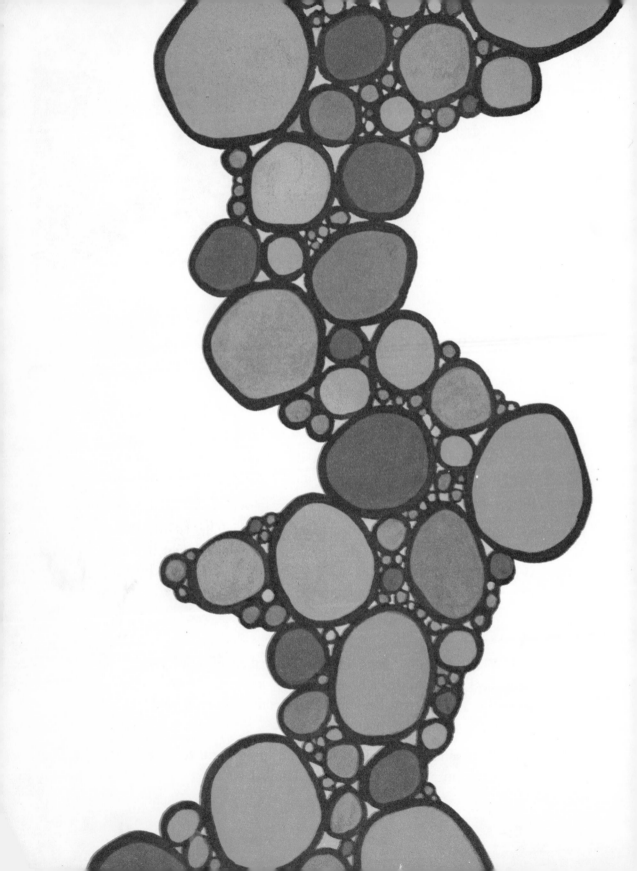

CHAPTER **8**

1. Spelling Reform in the United States

The following sentence might have appeared in an American newspaper around 1790.

> Hans Klein, a noted critick of musick and the theatre, was the guest of honour at a dinner given here last night.

■ Which words in the sentence have different spellings in America today?

A number of people have tried to reform English spelling through the years. One who had some success was Noah Webster, the great dictionary maker. Beginning in 1792 Webster wrote several spelling books and dictionaries. In them he made suggestions for simplifying the spelling of some English words.

In the news item above are four words that Webster succeeded in simplifying for Americans. But the public didn't accept all of his suggestions. Here are some that were not accepted.

lether	yeer	karacter
juce	wimmen	lepard
rong	tung	nabor

■ How are these words spelled today?

■ Would the suggested changes have made these words easier to spell?

For Discussion

A. The following groups contain some words as they appeared before Webster's time. How are these words spelled in America today? What general rule can you state for the spelling changes that were made in each group?

1	2	3
magick	errour	centre
publick	colour	fibre
tragick	labour	sepulchre

B. Here are nine more words whose spellings Webster succeeded in changing. Each one appears as it was spelled before Webster's time. How is each word spelled in America today?

1. cheque	**4.** tyre	**7.** neighbour
2. calibre	**5.** waggon	**8.** storey
3. flavour	**6.** gaol	**9.** frolick

C. The spellings below represent some of Webster's suggestions that were not accepted. What general rule can you state for the suggested changes in each group?

1	2	3
thred	granit	crum
lether	examin	ritten
fether	giraff	det

D. Here are some words whose spellings have been simplified since Webster's time, within the last one hundred years. How is each word spelled in America today?

1. hyaena	**3.** develope	**5.** aeroplane
2. catalogue	**4.** programme	**6.** axe

ON YOUR OWN

Imagine you are on a committee in charge of simplifying spelling. Jot down a few suggestions you would make and discuss them with the class. These groups of words may give you some ideas.

1	2	3
dollar	cage	calm
bitter	keep	thumb
actor	chorus	solemn

2. Noun-forming Suffixes

Look at the pairs of matching sentences in groups A and B. Notice the words in color in A. What suffix would you have to add to each word before you could use it as a noun in the matching sentence in B?

A	B
1. The boys collect stamps.	They have a stamp —.
2. I will donate some money.	It will be a small —.
3. He will predict the weather.	His — may be wrong.

The suffix *–ion* is called a **noun-forming suffix** because it changes certain words to nouns.

English contains thousands of nouns that are made by adding suffixes like *–ion* to other words. To discover some other noun-forming suffixes, try this. Add a suffix to each word in color and use the new word to complete the matching sentence in D.

C	D
4. The actors will perform tonight.	We will watch their —.
5. The day was very humid.	The — was high.
6. The train should depart at six.	Its — may be late.
7. The sun was bright.	Its — hurt our eyes.

Think about the nouns you used to complete the sentences in this lesson. How are all of these nouns alike?

For Discussion

To each word below, add the suffix that follows. What new word did you make? Try to use each new word as a noun in a sentence of your own. Which suffixes are noun-forming suffixes? Which suffix is not a noun-forming suffix? How can you tell?

1. loyal + –ty
2. deep + –en
3. amaze + –ment
4. free + –dom

244

For Practice

For More Practice
See Page 391

Oral Add a noun-forming suffix to each word in italics. Use the noun you make to complete the second sentence.

1. The doctor must *act* quickly.
   Quick — is important.
2. How can we *enter* the building?
   We must find the —.
3. Our experiment may *fail*.
   We will learn from our —.
4. That animal may *starve*.
   It may die of —.
5. King Solomon was *wise*.
   He was known for his great —.
6. Tyrone will *assist* his father.
   He will be his father's —.
7. Did Roger *invent* this gadget?
   Yes, it is Roger's —.
8. Dean is a *friendly* boy.
   He is liked because of his —.
9. The speaker seemed *sincere*.
   The audience respected his —.

Written Complete each sentence below with a noun made from the word in parentheses.

1. Every car was checked for — before it was driven. (safe)
2. The — outside woke the baby. (disturb)
3. My brother asked his — for a raise. (employ)
4. Our gift for Dad was a set of camping —. (equip)
5. Andrea felt the — of the kitten's fur. (soft)
6. Edward worked hard for his college —. (educate)
7. The scientists made an important —. (discover)

245

3. Verb-forming Suffixes

Look at the pairs of matching sentences in A and B. Notice the words in color in A. What suffix would you have to add to each word before you could use it as a verb in the matching sentence in B?

A	B
1. Pedro has a good memory.	He will — his speech.
2. This house is not modern.	We can — it.
3. A snowflake is a crystal.	Water will — to form snow.

The suffix –*ize* is called a **verb-forming suffix** because it changes certain words to verbs.

English contains many verbs that are made by adding suffixes like –*ize* to other words. To discover some other verb-forming suffixes, try this. Add a suffix to each word in color and use the new word to complete the matching sentence in D.

C	D
4. The water isn't pure.	Chlorine will — it.
5. The concrete isn't hard.	It will — soon.

Think about the verbs you used to complete the sentences in this lesson. How are all of these verbs alike?

For Discussion

To each word below, add the suffix that follows. What new word did you make? Try to use each new word as a verb in a sentence of your own. Which suffixes are verb-forming suffixes? Which suffixes are not verb-forming suffixes? How can you tell?

1. weak + –en
2. music + –al
3. beauty + –fy
4. violin + –ist

For Practice

Oral Change each word in italics to a verb by adding a verb-forming suffix. Use the verb to complete the second sentence.

1. The paint is *bright* yellow.
   It will — the kitchen.
2. The farms have *fertile* soil.
   Farmers — the soil each year.
3. This coat is the wrong *length*.
   The tailor will — it.
4. That child deserves *sympathy*.
   We should — with him.
5. The sky will soon be *dark*.
   Storm clouds will — the sky.
6. The speaker will give a *summary*.
   He will — his ideas.
7. The street isn't *wide* enough.
   The city should — it.
8. Every plant belongs to a *class*.
   Scientists — the various plants.
9. The lion is a *symbol* of courage.
   What does the lamb —?

For More Practice
See Page 392

Written Complete each sentence below with a verb formed from the word in parentheses.

1. The ghost story didn't — Kezia. (fright)
2. Electric appliances — housework. (simple)
3. I will add some bleach to — the clothes. (white)
4. Boiling the water will — it for drinking. (sterile)
5. The rising wind will — the surface of the lake. (rough)
6. The librarian will — these cards. (alphabet)
7. The defendant failed to — his actions. (just)
8. Some starch will — that collar. (stiff)
9. Can you — this bar of iron? (magnet)
10. I must — this room. (straight)

247

4. Combining Sentences with Relative Clauses

Read the sentences below. In each group, two sentences have been combined to form one sentence.

	A		B
1.	The boy lives next door. The boy sells minnows.	⇒	The boy **who lives next door** sells minnows.
2.	The girl is singing. The girl is my sister.	⇒	The girl **who is singing** is my sister.
3.	The men poured the concrete. The men were resting.	⇒	The men **who poured the concrete** were resting.

Each word group in color in *B* is a **relative clause.** The word *who* that begins each relative clause is a **relative pronoun.**

Now study the sentences again. Notice how two sentences were combined to form one sentence that has a relative clause.

- Which sentences in *A* were changed to relative clauses in *B*?
- Which noun phrases in *A* were changed to the relative pronoun *who* in *B*?
- Where was each relative clause inserted to make the new sentence?

Next, notice that the sentences in each pair in *A* are alike in one way. Both sentences contain the same noun phrase.

- What two noun phrases are the same in each pair of sentences in *A*?

Think about what you have learned. When can two sentences be combined to form one sentence with a relative clause? How can the two sentences be combined?

Explain how you could combine the two sentences below by using a relative clause beginning with *who*.

The child was lost.
The child found a policeman. } ⇒ The child — — — found a policeman.

For More Practice
See Page 392

Oral Combine each pair of sentences below. Make the first one a relative clause inside the second one. Begin your relative clause with *who*.

1. The mailman brings our mail.
   The mailman has a dachshund.

2. The doctor lives next door.
   The doctor studied at Harvard.

3. The policeman patrols our street.
   The policeman found a lost dog.

4. The dentist fixed my teeth.
   The dentist has three diplomas.

5. Some girls live on our block.
   Some girls are selling cookies.

6. The boy brings our newspapers.
   The boy won a contest.

7. A man knows my father.
   A man fixed my bicycle.

8. A farmer works hard.
   A farmer reaps a good harvest.

Written Combine each pair of sentences. Make the first one a relative clause inside the second one. Begin your relative clause with *who*.

1. The player hit the winning run.
   The player was the pitcher.

2. The man designed that bridge.
   The man is my father.

3. The artist painted that picture.
   The artist studied in Paris.

4. The child is hiding.
   The child is afraid of the storm.

5. The lifeguard rescued the child.
   The lifeguard received a reward.

6. My pen pal lives in Ireland.
   My pen pal will visit America.

7. An old man lived upstairs.
   An old man played the violin.

8. The astronaut walked on the moon.
   The astronaut left a flag there.

5. Relative Clauses Beginning with *Who* and *Which*

Read the sentences below. Notice how two sentences have been combined to form one sentence that contains a relative clause.

---

1. The man buried the gold. ⎫
2. The man was a pirate. ⎬ ⟹   3. The man **who buried the gold** was a pirate.

- ■ Which sentence, *1* or *2*, was changed to a relative clause in sentence *3*?

- ■ What noun phrase was changed to the relative pronoun *who* in sentence *3*?

Now compare the following sentences with the ones above. Again, two sentences have been combined to form one sentence that contains a relative clause.

---

4. A plane flew above us. ⎫
5. A plane landed nearby. ⎬ ⟹   6. A plane **which flew above us** landed nearby.

- ■ Which sentence, *4* or *5*, was changed to a relative clause in sentence *6*?

- ■ What noun phrase was changed to the word *which*?

The word *which*, like *who*, is a relative pronoun when it replaces a noun phrase and begins a relative clause.

Now look at the example sentences again to discover the difference between the relative pronouns *who* and *which*.

- ■ Which relative pronoun replaces a noun phrase that names a person?

- ■ Which relative pronoun replaces a noun phrase that names a thing?

What relative clauses can you use to fill the blanks below? Would you use *who* or *which* to begin each clause? Why?

1. The money is on the table.
   The money belongs to Ann. } ⇒ The money — — — — — belongs to Ann.

2. The man rang our doorbell.
   The man was a stranger. } ⇒ The man — — — — was a stranger.

3. The player struck out.
   The player is my brother. } ⇒ The player — — — is my brother.

For More Practice
See Page 393

Oral Combine each pair of sentences. Make the first one a relative clause inside the second one. Begin the clause with *who* or *which*.

1. The kite wouldn't fly.
   The kite was torn.

2. The plane is due at four.
   The plane will be late.

3. The reporter wrote that story.
   The reporter is my uncle.

4. The children had no raincoats.
   The children got wet.

5. The instrument belongs to Ed.
   The instrument is a mandolin.

6. The supper was waiting for us.
   The supper looked delicious.

7. The stairs led to the attic.
   The stairs were steep and narrow.

8. The boy brought the message.
   The boy was tired.

Written Combine each pair of sentences below with *who* or *which*. Make the first sentence a relative clause inside the second sentence.

1. The teacher walked into the room.
   The teacher was a substitute.

2. The people had tickets.
   The people boarded the plane.

3. The letter came this morning.
   The letter brought good news.

4. The river crossed our trail.
   The river was deep and swift.

5. A needle fell into a haystack.
   A needle was lost.

6. The man rode in a convertible.
   The man is our mayor.

7. The wind blew in our faces.
   The wind was cold.

8. The plant is on the windowsill.
   The plant needs water.

6. Relative Clauses Beginning with *That*

Read the sentences below. Notice that sentences *1* and *2* have been combined in two different ways.

1. The man trains seals.
2. The man is my father. $\Rightarrow$

3. The man who trains seals is my father.
4. The man that trains seals is my father.

■ Which sentence, *1* or *2*, was changed to a relative clause in sentences *3* and *4?*

■ What noun phrase was changed to *who* in sentence *3* and to *that* in sentence *4?*

■ Does the noun phrase name a person, or a thing?

Next, read the following sentences. Notice that sentences *5* and *6* have been combined in two different ways.

5. The tree fell.
6. The tree was an oak. $\Rightarrow$

7. The tree which fell was an oak.
8. The tree that fell was an oak.

■ Which sentence, *5* or *6*, was changed to a relative clause in sentences *7* and *8?*

■ What noun phrase was changed to *which* in sentence *7* and to *that* in sentence *8?*

■ Does the noun phrase name a person, or a thing?

The word *that*, like *who* and *which*, is a relative pronoun when it replaces a noun phrase and begins a relative clause.

Think about what you have learned. What are the three relative pronouns that may begin a relative clause? Which one can replace any noun phrase, whether it names a person or a thing?

For Discussion

How could you combine each pair of sentences below by using a relative clause beginning with *that*? What other relative pronoun could you use in each sentence?

1. The bridge spanned the river. } ⇒ The bridge — —
   The bridge collapsed.   — — collapsed.

2. The boy fell off the porch. } ⇒ The boy — — —
   The boy broke his arm.   — — broke his arm.

For Practice

For More Practice
See Page 393

Oral Combine the pairs of sentences below in two ways, first with *who* or *which* and then with *that*. Make the first sentence in each pair a relative clause inside the second sentence.

1. The apple fell on Newton's head.
   The apple became famous.
2. The player hit a home run.
   The player autographed my ball.
3. The man changed our tire.
   The man was a stranger.
4. The boots needed polishing.
   The boots were my father's.
5. The guests arrived early.
   The guests stayed late.
6. The letter came from my pen pal.
   The letter was interesting.
7. A flower blooms at Christmas.
   A flower is a poinsettia.

Written Write each sentence, filling the blank with a relative clause beginning with *that*.

1. The flowers — are artificial.
2. A song — is on the radio.
3. The fireman — won a medal.
4. The guard — let us go in.
5. The child — laughed happily.
6. The armor — was shiny.

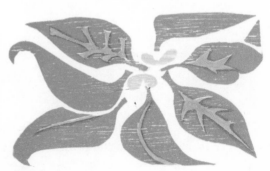

7. Using Apostrophes in Contractions

Read the words below. Notice the spelling of each of the contractions.

A	**B**
1. he + had → he'd	1. does + not → doesn't
2. we + would → we'd	2. is + not → isn't
3. I + am → I'm	3. has + not → hasn't
4. we + will → we'll	4. should + not → shouldn't
5. you + are → you're	5. will + not → won't

- What kind of word is combined with a verb or an auxiliary to form each contraction in A?

- What word is combined with a verb or an auxiliary to form each contraction in B?

- What letter or letters does the apostrophe replace in each contraction?

- Which one of the contractions in B has an irregular spelling?

Now read the sentences in each pair below. Notice the words printed in color.

1. It's getting dark now.	The dog ate its supper.
2. You're late.	Your lunch is ready.
3. They're coming.	They drove their car.
4. Who's there?	Whose book is that?

- Do the words in color in each pair have the same sounds, or do they have different sounds?

- Do these words have the same spellings or different spellings?

- Which word in each pair is a contraction? How can you tell?

Contractions are used often, especially in speaking. When you use a contraction in writing, you should remember the apostrophe. What rule can you make to tell where the apostrophe belongs?

For Discussion

Explain why the same contraction has two different meanings in each pair of sentences below.

1. If I were you, I'd tell the truth.
   When Alex came, I'd already gone home.

2. Jim says that he's eaten lunch.
   Jim says that he's tired.

For Practice

For More Practice
See Page 394

Written **A.** Write the contraction you can make from each pair of words below. Use the rule you made to help you decide where the apostrophe belongs in each contraction.

1. there is
2. here is
3. where is
4. who has
5. who is
6. who will

B. Rewrite the following sentences. Use contractions wherever you can.

1. John will not play baseball with us today.
2. He does not feel very good.
3. He is going to sit on the bench.
4. I will be playing shortstop.
5. You are welcome to come and watch.
6. It is our last game this season.

C. Make up a short sentence to show how you would use each word below.

1. it's
2. its
3. they're
4. their
5. you're
6. your
7. who's
8. whose

255

8. Using Apostrophes in Possessive Nouns

Read the sentences below. Find the noun in each sentence that expresses the idea of ownership.

> Mark's bicycle is broken.
>
> I found the student's book.

Nouns that express the idea of ownership or possession are called **possessive nouns.**

- ■ What ending appears on each possessive noun in the sentences above?

Now study the possessive nouns in each group below to discover how they are spelled.

A	B	C
a girl's coat	some girls' coats	those women's hats
that man's shoes	those robins' nests	the men's shoes
a lady's hat	the ladies' hats	the children's toys

- ■ Which group contains the possessive forms of some singular nouns?

- ■ Which group contains the possessive forms of some plural nouns that end in $-s$?

- ■ Which group contains the possessive forms of some plural nouns that do not end in $-s$?

LADIES' HATS   MEN'S HATS

One important use of the apostrophe is in spelling the possessive form of nouns. What rule can you make for spelling the possessive form of a singular noun? What two rules can you make for spelling the possessive form of a plural noun?

For More Practice
See Page 394

For Discussion

A. Read the following sentences aloud. Which two sentences sound exactly alike? How are these two sentences different in writing? Why are they different?

1. The bird had a cage. Someone opened the bird's cage.
2. The birds had a cage. Someone opened the birds' cage.

B. Where does the apostrophe appear in each possessive form below? Why does the apostrophe appear in two separate places in the two possessive forms?

1. My mother joined the ladies' club.
2. My mother joined the women's club.

For Practice

Oral Tell where you would put an apostrophe in writing each of the possessive forms below.

1. the teachers pencil
2. Angelas stamp collection
3. a boys jacket
4. some boys jackets
5. a mans suit
6. some mens suits

Written Each of the following sentences expresses an idea of ownership. Write a noun phrase containing a possessive noun that expresses the same idea. Be sure to follow the rules for spelling possessive nouns.

1. My uncle has a truck.
2. Christine has a new dress.
3. Our neighbor has a garden.
4. Our neighbors have a garden.
5. The catcher has a mitt.
6. Policemen have whistles.
7. The girls have raincoats.
8. The doctor has an office.
9. The students have lunch boxes.
10. The children have lunch boxes.

257

9. For Review

Read and discuss the questions below.

A. What are noun-forming suffixes? Verb-forming suffixes? Which words below end with noun-forming suffixes? With verb-forming suffixes? How did you decide?

1. action   performance   **2.** memorize   purify
      amazement   departure   harden

B. Which pair of sentences below can be combined by turning the first sentence into a relative clause? Why won't the same process work with the other pair of sentences?

1. The boy lives here.   **2.** Those men are famous.
      The boy mows our lawn.   Those scientists study space.

C. Which pair of sentences below can be combined by using a relative clause beginning with *who?* With *which?* What other relative pronoun could you use in each sentence?

1. The girls had no boots.   **2.** The jet is due now.
      The girls got wet.   The jet will be late.

D. What word in each sentence below is a contraction and needs an apostrophe? Explain how you decided.

1. Youre not going to leave your books there, are you?
2. Its time the kitten had its supper.
3. Whos able to tell whose book this is?

E. How do you decide where to use an apostrophe in writing a possessive noun? Refer to these examples in your answer.

Singular Nouns	Plural Nouns ending in *s*	Plural Nouns without *s* at the end
girl's	girls'	children's
lady's	ladies'	men's

258

Read the directions for each exercise below. Follow the directions, writing your answers on your own paper.

A. Write each sentence below. Add a noun- or a verb-forming suffix from the box to the word in parentheses. Then for each sentence write **noun** or **verb** to show what word you made.

1. The climber checked his — (equip).
2. This chemical helps to — (soft) the metal.
3. A recent — (invent) helps lessen air pollution.
4. They decided to — (modern) the old house.

> –ion
> –ize
> –en
> –ment

B. Combine each pair of sentences below by making the first one a relative clause inside the second. Begin the clauses with *who* or *which*.

5. The ice covered the lagoon.
   The ice began to break.
6. The man is wearing a striped shirt and a bow tie.
   The man is a hypnotist.

C. Combine each pair of sentences below by making the first one a relative clause inside the second. Begin the clauses with *that*.

7. The artist is sketching a child.
   The artist is my sister.
8. The car will be shown at the exhibit.
   The car is a valuable model.

D. The sentences below contain some contractions and some possessive nouns. Write the sentences, using apostrophes where they are needed.

9. Whats in those boys boxes?
10. Isnt that a girls ring lying on the floor?

11. Talking about Heroes

People in every nation and in every time have had heroes. The oldest hero tale to come down to us in English is *Beowulf*, a story in verse about a noble warrior and prince of the Geats. In the story Beowulf sails to Denmark to the aid of King Hrothgar, whose warriors are being killed and eaten by Grendel, a superhuman monster. The poet introduces the hero in these lines.

> Now there lived overseas
> In the land of the Geats a youth of valiance abounding,
> Mightiest yet mildest of men, his name Beowulf,
> Who, hearing of Grendel and minded to destroy him,
> Built a boat of the stoutest timber and chose him
> Warriors, fourteen of the best.

Now listen as your teacher reads the story of Beowulf's encounter with Grendel. It is night. Beowulf and his men are lying in Heorot, the great hall of King Hrothgar. Only Beowulf is awake, watching for the enemy.

> Over the misty moor
> From the dark and dripping caves of his grim lair,
> Grendel with fierce ravenous stride came stepping.
> A shadow under the pale moon he moved,
> That fiend from hell, foul enemy of God,
> Toward Heorot. He beheld it from afar, the gleaming roof
> Towering high to heaven. His tremendous hands
> Struck the studded door, wrenched it from the hinges
> Till the wood splintered and the bolts burst apart.
> Angrily he prowled over the polished floor,
> A terrible light in his eyes—a torch flaming!
> As he scanned the warriors, deep-drugged in sleep,
> Loud loud he laughed, and pouncing on the nearest
> Tore him limb from limb and swallowed him whole,
> Sucking the blood in streams, crunching the bones.

Half-gorged, his gross appetite still unslaked,
Greedily he reached his hand for the next—little reckoning
For Beowulf. The youth clutched it and firmly grappled.

Such torture as this the fiend had never known.
In mortal fear, he was minded to flee to his lair,
But Beowulf prisoned him fast. Spilling the benches,
They tugged and heaved, from wall to wall they hurtled.
And the roof rang to their shouting, the huge hall
Rocked, the strong foundations groaned and trembled.
Then Grendel wailed from his wound, his shriek of pain
Roused the Danes in their hiding and shivered to the stars.
The warriors in the hall spun reeling from their couches,
In dull stupor they fumbled for their swords, forgetting
No man-made weapon might avail. Alone, Beowulf
Tore Grendel's arm from his shoulder asunder,
Wrenched it from the root while the tough sinews cracked.
And the monster roared in anguish, well knowing
That deadly was the wound and his mortal days ended.
Wildly lamenting, away into the darkness he limped,
Over the misty moor to his gloomy home.
But the hero rejoiced in his triumph and wildly waved
In the air his blood-soaked trophy.

                       And the sun,
God's beacon of brightness, banishing night,
Made glad the sky of morning. From near and far
The Danes came flocking to Heorot to behold
The grisly trophy—Grendel's giant arm
Nailed to the wall, the fingertips outspread,
With nails of sharpened steel and murderous spikes
Clawing the roof. Having drunk their fill of wonder,
Eagerly they followed his track to the lake, and there
Spellbound they stared at the water welling with blood,
Still smoking hot where down to the joyless deep
He had dived, downward to death. And they praised Beowulf
And swore that of all men under the sun, beyond measure
Mightiest was he and fittest to govern his people.

                      —Translated by IAN SERRAILLIER

262

Now read the story silently, thinking about these questions.

- What kind of man was Beowulf? How do you think his deeds made him a hero?

- Are heroes today admired for the same kinds of deeds and qualities?

For Discussion

A. What was Beowulf like? Was he admired for any qualities besides physical strength?

B. What people of modern times might be called heroes? How are they like Beowulf? How are they different? Can you think of any reason why today's heroes might be different in some ways from the heroes of long ago?

C. Individuals differ in the qualities they admire most in other people. Think about the people you admire from history, literature, or public life. Who are your own personal heroes? Why?

Activities

Separate into groups of about five members each. Let each group select one of the hero stories listed below. Read about the hero your group chose. Then, as a group, prepare to present that hero to your class. Since most heroes had several adventures told about them, one good idea is to let each person prepare to tell one adventure. Use whatever maps, pictures, and other visual aids you think will help make your stories interesting.

1. Further Adventures of Beowulf
2. The Wanderings of Odysseus (Ulysses)
3. The Story of Siegfried
4. The Story of Roland
5. The Story of Robin Hood
6. King Arthur and the Knights of the Round Table

12. Dramatizing a Hero Story

The Volsung kings are the heroes of some wonderful tales that were first told many, many years ago in Iceland. It was said that the first of the Volsung kings was descended from the god Odin. The following story is about Sigmund, a young Volsung prince. As you read the story, decide how you can tell that Sigmund is a hero.

Long years ago, before the evil days had dawned, King Volsung ruled over all the land which lies between the sea and the country of the Goths. The days were golden; and the good Frey dropped peace and plenty everywhere, and men went in and out and feared no wrong. King Volsung had a dwelling in the midst of fertile fields and fruitful gardens. Fairer than any dream was that dwelling. The roof was thatched with gold, and red turrets and towers rose above. The great feast hall was long and high, and its walls were hung with sunbright shields; and the door nails were of silver. In the middle of the hall stood the pride of the Volsungs,—a tree whose blossoms filled the air with fragrance, and whose green branches, thrusting themselves through the ceiling, covered the roof with fair foliage. It was Odin's tree, and King Volsung had planted it there with his own hands.

On a day in winter King Volsung held a great feast in his hall in honor of Siggeir, the King of the Goths, who was his guest. And the fires blazed bright in the broad chimneys, and music and mirth went round. But in the midst of the merrymaking the guests were startled by a sudden peal of thunder, which seemed to come from the cloudless sky, and which made the shields upon the walls rattle and ring. In wonder they looked around. A strange man stood in the doorway, and laughed, but said not a word. And they noticed that he wore no shoes upon his feet, but that a cloud-gray cloak was thrown over his shoulders, and a blue hood was drawn down over his head. His face was half hidden by a heavy beard; and he had but one eye, which twinkled and glowed like a burning coal. And all the guests sat moveless in their seats, so awed were they in the presence of him who stood at the door; for they knew that he was none other than Odin the All-Father, the king of gods and men. He spoke not a word, but straight into the hall he strode, and he paused not until he stood beneath the blossoming branches of the tree. Then, forth from beneath his cloud-gray cloak, he drew a gleaming sword, and struck the blade deep into the wood,—so deep that nothing but the hilt was left in sight. And, turning to the awe-struck guests, he said, "A blade of mighty worth have I hidden in this tree. Never have the earth folk wrought better steel, nor has any man ever wielded a more trusty sword. Whoever there is among you brave enough and strong enough to draw it forth from the wood, he shall have it as a gift from Odin." Then slowly to the door he strode again, and no one saw him any more.

And after he had gone, the Volsungs and their guests sat a long time silent, fearing to stir, lest the vision should prove a dream. But at last the old king arose, and cried, "Come, guests and kinsmen, and set your hands to the ruddy hilt! Odin's gift stays, waiting for its fated owner. Let us see which one of you is the favored of the All-Father." First Siggeir, the King of the Goths, and his earls, the Volsungs' guests, tried their hands. But the blade stuck fast; and the stoutest man among them failed to move it. Then King Volsung, laughing, seized the hilt, and drew with all his strength; but the sword held still in the wood of Odin's tree. And one by one the nine sons of Volsung tugged and strained in vain; and each was greeted with shouts and laughter, as, ashamed and beaten, he wended to his seat again. Then, at last, Sigmund, the youngest son, stood up, and laid his hand upon the ruddy hilt, scarce thinking to try what all had failed to do. When, lo! the blade came out of the tree as if therein it had all along lain loose. And Sigmund raised it high over his head, and shook it, and the bright flame that leaped from its edge lit up the hall like the lightning's gleaming; and the Volsungs and their guests rent the air with cheers and shouts of gladness. For no one among all the men of the mid-world was more worthy of Odin's gift than young Sigmund the brave.

—JAMES BALDWIN

- In what ways can you tell that Sigmund was a hero?

- Do you think he had shown the qualities of a hero before he drew the sword from Odin's tree? How can you tell?

One way to bring a story to life is to dramatize it. To do this, you do not need to have a script. Just make up the words while you act out the story. What characters would you need in order to dramatize the story of Sigmund?

For Discussion

Decide how you and your classmates would dramatize the story about Sigmund.

1. What characters would you need? Which ones would have the main speaking parts?

2. How can the minor characters also take part with both words and actions?

3. What are some simple props and sound effects that you can use?

Activities

Dramatize the story of Sigmund.

1. Decide what part each member of the class will take.

2. Discuss the actions of the main characters and the minor characters.

3. Decide what the main characters should say, but do not plan their exact words.

4. Decide what props and sound effects you will use.

13. Writing a Journal Entry

The pages of history are filled with real hero stories. Stop and think about it. What explorers do you know about who deserve to be called heroes? What doctors and nurses? What political leaders? What aviators?

Some of the most courageous and colorful men in the story of our country were the mountain men who came to the Rockies to trap beaver. You may know some of their names. Jim Bridger, John Colter, Kit Carson, and Jed Smith are among the most famous.

The stories of these men tell of strength, endurance, courage, wit, and love of freedom and adventure. They faced hunger, thirst, prairie fires, disease, and wild animals in the daily struggle for survival in the wilderness. They had to be heroes because their way of life demanded heroism.

Kit Carson was able to think fast in emergencies. One time he had a hair-raising encounter with two grizzly bears. Suppose he had kept a **journal,** a day-by-day record of things that happened to him. He might have written the following entry.

Today I was hunting elk in the Medicine Bow Mountains when suddenly two grizzlies stood right in front of me. They looked mighty angry. Their jaws were open and their claws were stretched toward me. There was no time to shoot, so I quickly climbed a nearby aspen tree. I barely escaped the vicious claws of one of the grizzlies. The slender bough bent almost within his reach. I was so close that he got one of my moccasins with a swipe of his paw. I broke off a branch and gave his nose a hard smack. The pain angered him. With a roar he grabbed the tree and shook it hard.

I was swaying wildly back and forth. expecting the tree to break at any moment. But suddenly the grizzlies noticed some elk. As quickly as they had appeared, they ran off in search of the new prey. That was the narrowest escape I've had yet.

Think about the event that is described in the imaginary journal entry.

- How does the event show something about the life of a mountain man?
- What does the event suggest about the heroism of a mountain man?

Think about your favorite heroes from history. Why do you consider them heroes? Suppose one of your favorite heroes kept a journal. What kinds of events might he or she have recorded?

For Discussion

Suppose you were going to write an imaginary entry in the journal of a hero from history.

1. What hero would you choose? Why?
2. What events happened in the hero's life that would make an interesting journal entry?
3. What events do you think might have happened in the hero's life even though history doesn't actually record them?

Activities

A. Write an imaginary entry in the journal of a hero from history. The event you write about may be either one that really happened or one that might have happened.

B. Read your journal entry aloud to the rest of the class.

14. Listening to Poetry

Listen as your teacher reads the following poem to you.

AN INDIAN SUMMER DAY ON THE PRAIRIE

IN THE BEGINNING

The sun is a huntress young,
The sun is a red, red joy;
The sun is an Indian girl
Of the tribe of the Illinois.

MID-MORNING

The sun is a smoldering fire
That creeps through the high gray plain,
And leaves not a bush of cloud
To blossom with flowers of rain.

NOON

The sun is a wounded deer
That treads pale grass in the skies,
Shaking his golden horns,
Flashing his baleful eyes.

SUNSET

The sun is an eagle old;
There in the windless west
Atop of the spirit-cliffs,
He builds him a crimson nest.

—VACHEL LINDSAY

Listen as your teacher reads the poem again.

- Why did Vachel Lindsay divide the poem into four parts?

- What comparisons did the poet use to picture the sun at different times of day?

For Discussion

A. What is Indian summer? Why can you understand the poem better if you know what Indian summer is?

B. What colors are mentioned in the poem? How does the color of the sun change as the day passes?

C. What kind of sun do you picture in each comparison? Which comparisons picture the sun as a living thing?

D. Why, do you think, is the first part called "In the Beginning" instead of "Dawn"?

Activities

Your class may want to read this poem together. Practice reading it several times until it sounds good to you. If there is a tape recorder available, you may want to record your reading and then listen to it. Here is one way you could read the poem.

1. The four subtitles may be read by one person.
2. The rest of the poem may be read as follows.
   "In the Beginning": girls in unison
   "Mid-Morning": one girl
   "Noon": one boy
   "Sunset": boys in unison

CHAPTER 9

1. Capitalization and Punctuation

Here is an example of early Greek writing. Even if you don't know how to read Greek, you can probably see some ways in which early writing like this differs from modern writing.

Now read the following sentences. They are written in much the same way as the early Greek writing above.

THEGREEKPOETSTOLDLONGEXCITING
TALESSOMEOFTHESETALESWEREABOUT
THETROJANWARANDTHEWANDERINGSOF
THEHEROODYSSEUS

- What practices of modern writing were not yet invented at the time the early Greek writing was done?

- Do you think these later developments in writing are helpful to readers? If so, how?

Writing was invented hundreds of years before the practices of word division, capitalization, and punctuation were introduced. It wasn't until the seventh century A.D. that it became the regular practice to leave spaces between words. It wasn't until the tenth century that it became customary to begin each sentence with a capital letter and end it with a mark of punctuation.

Think about the practices of word division, capitalization, and punctuation. How did each of these practices represent an improvement in the writing system?

A. Listen as your teacher reads the following paragraph. How does your teacher's voice show where one sentence ends and another begins? How would you show the same things in writing?

THEGREEKSLOVEDCONTESTSOFALLKINDSEVERY
FIVEYEARSTHEYHELDASERIESOFCONTESTSAT
ATOWNCALLEDOLYMPIATHEYGAVEPRIZESTO
THEMENWHOWEREBESTATRUNNINGJUMPING
THROWINGTHEIRSPEARSANDRACINGTHEIRHORSES
THEYALSOGAVEPRIZESTOTHEBESTWRITERSOF
POETRYANDMUSIC

B. Listen as your teacher reads the paragraph below. You will discover one more way in which some very early Greek writing differed from modern writing. After your teacher finishes reading, explain why this kind of writing is well named. What reason can you think of that might explain why the Greeks gave up the practice of writing this way?

SOMEVERYEARLYGREEKWRITINGWENTFROMLEFT
MORFNEHTTFELOTTHGIRMORFNEHTTHGIROT
LEFTTORIGHTANDSOFORTHTHISKINDOFWRITING
TAHTDROWKEERGANODEHPORTSUOBDELLACSI
MEANSTURNINGLIKEOXENINPLOWING

ON YOUR OWN

A. Rewrite the paragraph in part *A* of For Discussion. Use capital letters and punctuation marks wherever necessary.

B. The nursery rhyme below is written without punctuation. Read it and decide how you could punctuate it so that it makes sense. You may want to use the rhyme to puzzle your sister or brother.

> Every lady in the land
> Has twenty nails on each hand
> Five and twenty on hands and feet
> This is true without deceit

2. Adjective-forming Suffixes

Look at the pairs of matching sentences in groups A and B. Notice the words in color in A. What suffix would you have to add to each word before you could use it as an adjective in the matching sentence in B?

A	**B**
1. The key was covered with rust.	The key was very —.
2. The orange was full of juice.	The orange was very —.
3. The soup had too much salt.	The soup was very —.

The suffix –y is called an **adjective-forming suffix** because it changes certain words to adjectives.

English contains many adjectives that are made by adding suffixes like –y to other words. To discover some other adjective-forming suffixes, try this. Add a suffix to each word in color in C, and use the new word to complete the matching sentence in D.

C	**D**
4. The story had humor.	The story was very —.
5. He behaved like a child.	His behavior was very —.
6. The student showed respect.	The student was very —.
7. Did you enjoy the play?	Yes, the play was very —.

Think about the adjectives you used to complete the sentences in this lesson. How are all of these adjectives alike?

276

To each word below, add the suffix that follows. What new words did you make? Try to use each new word as an adjective by completing the sentence, "This is very —." Which suffixes are adjective-forming suffixes? Which suffix is not an adjective-forming suffix? How can you tell?

1. danger + –ous
2. agree + –able

3. care + –less
4. mother + –hood

For More Practice
See Page 394

Oral Add an adjective-forming suffix to each word in italics. Use the adjective you make to complete the second sentence.

1. The water was full of *soap*.
   The water was —.

2. We can put this box to *use*.
   The box will be —.

3. The cat had no *home*.
   The cat was —.

4. We all *hope* the team will win.
   Everyone in town is —.

5. He faced danger without *fear*.
   He was — in the face of danger.

6. Do you *like* the new boy?
   Yes, he is very —.

Written Complete each sentence with an adjective made from the word in parentheses.

1. The venom of a rattlesnake is —. (poison)

2. The sky was —. (storm)

3. That vase is —. (break)

4. The — children were hiding under the bed. (fear)

5. Ferdinand regretted his — action. (self)

6. The journey was long and —. (danger)

7. The dress is not —. (fashion)

8. The traveler was tired and —. (thirst)

9. Bright colors are — to small children. (attract)

10. The book was old and —. (dust)

277

3. Adverb-forming Suffixes

Look at the pairs of matching sentences in groups A and B. All the words in color in A are adjectives. What suffix would you have to add to each word before you could use it as an adverb in the sentence in B?

A	B
1. The river was swift.	The river flowed —.
2. We were glad to see him.	We welcomed him —.
3. The wood-carver was skillful.	He carved the statue —.
4. The happy children played.	The children played —.
5. He is a reckless driver.	He drives —.

The suffix *–ly* is called an **adverb-forming suffix** because it changes certain adjectives to adverbs. A large number of the adverbs in English are made with the suffix *–ly*. Now read the sentences in B once more.

■ Are the adverbs made with *–ly* adverbs of place, adverbs of time, or adverbs of manner? How can you tell?

Two other adverb-forming suffixes are *–wise* and *–ward* (or *–wards*). Add one of these suffixes to each word in color in C. Then use the new words to complete the matching sentences in D.

C	D
6. They looked toward home.	They looked —.
7. Turn the handle in the same direction as the hands of a clock.	Turn the handle —.

Think about the adverbs you used to complete the sentences in this lesson. How are all of these adverbs alike?

For Discussion

The suffix *–ly* is used to make many adverbs. It is also used to make certain adjectives. Add *–ly* to each of the following words.

278

What new word did you make? Is the new word an adjective, or is it an adverb? To prove your answer, use each new word in a sentence of your own.

1. courteous   **2.** love   **3.** friend   **4.** sad

For Practice

For More Practice
See Page 395

Oral   **A.** Change each word in italics to an adverb by adding the adverb-forming suffix *–ly*. Use the adverb to complete the second sentence.

1. The candidate was *hopeful*.
The candidate talked —.

2. Robin gave me a *sweet* smile.
Robin smiled —.

3. We were *eager* to play.
We waited — to start the game.

4. Cats are *graceful*.
My cat Toby moves —.

5. Mr. Fitzhugh was *angry*.
He slammed the door —.

6. The firemen were *courageous*.
They fought the blaze —.

7. The doctor's face looked *sober*.
He broke the bad news —.

8. The miser was *greedy*.
He hoarded his gold —.

9. The answer was *correct*.
Timothy answered —.

B. Use either *–wise* or *–ward* (or *–wards*) to form an adverb from each word below. Then use the adverb in a sentence of your own.

1. down   3. clock
2. back   4. other

Written   Complete each sentence below with an adverb formed from the word in parentheses.

1. The squire served the knight —. (faithful)

2. Please come —. (quick)

3. The flag waved —. (proud)

4. The boys stepped — into the dark cave. (cautious)

5. She cut the cloth —. (length)

6. The ship turned —. (land)

7. — he was sorry he had spoken. (after)

279

4. Adjectives in the Noun Phrase

Look at the sentences below. Notice that both sentences contain the same noun phrase. In addition, one sentence contains an adjective used as a completer after a form of the verb *be*.

The dog followed me home.
The dog was small.

■ What noun phrase appears in both sentences?

■ Which sentence contains an adjective after *be*? What is the adjective?

Now notice the way these sentences can be combined.

1. The dog followed me home. ⎫
2. The dog was **small**.   ⎬ ⟹   3. The **small** dog
                                        followed me home.

■ What part of sentence *1* appears in sentence *3*?

■ What part of sentence *2* becomes part of a noun phrase in sentence *3*?

■ Where does the adjective from sentence *2* appear within the noun phrase in sentence *3*, before the noun or after it?

Think about what you have learned. When can two sentences be combined to form one sentence containing an adjective that is part of a noun phrase?

For Discussion

How can you combine these sentences to form one sentence containing an adjective that is part of a noun phrase?

280   **1.** Her hair hung to her waist.   **2.** Her hair was shiny.

For More Practice
See Page 395

For Practice

Oral Combine each pair of sentences below. Make one sentence containing an adjective that is part of a noun phrase.

1. The knight drew his sword.
   The knight was brave.

2. The stranger stood at the door.
   The stranger was tall.

3. The barn needed paint.
   The barn was old.

4. The class became quiet.
   The class was unruly.

5. The truck bumped along slowly.
   The truck was rickety.

6. The soap smelled spicy.
   The soap was green.

7. The street led to the beach.
   The street was narrow.

8. The voyage ended at last.
   The voyage was long.

Written From each pair of sentences, write one sentence. Your sentence should contain an adjective that is part of a noun phrase.

1. The siren broke the stillness.
   The siren was shrill.

2. The fish escaped the hook.
   The fish was silvery.

3. The path followed the creek.
   The path was shady.

4. The mechanic worked hard.
   The mechanic was skillful.

5. The wind blew sand in our eyes.
   The wind was hot.

6. The moth rested on a twig.
   The moth was frail.

7. The children ran home.
   The children were hungry.

8. The apple tasted delicious.
   The apple was juicy.

281

5. Verbs in the Noun Phrase

Read the two pairs of sentences below. Notice that both sentences in each pair contain the same noun phrase. In addition, one sentence in each pair contains a verb used with an auxiliary.

A	**B**
The dog appeared at the door.	A lamp lay on the rug.
The dog was shivering.	A lamp was broken.

- What noun phrase appears in both sentences in *A?* In both sentences in *B?*

- Which sentence in *A* contains the *ing* form of a verb? Which sentence in *B* contains the *en* form of a verb?

Sentences like the ones in each pair above can be combined to form a third sentence.

The dog appeared at the door.
The dog was shivering. $\Big\} \Rightarrow$ The shivering dog appeared at the door.

The lamp lay on the rug.
The lamp was broken. $\Big\} \Rightarrow$ The broken lamp lay on the rug.

- What verb in the second sentence in each pair becomes part of a noun phrase in the new sentence?

- Where does the verb appear within the noun phrase, before the noun or after it?

You have seen that two sentences can be combined to form one sentence containing a verb that is part of a noun phrase. What are the two verb forms that can be used this way?

How can you combine these sentences to form one sentence containing a verb that is part of a noun phrase? Where will the verb appear, before the noun or after it?

1. The cattle raced down the valley.
2. The cattle were stampeding.

For Practice

For More Practice
See Page 396

Oral Combine each pair of sentences to form one sentence. Your sentence should contain a verb that is part of a noun phrase.

1. The log struck our canoe.
   The log was drifting.

2. The child sat on the curb.
   The child was weeping.

3. A crow perched on the sill.
   A crow was talking.

4. The speaker entertained us.
   The speaker was smiling.

5. The collar became uncomfortable.
   The collar was starched.

6. The leaves burned quickly.
   The leaves were withered.

7. The telephone woke me.
   The telephone was ringing.

8. The fender on my bicycle will be replaced.
   The fender was dented.

9. The kite fell to the ground.
   The kite was broken.

10. The frog sat on a lily pad.
    The frog was sleeping.

Written From each pair of sentences, write one sentence. Your sentence should contain a verb that is part of a noun phrase.

1. The geese flew above us.
   The geese were migrating.

2. The marshmallows taste good.
   The marshmallows are toasted.

3. The army marched homeward.
   The army was defeated.

4. That shutter should be fixed.
   That shutter is rattling.

5. The rabbit scurried into the black-berry bushes.
   The rabbit was startled.

6. That dog wants to come in.
   That dog is barking.

7. The snake frightened Emily.
   The snake was hissing.

8. The car could not be found.
   The car was stolen.

9. The candle gave little light.
   The candle was flickering.

10. His ankle hurt.
    His ankle was sprained.

283

6. Other Words in the Noun Phrase

Look at the sentences in A. Notice that both sentences contain the same noun phrase. In addition, one sentence contains an adverb used as a completer after the verb *be*.

Now look at the sentences in B. Notice again that both sentences contain the same noun phrase. In addition, one sentence contains the verb *be* plus a prepositional phrase.

A
The noise frightened us.
The noise was upstairs.

B
A boy rode past.
A boy was on a bike.

Sentences like those in each pair above can be combined to form a third sentence.

The noise frightened us.
The noise was **upstairs.** $\}$ $\Rightarrow$ The noise **upstairs** frightened us.

A boy rode past.
A boy was **on a bike.** $\}$ $\Rightarrow$ A boy **on a bike** rode past.

- What part of the second sentence in each pair becomes part of a noun phrase in the new sentence?

- Where does the adverb or prepositional phrase appear within the noun phrase, before the noun or after it?

You have discovered that you can combine two sentences to form one sentence containing an adverb or a prepositional phrase that is part of a noun phrase. When can two sentences be combined in this way?

For More Practice
See Page 396

For Discussion

How can you combine the sentences in each pair below to form one sentence? The new sentence should contain a one-word adverb or a prepositional phrase that is part of a noun phrase.

1. The clock chimes loudly.
   The clock is on the wall.

2. The river overflowed.
   The river was nearby.

For Practice

Oral Combine each pair of sentences. Your new sentence should contain a one-word adverb or a prepositional phrase that is part of a noun phrase.

1. The tree blossomed.
   The tree was behind our house.

2. A hole let in the rain.
   A hole was in our tent.

3. The stores open at nine.
   The stores are downtown.

4. The snake slithered away.
   The snake was under the porch.

5. A troll frightened everyone.
   A troll was beneath the bridge.

6. The people came to dinner.
   The people were downstairs.

Written From each pair of sentences, write a single sentence. Your new sentence should contain a one-word adverb or a prepositional phrase that is part of a noun phrase.

1. The dog barked all night.
   The dog was in the kennel.

2. The crowd began to cheer.
   The crowd was around the speaker.

3. The daisies wilted.
   The daisies were in the vase.

4. Jets drowned out our voices.
   Jets were overhead.

5. The trunk smelled musty.
   The trunk was in the attic.

6. The ladybug flew away.
   The ladybug was on your collar.

7. The air was bitterly cold.
   The air was outside.

8. The noise startled us.
   The noise was below.

7. Using Capital Letters in Proper Nouns

Look at the proper nouns below.

Denver	Brookfield Zoo	New York City
Charles	United Kingdom	Empire State Building
April	Lake Street	Golden Gate Bridge
Thursday	Coast Guard	St. John's Cathedral

- How many words does each proper noun contain?

- What rule can you make for writing proper nouns?

Next, look at the proper nouns in this group.

> Cave of the Mounds
> Museum of Science and Industry
> Meyer and Sons

- What can you add to the rule you made for writing proper nouns?

Now look at some names that contain titles of respect.

> Uncle Ben
> Senator Brooke
> Professor Silverstein

- What rule can you make for writing titles of respect?

For Discussion

Tell which of the words below should begin with a capital letter. Explain why.

1. arthur
2. trinity church
3. aunt sarah
4. house of representatives
5. pine mountain school
6. grand canyon of the colorado river

For Practice

Written A. Write each of these word groups on your paper. Use capital letters wherever they are needed.

1. laurel creek
2. some navaho indians
3. first avenue
4. st. mark's church
5. crater lake
6. sunday afternoon
7. his horse jennie
8. the milky way
9. marshall field and company
10. department of the interior

B. Rewrite each of the following sentences, replacing the words in italics with a proper noun.

1. Jim belongs to *a boys' club*.
2. School is closed for *a holiday*.
3. My sister is studying *a foreign language*.
4. My father flew to *a city*.
5. Our school is on *a street*.
6. Will you call *the dog*?
7. Margaret wrote to *her teacher*.
8. Al belongs to *a political party*.
9. Meg goes to *a junior high school*.
10. I bought these strawberries in *a grocery store*.

C. Rewrite each sentence below, using the word in italics as a title of respect before someone's name.

1. The jury greeted the *judge*.
2. Everyone welcomed the *private*.
3. The palace is the home of the *queen*.
4. I called my *aunt* long distance.
5. Write to your *representative*.
6. Everyone liked the *professor*.
7. A message came from the *bishop*.
8. The people reelected the *mayor*.
9. That man is a *colonel*.
10. Here comes the *senator*.

287

8. More about Capital Letters

It is important to know when to use capital letters, but it is equally important to know when *not* to use them. Compare the words printed in color in the two groups below.

A	B
1. the Oregon Trail	the trail to Oregon
2. the City of New York	a city in New York
3. the Illinois River	an Illinois river
4. Uncle Bert	my uncle
5. the Prudential Building	a building in Chicago
6. Thanksgiving Day	a November day
7. New York University	a university in New York
8. Queen Elizabeth II	an English queen
9. San Francisco Bay	a bay in California

■ Why are capital letters used to begin the words printed in color in *A?*

■ Why aren't capital letters used to begin the same words in *B?*

In the sentences below, the nouns printed in color name divisions of time. Study these nouns carefully.

10. They will come on Tuesday.
11. They will come in July.
12. They will come in the summer.

■ Are the names of days of the week and months of the year common nouns, or are they proper nouns?

■ Are the names of seasons common nouns, or are they proper nouns?

■ What rule can you make for capitalizing words that name divisions of time?

Tell which of the words in italics should begin with a capital letter. Explain why.

1. A *city* in *oklahoma* is *oklahoma city*.
2. A *planetarium* in *chicago* is the *adler planetarium*.
3. A *judge* from *harlan county* is *judge allweiss*.
4. He came to our town in the middle of *winter*, on a cold *monday* in *january*.

For
Practice

For More Practice
See Page 397

Oral For each sentence below, make up a sentence in which the word in italics would not be capitalized.

1. We saw the *Garden* of the Gods.
2. The battle was fought near Blenheim *Palace*.
3. The travelers stayed at the Ocean View *Inn*.
4. Last Saturday the boys played tennis in Lincoln *Park*.
5. The house was on Ridge *Road*.
6. The speaker was *Governor* Yates.
7. We saw the Big *Dipper*.
8. School began after Labor *Day*.
9. The service was held in the First Baptist *Church*.

Written A. Write each of these word groups on your paper. Use capital letters wherever they are needed.

1. a country in europe
2. the arctic circle
3. a general in the united states army
4. general eisenhower
5. one morning in spring
6. a wednesday morning in may

B. Write two sentences using each word below, first as a common noun, then as part of a proper noun.

1. city   4. club
2. river   5. day
3. street   6. captain

289

Read and discuss the questions below.

A. How is the writing of today different from early Greek writing? Use these examples in explaining your answer.

1. EARLYGREEKWRITINGLOOKED
   SOMETHINGLIKETHIS

2. Modern writing looks like this.

B. What are adjective-forming suffixes? What are adverb-forming suffixes? Which group below contains words that are made with adjective-forming suffixes? With adverb-forming suffixes? How did you decide?

1	2
frosty	suddenly
joyful	lengthwise
agreeable	seaward

C. The sentences in each pair below can be combined to form a new sentence. Which pair would make a new sentence containing an adjective in the noun phrase? A one-word adverb in the noun phrase? A prepositional phrase in the noun phrase? A verb in the noun phrase? How did you decide?

1. The light bulb flickered.
   The light bulb was *above*.

2. The robins ate hungrily.
   The robins were *young*.

3. The wren flew away.
   The wren was *singing*.

4. A man rode past.
   A man was *on a horse*.

D. In the sentences below, why are some of the italicized words capitalized? Why aren't the other italicized words capitalized?

1. We visited St. Paul's *Cathedral* in *London* last *summer*.
2. The *doctor* I saw on *Tuesday* is *Doctor* Allen.
3. A government *department* is the *Department of Justice*.

Read the directions for each exercise below. Follow the directions, writing your answers on your own paper.

A. Write the following sentences. Add an adjective- or an adverb-forming suffix from the box to each word in parentheses. Then for each sentence write **adjective** or **adverb** to show what kind of word you made.

1. The cat's fur felt —. (silk)
2. Our hostess greeted us —. (courteous)
3. After months of travel, Eloise was glad to turn — at last. (home)
4. The chair was soft and —. (comfort)

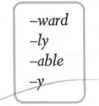

–ward
–ly
–able
–y

B. Combine the sentences in each pair. Make the word or words in italics part of a noun phrase in the first sentence. Then identify the part in italics by writing **adjective, verb, adverb,** or **prepositional phrase.**

5. Snow made the path muddy.
   Snow was *melting*.

6. The house was empty.
   The house was *on the mountainside*.

7. The colt ran around the corral.
   The colt was *frisky*.

8. The rooms need painting.
   The rooms are *upstairs*.

C. Write the following sentences. Use capital letters wherever they are needed.

9. Last winter I visited aunt martha in atlanta.
10. My uncle was a professor at the university of iowa.
11. My sister ann attended central junior high school.
12. School began on the day after labor day.

291

11. Talking about Books

One night Archy the cockroach typed the following book review and left it in his boss's typewriter.

```
         book review

boss a new book
has appeared
which should be
read by every one
it is entitled
the cockroach
its life history
and how to deal
with it and
the author
is frederick laing
who is assistant
in the department
of entomology in the
british museum
of natural history
it is one of the
best books i ever
tasted i am eating
the binding from
a copy with
a great deal of
relish and
recommend it
to all other
insects yours
truly

            archy
```

Archy, a cockroach with the soul of a poet, was created by a writer named Don Marquis. Every night Archy jumped on the keys of his boss's typewriter and typed free verse poems like the one on the opposite page. Archy wasn't heavy enough to use the shift key. For that reason his poems do not have capital letters.

Next, read Archy's review again, and answer the following questions.

- Why was Archy especially interested in the book he was reviewing?

- How did he express his opinion of the book in the last part of the review?

You have probably given some book reviews or book reports of your own. Sometimes you prepare them for class according to the instructions of your teacher. But sometimes, like Archy, you may simply tell a friend why he would enjoy a book you have read.

- If you wanted to interest a friend in reading a book, what are some things you would tell him about it?

- How is telling a friend about a book similar to giving a book report?

For Discussion

A. In the lessons to follow, you will discover several ways in which you can share a book you have read with someone else. Before you look ahead, think of at least one way to tell others about a book without giving away the outcome of the story. Think about some ways of picturing the book as well as some ways of talking or writing about it. Discuss your ideas with your class.

B. The dust jackets below belong to books that are favorites of many young people. Which of the books have you read? Which ones did you like? What are some other books that you would put on a list of favorites for young people? Why?

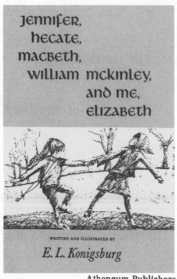

JENNIFER, hecate, macBeth, william mckinley, and me, elizabeth

WRITTEN AND ILLUSTRATED BY
E. L. Konigsburg

Atheneum Publishers

Charlotte's Web

by E.B. WHITE
Author of STUART LITTLE
Pictures by GARTH WILLIAMS

Harper & Row, Publishers

Holt, Rinehart and Winston, Inc.

THE BOOK OF THREE

BY LLOYD ALEXANDER

...and now Miguel

By JOSEPH KRUMGOLD
ILLUSTRATED BY JEAN CHARLOT

Thomas Y. Crowell Company

294

12. Dramatizing a Scene from a Book

It was a beautiful Saturday morning, but Tom Sawyer couldn't enjoy it. Instead of going swimming with his friends, he had to stay home and whitewash the fence. He was a melancholy boy until, as Mark Twain put it, "an inspiration burst upon him." Soon Ben Rogers came by and spoke to Tom.

"Hello, old chap, you got to work, hey?"

Tom wheeled suddenly and said:

"Why, it's you, Ben! I warn't noticing."

"Say—*I'm* going in a-swimming, *I* am. Don't you wish you could? But of course you'd druther *work*—wouldn't you? Course you would!"

Tom contemplated the boy a bit, and said:

"What do you call work?"

"Why, ain't *that* work?"

Tom resumed his whitewashing, and answered carelessly:

"Well, maybe it is, and maybe it ain't. All I know is, it suits Tom Sawyer."

"Oh come, now, you don't mean to let on that you *like* it?"

The brush continued to move.

"Like it? Well, I don't see why I oughtn't to like it. Does a boy get a chance to whitewash a fence every day?"

That put the thing in a new light. Ben stopped nibbling his apple. Tom swept his brush daintily back and forth—stepped back to note the effect—added a touch here and there—criticized the effect again—Ben watching every move and getting more and more interested, more and more absorbed. Presently he said:

"Say, Tom, let *me* whitewash a little."

Tom considered, was about to consent; but he altered his mind:

"No—no—I reckon it wouldn't hardly do, Ben. You see, Aunt Polly's awful particular about this fence—right here on the street, you know—but if it was the back fence I wouldn't mind and *she* wouldn't. Yes, she's awful particular about this fence; it's got to be done very careful; I reckon there ain't one boy in a thousand, maybe two thousand, that can do it the way it's got to be done."

"No—is that so? Oh come, now—lemme just try. Only just a little—I'd let *you*, if you was me, Tom."

"Ben, I'd like to, honest injun; but Aunt Polly—well, Jim wanted to do it, but she wouldn't let him; Sid wanted to do it, and she wouldn't let Sid. Now don't you see how I'm fixed? If you was to tackle this fence and anything was to happen to it—"

"Oh, shucks, I'll be just as careful. Now lemme try. Say—I'll give you the core of my apple."

"Well, here—No, Ben, now don't. I'm afeard—"

"I'll give you *all* of it!"

Tom gave up the brush with reluctance in his face, but alacrity in his heart.

—MARK TWAIN

Later Tom traded his job for a kite from Billy Fisher and a dead rat from Johnny Miller.

One way to interest someone else in a book is to dramatize a scene from it. Read the scene until you understand it thoroughly. Then act it out, making up the words and actions as you go.

Suppose you decided to act out the whitewashing scene.

- What characters would you need?
- What actions could the characters perform?
- What simple props could you use?

For Discussion

A. Plan to dramatize the whitewashing scene. Decide who will play each part. Decide what props you will need and who will bring them to class. Plan to act out the scene freely, making up your own words for the dialogue between Tom and Ben. You may also want to add dialogue between Tom and the other two boys, Billy Fisher and Johnny Miller. Suppose you wanted to use even more characters. How could you easily add some?

B. Think of some scenes from books you have read recently. Which scenes would be good ones to dramatize? Why?

Activities

A. Dramatize the whitewashing scene. Follow the plans you made in For Discussion.

B. Separate into groups to dramatize scenes from other books you have read. Each group should plan and act out one scene. Practice it two or three times in your group. Then, if you wish, present it to the rest of the class.

C. If you prefer, make puppets and present the scene you chose in the form of a puppet play.

13. Playing a Role

One way to tell about a book is to play the role of the main character. Dress as much like the main character as you can. Then tell an interesting part of the story just as if it happened to you. For example, you might begin your story something like this.

Scout Knife

Spy Glasses

Dark Blue Sweatshirt

Belt

Leather Pouch (for Notebook)

Canteen

Flashlight

Leather Pen Case

Ancient Blue Jeans

Sneakers

My name is Harriet M. Welsch. I am the main character in the book *Harriet the Spy*, by Louise Fitzhugh.

One day when I came to school, no one spoke to me. In fact, everyone looked at me with mean eyes. I knew they had a plan, and that I was going to get it. I also knew why.

The day before when we were playing tag, I had lost my notebook. One of the other kids found it. Before I knew it was missing, they had all read it. In it were my notes about all of them. I want to be a writer, so I take notes about everyone I meet and know. Here's an example from the notebook I lost. I wrote this about Sport, my best friend.

SOMETIMES I CAN'T STAND SPORT. WITH HIS WORRYING ALL THE TIME AND FUSSING OVER HIS FATHER, SOMETIMES HE'S LIKE A LITTLE OLD WOMAN.

- Do you think the speaker has chosen a good part of Harriet's story to tell? Would it be a good idea to tell the rest of the story, including what happens at the end of the book?

- Does the speaker refer to Harriet as *I* or as *she*? Why?

For Discussion

What books have you read recently that you could tell about by playing the role of one of the characters? Why are these books good choices for role-playing?

Activities

A. Plan to play the role of a character from a book you have read recently.

1. Decide what character you will pretend to be.

2. Choose one incident or adventure from the book. Plan to tell the story as if it happened to you.

3. Plan and prepare a simple costume. The descriptions and the pictures in the book may give you some good ideas. If you wish, plan to use some props also.

B. Present your story to the class.

14. Picturing a Book

A story that takes place in China is *The House of Sixty Fathers*. Read some paragraphs from the beginning of Chapter 1, called "Rain on the Sampan."

Rain raised the river. Rain beat down on the sampan where it lay in a long row of sampans tied to the riverbank. Rain drummed down on the mats that were shaped in the form of an arched roof over the middle of the sampan. It clattered hard on the four long oars lying on top of the roof of mats.

The rain found the bullethole in the roof of mats. Thick drops of water dripped through the bullethole onto the neck of the family pig, sleeping on the floor of the sampan. . . .

Rain raised the river. The sampan swayed and bobbed on the rising water. Voices drifted from the other sampans in the long row of sampans and muttered among the drumming rain. Tien Pao closed his eyes and almost slept, and yet he didn't sleep. He sat sagged against the mats, dreamily remembering the hard days just past, the hard journey.

—MEINDERT DEJONG

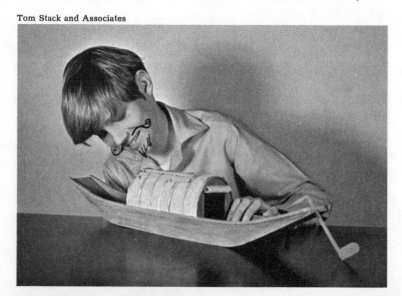

Later Tien Pao was separated from his parents when the sampan accidentally came loose from the riverbank and was swept far down the river. The story goes on to tell about the exciting adventures that followed.

Sometimes you may want to picture a story instead of telling it. The boy in the picture is holding a model of a sampan. Ideas for the model came from descriptions and pictures in *The House of Sixty Fathers*.

■ What materials might have been used in making the model?

■ How could the model help you to picture what happened in the story?

For Discussion

Here are some ways of picturing a story. What book have you read recently that you could report on in one of these ways? Can you think of other ways of picturing a book?

1. Draw or paint a dust jacket for the book.
2. Make a diorama picturing a scene from the book.
3. Make a poster, collage, or bulletin-board display.
4. Make a mobile picturing characters or objects from the story.
5. With others who have read the same book, create a mural or a series of pictures about the story.
6. Make puppet figures of characters from the book.

Activities

A. Choose a book to report on by picturing the story. Use one of the ideas in For Discussion or an idea of your own.

B. Arrange a display of the reports. Invite your parents or the members of another class to see the display.

15. Writing about a Book

Nearly everyone likes to pretend. One of the pleasures people get from books is a kind of pretending. As you read, you imagine yourself as one of the characters. You can do some of this kind of pretending when you write about a book you have read. Read the example that follows.

My name is True Son. I am the main character in the book *The Light in the Forest*, by Conrad Richter.

My name is also Johnny Butler. You see, I was born the son of Mr. and Mrs. Butler. When I was four years old, I was captured by Indians. I lived with my Indian father Cuyloga and my Indian mother Quaquenga for eleven years. Then I was forced to go back to the home of my white parents, where I am living now.

I loved my life as an Indian. I loved the freedom of being close to the rivers and earth and sky. I was proud of my strong, brave father. For years I played and laughed with my friends Half Arrow and Little Crane.

The ways of the white man are strange to me, and I don't like them. I don't like to stay in a house that is closed tight against the fresh, living air. I feel bound in by the stiff clothes and shoes I have to wear. The Butlers are my real parents, but sometimes I wonder. Am I more white man or Indian?

Suppose you wanted to write this kind of report about a book you read. To find out how to do it, answer these questions.

- ■ What character does the writer of the report pretend to be?
- ■ In which paragraphs does he introduce himself?
- ■ In which paragraphs does he explain a major problem he faced in the story? What was the problem?

For Discussion

What book character would you like to pretend to be? Is he or she the main character of the book, or a minor character? What problem does the character face?

Activities

A. Plan and write a book report in which you imagine yourself as one of the characters. Write about something that happened to you in the story, or describe a problem you faced. Use the pronoun *I*. Try not to give away the outcome of the book.

B. Present your report to the rest of the class in one of the ways suggested below.

1. Read your paper aloud to the class.
2. Post your paper on a class bulletin board.
3. Prepare a copy for a class book of reports.

16. Listening to Poetry

Listen as your teacher reads the following poems to you.

WATER-FRONT STREETS

The spring is not so beautiful there—
    But dream ships sail away
To where the spring is wondrous rare
    And life is gay.

The spring is not so beautiful there—
    But lads put out to sea
Who carry beauties in their hearts
    And dreams, like me.

                —Langston Hughes

DREAMS

Hold fast to dreams
For if dreams die
Life is a broken-winged bird
That cannot fly.

Hold fast to dreams
For when dreams go
Life is a barren field
Frozen with snow.

            —Langston Hughes

Now listen as your teacher reads the poems again. Think about these questions.

- What kind of dreams are the two poems about?
- Do you have dreams like these?
- Do you think that dreams are as important to people as Langston Hughes says they are in these poems?

For Discussion

A. Read the first line of "Water-Front Streets." Where is spring "not so beautiful," and why?

B. What are the "dream ships" in the second line of "Water-Front Streets"?

C. What are the two comparisons in "Dreams"? Why did Langston Hughes use comparisons to say what he wanted to say about dreams? (To find out, try to say the same things without using comparisons.)

Activities

A. If you live in the city, make a collection of city poems like "Water-Front Streets."

B. The poem "Dreams" is an especially easy one to learn by heart. If you wish, learn the poem by reading it to yourself several times. Then share it with someone else, either at school or at home.

C. If you enjoyed these poems, find and read some others by Langston Hughes. Share your favorite one with the class by reading it aloud.

CHAPTER 10

1. The Story of the Alphabet

The chart on the opposite page tells some of the long story of the alphabet you use to write English. Scholars believe the story goes back to ancient Egypt. The Egyptians developed a kind of picture writing called **hieroglyphics.** Later the Phoenicians invented an alphabet. Now look at the chart.

- What evidence can you find that the Phoenician letter forms developed from hieroglyphics?

The Phoenicians were a great seafaring people who traded far and wide all over the Mediterranean Sea. They carried their writing system to other countries, including Greece. As a result, the Greeks began to use the Phoenician letters to write their own language. Now study the chart again.

- Which Greek letters are much like the Phoenician letters? Which ones are quite different?
- What are some letters that the Greeks added?

The Romans adopted the Greek alphabet, making further changes. Finally, the Roman alphabet was used to write English. Study the chart once more.

- Which Greek letter forms were changed only slightly by the Romans?
- What letters not in the Roman alphabet are used today to write English?

For Discussion

Find evidence in the chart for these statements.

1. The Phoenicians named some of their letters for objects pictured in Egyptian hieroglyphics.
2. The Greeks borrowed the names as well as the forms of some Phoenician letters.

308

FROM HIEROGLYPHICS TO LETTERS

EGYPTIAN HIEROGLYPHICS		PHOENICIAN LETTERS		GREEK LETTERS		ROMAN LETTERS	MODERN LETTERS
	(ox)		aleph (ox)		alpha	A	A
	(house)		beth (house)		beta	B	B
	(corner)		gimel (camel)		gamma	C	C
	(door)		daleth (door)		delta	D	D
	(high)		he		epsilon	E	E
	(peg)		wau (peg)		digamma	F	F
						G	G
	(fence)		cheth (fence)		eta	H	H
	(hand)		yod (hand)		iota	I	I
							J
	(palm)		kaph (palm)		kappa	K	K
	(cord)		(crook)		lambda	L	L
	(water)		mem (water)		mu	M	M
	(snake)		nun (fish)		nu	N	N
	(eye)		ayin (eye)		omicron	O	O
	(mouth)		pe (mouth)		pei	P	P
			koph (monkey)		koppa	Q	Q
	(head)		resh (head)		rho	R	R
	(mountains)		shin (mountains)		sigma	S	S
	(cross)		tau (mark)		tau	T	T
							U
					upsilon	V	V
							W
					khei	X	X
						Y	Y
			zayin (balance)		zeta	Z	Z

2. Rules for Adding Suffixes

Study the two groups of words below. Notice the words that end with the letter *y*. Then observe what happens to the spelling of each word when you add a suffix.

A	**B**
employ + –er → employer	lonely + –ness → loneliness
enjoy + –able → enjoyable	merry + –ment → merriment
pay + –ment → payment	try + –al → trial

- Which group contains words that have a vowel letter before the final *y*? A consonant letter before the final *y*?

- In which words do you keep the *y* when you add a suffix? In which words do you change *y* to *i* when you add a suffix?

Next, study two more groups of words. Notice the words that end with an *e*. The final *e* in these words does not stand for a sound. See what happens when you add suffixes.

C	**D**
like + –ness → likeness	erase + –able → erasable
hope + –ful → hopeful	vote + –er → voter
retire + –ment → retirement	write + –ing → writing

- Which group contains suffixes that begin with a consonant letter? What happens to the final *e* in a word when one of these suffixes is added?

- Which group contains suffixes that begin with a vowel letter? What happens to the final *e* in a word when one of these suffixes is added?

Look once more at the four groups of words above. What two spelling rules can you make for adding a suffix to words ending in *y*? What two spelling rules can you make for adding a suffix to words ending in an *e* that does not stand for a sound?

Study the word groups below. For each group, what rule explains what happens to the spelling when a suffix is added to a word ending in *y* or *e*?

1	2	3	4
rudeness	famous	betrayal	beautiful
careful	education	employment	penniless
advancement	lining	destroyer	envious

**For
Practice**

For More Practice
See Page 398

Written A. Join each word and suffix to make another word. Use two of the rules you have studied to help you spell the new words.

1. busy + –ly
2. dry + –ness
3. play + –er
4. likely + –hood
5. icy + –ness
6. library + –an
7. duty + –ful
8. homely + –ness
9. boy + –ish
10. joy + –ful

B. Join each word and suffix to make another word. Use two of the rules you have studied to help you spell the new words.

1. false + –ify
2. false + –ness
3. rehearse + –al
4. create + –ion
5. grace + –ful
6. loose + –en
7. juice + –y
8. late + –ly
9. write + –er
10. place + –ment

ON YOUR OWN

How are the words below exceptions to one of the spelling rules? Can you guess why these words don't follow the rule? If they did, what spellings would result?

study + –ing → studying   forty + –ish → fortyish

3. More about Adding Suffixes

Each word below ends with a single consonant letter.

ship   red   sun

- How many syllables does each word have?
- Is the final consonant letter in each word preceded by one vowel letter or two?

Now observe what happens when suffixes are added to one-syllable words like these.

A   **B**

ship + –er → shipper   ship + –ment → shipment
red + –est → reddest   red + –ness → redness
sun + –y → sunny   sun + –ward → sunward

- Which group contains suffixes that begin with a vowel letter? With a consonant letter?
- What happens to the final consonant when you add a suffix beginning with a vowel letter?

Next, study some more words that end in one consonant letter preceded by one vowel letter. Each word has two syllables.

C   **D**

admít + –ed → admitted   joúrnal + –ist → journalist
propél + –er → propeller   póison + –ous → poisonous
regrét + –able → regrettable   fávor + –able → favorable

- Which two-syllable words are stressed on the first syllable? On the second syllable?
- In which of these words do you double the final consonant letter when you add a suffix beginning with a vowel letter?

You have discovered some rules for adding suffixes to words ending in one consonant letter. What are the rules?

In each box, why are the consonant letters doubled before the suffix in the words in column *1?* Why aren't they doubled in the words in column *2?*

1	2
robber	waiter
wrapped	boiling
swimming	sleepy

1	2
patrolled	marketing
beginner	perilous
committing	different

**For
Practice**

For More Practice
See Page 398

Written Join each word and suffix to make another word. Use the rules you have studied to help you spell the new words.

1. scar + –ed
2. swim + –er
3. prefer + –ed
4. repel + –ent
5. pilot + –ed
6. bob + –ed
7. regret + –able
8. drum + –er
9. occur + –ence
10. fog + –y
11. fat + –en
12. deaf + –en
13. expel + –ing
14. conceal + –ing

ON YOUR OWN

Read the sentences below. What spelling rules has the writer forgotten? What would you have to do to correct each sentence?

1. Brian lay on his back and starred at the stary sky.

2. Alex riped a bunch of grapes from the vine before they had rippened.

3. Peter hoped off the train, hopping that someone would be there to meet him.

313

4. Making Language Choices

Imagine you are writing a letter to a friend. You are telling about a carnival you went to last Saturday. Read the sentences below. Which way, *1* or *2*, would you choose to tell about the carnival act shown in the picture? Why?

1. A clown performed for us.
   A trained seal performed for us.
2. A clown **and** a trained seal performed for us.

Now answer these questions to see how the examples differ.

- Which example, *1* or *2*, has fewer words?
- What sentence parts are combined with the conjunction *and* in example *2*?

Often in writing you can make the kind of language choice shown above. You can choose to repeat words, as in example *1*. Or you can combine ideas and use fewer words, as in example *2*.

Other sentence parts besides noun phrases can be joined with a conjunction. Study the sentences below.

3. He saddled his horse.
   He rode to town.
4. He saddled his horse **and** rode to town.

314

5. The morning was cold.
   The morning was sunny.
6. The morning was cold **but** sunny.
7. Let's walk through the woods.
   Let's walk along the river.
8. Let's walk through the woods **or** along the river.

   ■ Which sentence contains a conjunction that joins verb phrases? Adjectives? Prepositional phrases?

   ■ What different conjunctions are used?

English often gives you choices, different ways of expressing the same ideas. This lesson is about one kind of choice you have. What is it?

For Discussion

A. If you wanted to express the following ideas, what sentences could you make using conjunctions? In what ways would your new sentences be different from the ones below?

1. Mother poured the orange juice.
   Mother buttered the toast.

2. Isaac knew that the key might be under the doormat.
   Isaac knew that the key might be on the windowsill.

B. Sometimes more than two sentences can be combined. How can you make one sentence from the three sentences in each example below?

1. The bacon was crisp.
   The bacon was tender.
   The bacon was juicy.

2. The train took us out of town.
   The train took us across five states.
   The train took us into the great city.

315

For Practice

Oral Use a conjunction to join sentence parts in each example.

1. Amos will order a hamburger.
   Amos will order a barbecue.

2. Sara will bake a pie.
   Sara will bake a cake.
   Sara will bake some cookies.

3. A gingham dog sat on the table.
   A calico cat sat on the table.

4. Roger will wash the car.
   Dean will wash the car.

5. You will find the letter in the mailbox.
   You will find the letter on the floor.

6. The fish nudged the bait.
   The fish didn't bite.

7. Lisa poured oil in the pan.
   Lisa dumped in the popcorn.

8. I sat by the pond.
   I put on my ice skates.

9. The sailor's story was strange.
   The sailor's story was true.

For More Practice
See Page 399

Written Write sentences using a conjunction to combine sentence parts in each example.

1. The girls stood on the pier.
   The girls waved to their families.

2. The winning team looked tired.
   The winning team looked happy.

3. I will call you tonight.
   I will call you tomorrow.

4. Mrs. Gamez weeded the flowers.
   Mrs. Gamez watered the flowers.

5. Fishing nets covered the pier.
   Lobster traps covered the pier.

6. Mr. Sislian gave Jill a book.
   Mr. Sislian gave me a record.

7. We drew the curtains back.
   We watched the rain fall.

8. The story told about a dragon.
   The story told about a prince.
   The story told about a small shepherd boy.

5. Some More Language Choices

Read the two short sentences below. Then notice how they can be combined to form several different sentences.

> Delmar needed money.
> He wrote to his father.

1. Delmar needed money, **and** he wrote to his father.
2. Delmar needed money, **so** he wrote to his father.
3. **When** Delmar needed money, he wrote to his father.
4. **Whenever** Delmar needed money, he wrote to his father.
5. **Because** Delmar needed money, he wrote to his father.
6. **As soon as** Delmar needed money, he wrote to his father.
7. **If** Delmar needed money, he wrote to his father.
8. **Before** Delmar needed money, he wrote to his father.

- Which sentences contain conjunctions that connect the two ideas?
- Which sentences contain subordinators that connect the two ideas?

Now think about the meaning that each connecting word gives to the sentence.

- Which of the words in color express an idea of time?
- What are some other ideas that the different connecting words express?

Here is another sentence made by combining the two ideas at the top of this page.

9. Delmar wrote to his father **whenever** he needed money.

- Which two of the nine numbered sentences have the same connecting word?
- Are the two sentences the same in meaning, or are they different?

317

The English language offers you many choices. Suppose you want to combine two short sentences with a connecting word. How can you decide which connecting word to use?

For Discussion

The short sentences in the box can be combined in several ways. What sentences can you make by connecting them with each of these words?

> 1. You are tired.
> 2. You should rest a while.

and   so   whenever   when   since   if

What different meanings do the new sentences express? How would a writer decide which word to use?

For Practice

For More Practice
See Page 399

Oral Make two or more new sentences by combining each pair of sentences with different connecting words. (Remember that you can change the order of the two short sentences if you want to.)

1. Irwin boarded the train.
   Jenny blew him a kiss.
2. You sing.
   I'll play the piano.
3. You shouldn't swim.
   There is no lifeguard.
4. John moved away.
   Our stamp club elected a new president.
5. I wrote to Marcia twice.
   She didn't answer.
6. The sun was very hot.
   The workmen didn't complain.
7. Alphonse comes home tonight.
   He will make some pizza.
8. The sink was plugged.
   We called a plumber.
9. The acrobat fell from the high wire.
   He wasn't injured.
10. The door was locked.
    We had to crawl in through the window.

Written Make two different sentences by combining each pair of sentences with two different connecting words.

1. The winner was announced.
   Matilda was unhappy.
2. Alan was happy.
   Tobias agreed to help him.

318

3. We questioned Peter.
   He refused to answer.

4. Your message is important.
   I will wake John up.

5. Sue's uncle visited her.
   He brought an unusual gift.

6. We stood.
   We could see the plane land.

7. The whistle blew.
   We boarded the train.

8. The sky was cloudy.
   We went for a walk.

ON YOUR OWN

As you read the paragraph below, notice that most of the sentences are very short. Decide which sentences could be combined. Then combine them, writing the new paragraph on your paper. You may join parts of sentences and whole sentences.

The sun was shining. Roger walked to the park. Dean walked to the park. They reached the ball diamond. The rest of the boys were already there. Everyone was eager to start the game. Clouds appeared suddenly on the horizon. Clouds moved swiftly across the sky. The rain began slowly. Soon it was raining hard. The boys were getting wet. They stopped their game. They looked for shelter. Nearby was a refreshment stand. They dashed over to it. They stood under the eaves. They stared sadly at the storm. They wished it would end. They could finish the game.

6. For Review

Read and discuss the questions below.

A. Which symbol shows where the story of the letter A probably began? What happened to the symbol over the centuries before it finally became the Roman letter A?

Egyptian	Phoenician	Greek	Roman
			A

B. What is the spelling rule for adding suffixes in each of the following examples?

1. Words ending in the letter *y*
   pay + –able → payable   copy + –er → copier
2. Words ending in an *e* that does not stand for a sound
   ripe + –ness → ripeness   explore + –ation → exploration
3. One-syllable words ending in a single consonant letter
   bat + –ing → batting   boat + –ing → boating
4. Two-syllable words ending in a single consonant letter
   regret + –ed → regretted   danger + –ous → dangerous

C. The following sentences show some choices that the English language gives you. For each group, what kind of choice would the writer have?

1. Alice laughed mysteriously. Vivian laughed mysteriously.
   Alice and Vivian laughed mysteriously.
2. Ed shot an arrow. Ed missed the target.
   Ed shot an arrow but missed the target.
3. You come to my house, and we can play scrabble.
   When you come to my house, we can play scrabble.
   If you come to my house, we can play scrabble.

Read the directions for each exercise below. Follow the directions, writing your answers on your own paper.

A. Join each word and suffix to make another word. Use the rules you have studied to help you spell the new words.

1. employ + –ee
2. funny + –est
3. run + –er
4. lone + –ly
5. mine + –ing
6. imagine + –ary
7. acquit + –al
8. journal + –ism
9. drop + –ed
10. bag + –age

B. Join the sentences in each pair below by connecting noun phrases, verb phrases, adjectives, or prepositional phrases.

11. The ballerina stood on her toes.
    The ballerina began to dance.
12. The cat often hides in the closet.
    The cat often hides under the bed.
13. The horse was old.
    The horse was frisky.
14. It's cold enough for a sweater.
    It's cold enough for a jacket.

C. Join the sentences in each pair below in two ways, first with a conjunction and then with a subordinator.

15. The weather was cold and damp.
    We stayed indoors all day.
16. The votes were counted.
    Sam knew he had lost the election.
17. The floodwaters weakened the bridge.
    It didn't fall.
18. It began to rain.
    The elf crept under a toadstool.

8. Talking about Folklore

Will it rain or won't it? How do you decide? Probably you listen to a weather report on radio or television. Long before there were weather reports, people made up sayings and rhymes about the weather. Here are some very old rhymes about rain.

Pale moon doth rain,
Red moon doth blow,
White moon doth neither rain nor snow.

The sharper the blast,
The sooner it's past.

Rain before seven,
Quit before eleven.

A sunshiny shower
Won't last half an hour.

Evening red and morning gray
Speed the traveler on his way;
Evening gray and morning red
Bring them down upon his head.

A rainbow in the morning
Is the shepherd's warning.
A rainbow at night
Is the shepherd's delight.

Red sky in the morning,
Sailors take warning;
Red sky at night,
Sailors' delight.

322

Rhymes like these are part of the **folklore** of the English-speaking people. Folklore is handed down by word of mouth from each generation to the next. It includes beliefs, sayings, rhymes, songs, and legends. Everyone knows some folklore. Everyone helps to preserve folklore and pass it on.

- Which of the rhymes on the opposite page are familiar to you?

- What other sayings or rhymes about weather can you think of?

For Discussion

Are any of the following rhymes familiar to you? What are some other rhymes that you know for predictions, wishes, and children's games?

Children's Games

Red Rover, Red Rover,
Let Johnny come over.

Wishes

Starlight, star bright,
First star I see tonight,
I wish I may, I wish I might
Have the wish I wish tonight.

Predictions

If you find a hairpin
Stick it in your shoe;
The next boy you walk with
Will be sure to marry you.

Activities

Find out what folk rhymes your parents and grandparents know. Besides the kinds included in this lesson, they might know rhymes containing medical advice, rhymes for farmers about when to plant corn, good-luck rhymes, magic spells, and charms. Report what you learn to the class.

9. Writing a *Why* Story

People have always looked at their world with wonder and asked the question *Why?* Folklore from all parts of the world contains stories that answer this question.

Here is a *why* story that comes from the Mpongwe people of the west coast of Africa.

Why Chicken Lives with Man

Long ago, as the birds flew over the world, they saw that men had a beautiful thing. It was a bright, blazing thing, very warm. Men cooked their food with it and sat beside it or around it to keep warm.

The birds thought life would be better if they too could have this thing. So they decided to send a messenger to Man to ask him for a little piece of it.

They thought Chicken was a good one to send because he was such a talker. So Chicken went. He flew far over the forest until he came to the towns of men.

He went into a town and walked around. He saw the blazing thing. He learned what it was called. "Fire," he heard men say.

He did not ask for a piece of it to take back to the birds right away, because there was so much food lying around men's dooryards that he started pecking and eating and forgot.

Men liked Chicken because he crowed at daybreak and woke them up. They let him run around in their dooryards and in and out of their houses. They threw him scraps.

So Chicken stayed with mankind. He never went back to the birds. He even forgot how to fly.

Most *why* stories explain something in nature that people have wondered about. Think about the story you just read.

■ What question does the story answer?

■ What answer does the story give?

For Discussion

A. What questions can you think of that you could answer in a *why* story? Here are a few examples to give you some ideas.

1. Why does the pine tree keep its needles?
2. Why do the tides ebb and flow?
3. Why does it snow?
4. Why do bears sleep all winter?
5. Why does the giraffe have a long neck?
6. Why does a caterpillar become a butterfly?

B. What answers can you think of for the questions in part A?

Activities

A. Write a *why* story of your own. Begin with a question from your class discussion, or think of another question to answer in your story.

B. If you wish, read your story aloud to your class. Or your teacher may arrange for you to share your stories with a class of younger children.

10. Writing about an Imaginary Animal

Some of the most wonderful characters in folklore are animals, both real and imaginary. For thousands of years, people have told stories about imaginary animals like the unicorn, the phoenix, and the dragon. From these stories, we have come to know some imaginary animals as well as we know the porpoise and the elephant.

No doubt you have read or seen pictures of the unicorn. In his book *The Most Wonderful Animals that Never Were*, Joseph Wood Krutch includes the following description. It was written in the seventh century by a Spaniard named Isidore.

He has the name unicorn because he has one horn four feet long in the middle of his forehead. And his horn is so strong and so sharp that it will pierce just anything. He often fights with the elephant and stabs him and throws him down. The most mighty hunters cannot capture him. But writers say that if a maiden sits down in the woods the unicorn will come and lay his head in her lap. And he will stay there quietly. Then he is taken by the hunter.

A story you may remember is "The Brave Little Tailor." To win the king's daughter, the tailor had to prove his heroism by capturing a unicorn. Here is how he did it.

The tailor took a halter and an ax and started for the woods, telling the party that was with him to wait outside. The unicorn came in sight immediately, and made for the tailor as if to gore him without ceremony.

"Steady, steady," cried the tailor. "Not so quick!"

He stood still and waited until the animal was quite close, and then sprang nimbly behind a tree. The unicorn made a frantic rush at the tree and gored it so firmly with his horn that he could not get it out again, and so was caught.

"Now I've got you, my fine bird," said the tailor, coming from behind the tree. He put the halter around the beast's neck, cut its horn out of the tree, and when all this was done led the animal home to the king.

—JACOB AND WILHELM GRIMM

Much more has been told about the unicorn. For example, according to legend, his horn was prized because it possessed magical powers to purify water and to heal.

Can you make up an imaginary animal? To start your imagination working, answer these questions about the unicorn.

- What real animal does the unicorn resemble?
- How is the unicorn different in appearance from any real animal?
- Besides his appearance, what else is unusual or magical about the unicorn?
- Suppose someone asked you how to capture a unicorn. What are two answers you could give him?

A. Some imaginary creatures have been a part of folklore for hundreds and even thousands of years. A few examples are the dragon, the basilisk, the manticore, the phoenix, and the griffin. Which of these have you read about? How could you describe them for someone else? What stories do you know in which an imaginary animal appears?

Basilisk

B. You may have heard about two modern creatures, the Loch Ness Monster of Scotland and the Abominable Snowman of the Himalayan Mountains in Asia. Whether these are real or imaginary, they have already become part of the folklore of the world. What do you know about them?

Manticore

Activities

A. Make up an imaginary animal and write a story about it. Begin your story by telling what the animal is called and what it looks like. Describe some unusual or magical qualities it has. Then you might tell how to catch the animal.

Phoenix

B. Trade stories with a classmate. Draw or paint a picture of the animal in your classmate's story, and let him do the same for your story. If your description is good, the animal in your classmate's picture may look something like the animal you saw in your imagination.

Griffin

328

11. Enjoying a Folk Song

You may be familiar with the following song from the Kentucky mountains. If so, your class may want to sing it now.

Down in the Valley

1. Down in the val — ley, Val—ley so low,
2. Build me a cas — tle, For—ty feet high,
3. Write me a let — ter, Send it by mail,

Hang your head o — ver, Hear the wind blow.
So I can see her As she goes by.
Send it in care of Bar—bour-ville jail.

Hear the wind blow, love, Hear the wind blow,
As she goes by, dear, As she goes by,
Bar—bour-ville jail, love, Bar-bour-ville jail,

Hang your head o — ver, Hear the wind blow.
So I can see her As she goes by.
Send it in care of Bar-bour-ville jail.

The oldest kind of folklore is probably the folk song. Folk songs grow out of the work and play, the laughter and sadness of people. Folk songs tell about things that happen, and how people feel about their lives. Many folk songs have come to us from other countries, but many others were first sung in America.

In one sense, folk songs aren't "finished." Through the years people sometimes add new stanzas, or make up new words for old tunes. Below are two stanzas that can be sung to the tune of "Down in the Valley." Your class may want to sing them now.

1. Once I went walking,
   Walking so far,
   When I met a man
   Who played a guitar.
   He played a guitar,
   He played a guitar,
   I met a man
   Who played a guitar.

2. He sang me a song
   Of when he was young,
   The funniest song
   I've ever heard sung.
   Ever heard sung,
   Ever heard sung,
   The funniest song
   I've ever heard sung.

Suppose you wanted to make up some new words of your own to sing to the tune of "Down in the Valley." Look again at the two stanzas on the opposite page.

- Which lines in each stanza repeat other lines?

- If you wanted to add more stanzas, what could they tell about?

For Discussion

What subjects can you think of for some new stanzas to be sung to the tune of "Down in the Valley"? For example, you might tell about a school activity, a pet, a game, a holiday celebration, or a place you have visited.

Activities

A. Make up one or more stanzas to sing to the tune of "Down in the Valley." Use rhyme if you want to, but it isn't necessary. Share your words with the class so that everyone can sing them together.

B. Think of another folk song and make up some new words to sing to that tune.

C. Your class may want to sing some folk songs that you know. Here are a few that may be familiar to you.

"The Erie Canal"

"Skip to My Lou"

"I've Been Working on the Railroad"

"Donkey Riding"

"Goodbye, Old Paint"

"Swing Low, Sweet Chariot"

12. Listening to Poetry

Listen as your teacher reads the following poem to you.

NEW YORK IN THE SPRING

Sometimes when I
am walking down the street
early in May
late in the afternoon
after it's rained
on the first hot day
of the hot summer
when the sidewalk
is still wet
and the grass smells new
the way it won't soon

When the dust is mud
and the sidewalk darkens
from the water
and the sun's not out yet
and it's cool and good
to be walking outside
after the rain

Before the dust flies in my face
and the sidewalk turns
white again
and so hot
it hurts my feet
right through my shoes
and reminds me about
the hot summer
and the sweat
and no cool air to breathe
and nowhere to go
away from the heat.

Before that

Before I take
another step
into the sun

For a moment
for a second

When the city smells cool

I forget about the space
between my teeth and I
laugh with my mouth open.

—David Budbill

332

Listen as your teacher reads the poem again.

- How does the speaker feel about the spring day he is describing?
- How does he feel about the summer days that will follow?
- What do you think makes him laugh?

For Discussion

A. Would the speaker notice the same details about spring if he lived in a suburb or in a small town or in the country? Find lines to support your answer.

B. Which of his five senses does the speaker use? Find lines to support your answer.

C. What is amusing about the last three lines of the poem? Do you like this ending? Why?

Activities

Practice reading "New York in the Spring" aloud. This poem has little punctuation, but you can read it well by letting the ideas help you decide where to pause or drop your voice. Usually you should pause very slightly at the end of each line.

For Individual Needs

Composition

1. Planning Before Writing

Suppose your class has been reading about colonial housing. Your teacher asks you to write a paragraph about the shelters which the colonists made before they built permanent homes. This might be your first attempt.

A

One kind of shelter was a wigwam which the colonists borrowed from the Indians. Eventually the colonists used wood, brick, and stone to make permanent shelters. Their most primitive shelters were dugouts.

By now you have discovered that something is wrong. Your paragraph has no plan. You will have to start over. This time you plan your writing before you begin to write. The plan you make consists of a topic and a list of details.

Early Colonial Shelters

Dugouts

Wigwams

Cabins

Cottages

Following this plan, you write the paragraph below.

B

The early colonists built temporary shelters for themselves and their families. The simplest were dugouts, pits dug in the ground with roofs of poles covered with bark. Another simple shelter was a type of wigwam borrowed from the Indians. The wigwam was not a cone-shaped tepee, but an oblong structure with a round roof. A third kind of shelter was a simple cabin built of vertical stakes driven into the ground with slender branches woven between. A fourth kind was a simple cottage. The frame was made of hewn planks or squared timbers, which were then covered with boards.

Points to Observe

⊙ Paragraph *A* does not have one clear topic.

⊙ Paragraph *B* is about one topic, and all the sentences help to support that topic.

⊙ The information in paragraph *A* is not arranged in a logical order.

⊙ The information in paragraph *B* is arranged in a logical order, from the simplest shelter to the most complex.

For Practice

A. Below are some topics and details for paragraphs. Choose one example and decide how you would arrange the details. Write a plan for a paragraph. Then write the paragraph.

Topic **1.** How fast various animals travel on land

        Cheetahs, 65 miles an hour

        Giant tortoises, 300 yards an hour

        Cats, 30 miles an hour

        Ostriches, 50 miles an hour

        Snakes, 2 miles an hour

        Elephants, 25 miles an hour

Topic **2.** Life of Jim Bowie

        Born in Georgia in 1799

        Served in Texan army, 1835 and 1836

        Died at Alamo in 1836

        Grew up in Louisiana

        Moved into Texas in 1828 and settled

        1832, early leader in fight of Texas
           for independence from Mexico

B. Make a plan for a paragraph on a topic that interests you. First write the topic and list three to six details under it. Then write the paragraph, following your plan.

337

2. Paragraphs in a Story

When you write a story, one problem you have is deciding when to indent and start a new paragraph. Notice the paragraphing in the story below.

In the Egyptian Room

Last Saturday afternoon my sister and I were visiting the Storm Museum. We became so interested in the mummies that we forgot the time. All at once the lights in the room dimmed twice and then went out.

It was pitch dark. I couldn't see Brenda, and she couldn't see me. I had visions of mummies all over the room unraveling themselves in the dark and reaching out toward us with cold, dead hands.

Then out of the darkness came a hoarse, muffled voice. "Who's there?"

At first, no one spoke. Then, in a frightened whisper, Brenda asked, "Who was that?"

"I don't know," I answered. "I hope it wasn't a mummy."

Suddenly the lights went on. An attendant was hurrying toward us. He looked angry as he led us out of the museum. He couldn't understand what we were doing there, since the museum had closed fifteen minutes before.

Points to Observe

Except in dialogue, there are no definite rules to tell you when to begin each new paragraph in a story. However, the example above may give you some ideas about how to paragraph your own writing.

○ When there is some kind of turning point or change in the story, a new paragraph begins.

○ In dialogue, a new paragraph begins whenever there is a new speaker.

For Practice

Oral The following sentences form the beginning of a story. Decide where you would indent and begin each new paragraph if you were writing the story. The sentences should make four or five paragraphs.

Fishing Trip

There I was, sleeping quietly, when all at once I heard, "Time to get up. Let's go!" I opened my eyes and blinked. Dad was standing at the foot of the bed, dressed for fishing. "Today's the day," he said. "Try to hurry and dress now. I'll have breakfast ready for you in five minutes. Will bacon and eggs be all right?" "I'll be right down," I answered. By this time I was fully awake. I struggled into my clothes. For months I had been looking forward to this day. Trout season was opening at 6:30 A.M.

Written Write the story below. Divide it into four, five, or six paragraphs.

Slow Rowing

Yesterday, Tom Clegg and I went fishing at Watuppa Lake. We spent an hour or so casting off Lander's Pier, but we didn't have any luck. Then I had what I thought was a good idea. "Why don't we rent a boat and row out to where the fish are biting?" I said. Tom replied, "I'm willing. Let's walk over to Napier's. We can get a boat there." After we had stowed all our gear aboard the boat, Tom took the oars. I sat up in front and started baiting my hook. "We'll soon be out on the lake where all the big fish are," I said. A few minutes later I looked up. I expected to find us already halfway out on the lake. Instead, we were still only about ten feet from the pier. Tom was rowing with all his might, but the boat seemed to be standing still. "What's the matter?" I called. Then I saw the trouble and laughed. "Tom, we forgot to untie the mooring line. It's still hitched to the dock."

3. Linking Sentences in Paragraphs

The paragraph below is arranged in time order. Notice the words and word groups in color. Think about what purpose they serve.

One night my friends and I decided to pop some corn at my house. I got out a large pan and some oil. Then Jean poured oil into the pan, and Maggie dumped in a cupful of corn. Soon everyone began to talk and laugh, filling the room with noise. We forgot all about the popcorn for a long time. Suddenly I remembered. I ran to the stove and lifted the lid from the pan. There lay the unpopped corn. No one had turned on the stove.

Points to Observe

⊙ Each word or word group in color suggests time order.

⊙ These words and word groups help to link the sentence ideas to each other and to the whole paragraph.

For Practice

Write a paragraph of your own about one of the topics suggested below.

1. Tell about something that happened, such as a storm, a game, or an interesting ride. Use three to five words or word groups to link the sentence ideas. Choose from the words and word groups below, or use others that suggest time order.

soon	at first	later	suddenly
then	at last	next	in a few minutes

2. Describe a landscape. Use three to five words or word groups to link the sentence ideas. Choose from the words and word groups below, or use others that suggest space order.

ahead	across the road	far away
nearby	above us	on our left

4. Using Specific Verbs

Notice the verb in color in each sentence below.
We hiked thirty miles across the island.
The rooster strutted around the farmyard.
The speaker finished his talk and strode from the platform.
The girls strolled home from school.
The lame man hobbled up the stairs.
The scouts marched in the Fourth of July parade.
The child toddled across the room.
Tom sauntered down the path by the lakeshore.

Points to Observe

⊙ Each verb in color has the same general meaning as the verb *walk*.

⊙ Each verb paints a clearer word picture than *walk* by suggesting a specific kind of walking.

For Practice

A. Write each sentence below. Fill the blank with one of these specific verbs with the same general meaning as the verb *ran: scurried, galloped, dashed, scampered, sprinted*.

1. The boy — across the street.
2. The runner — across the finishing line.
3. The squirrel — up a tree.
4. The horse — down the trail.
5. The mouse — across the attic floor.

B. Write each sentence below, using the verb in parentheses that is more specific.

1. The vase (broke, shattered) as it hit the tile floor.
2. Why are you (staring, looking) at me like that?
3. The hunters (followed, tracked) the tiger for two days.
4. The moisture caused the wood to (warp, bend).
5. It was so cold that we (shook, shivered).

5. Using Specific Adjectives

Notice the adjective in each pair of noun phrases below.

1. bad weather
   dismal weather

2. a bad temper
   a quick temper

3. a bad mistake
   a costly mistake

4. nice weather
   balmy weather

5. a nice smile
   a warm smile

6. a nice welcome
   a gracious welcome

Points to Observe

- The adjectives *bad* and *nice* have a general meaning and can be used to describe almost anything.

- Specific adjectives create clear, vivid word pictures.

For Practice

Write each sentence. Change each adjective in italics to one of the specific adjectives listed below.

clever	dazzling	enormous	interesting
thunderous	towering	graceful	slipshod
vigilant	delicious	tart	honey-colored

1. My pen pal wrote a *nice* letter.
2. Everyone enjoyed the *good* holiday dinner.
3. We admired the *large* sunflower.
4. The audience greeted the actors with *loud* applause.
5. The workmanship on this boat is *poor*.
6. The *smart* fox outwitted the hen.
7. The flavor of the lemon pie was too *strong*.
8. We gazed upward at the *big* redwood trees.
9. She had blue eyes and *light* hair.
10. Rover kept a *careful* guard over the children.
11. Amanda is a *good* dancer.
12. We blinked in the *bright* sunlight.

6. Using Specific Nouns

Compare the nouns in color in each pair of sentences below.

Before Revision	**After Revision**
1. There was a deep crack in the glacier.	1. There was a deep crevasse in the glacier.
2. At last we reached the top of the mountain.	2. At last we reached the summit of the mountain.
3. The group of wolves headed our way.	3. The pack of wolves headed our way.
4. He filled my glass right up to the top.	4. He filled my glass right up to the brim.

Points to Observe

- Before revision, the nouns in color are general.

- After revision, the nouns in color are specific.

- Specific nouns create clearer word pictures.

For Practice

Write each sentence. Improve it by changing the general noun in italics to a specific noun.

1. The door knocker was made of *metal*.
2. We had fried *fish* for supper.
3. Lightning split the giant *tree* in our backyard.
4. Look at that huge *animal!*
5. *Birds* nested in the orchard.
6. In her ring was a large *gem*.
7. The police began their search for the *lawbreaker*.
8. A new *boat* rested in the harbor.

343

7. Using Specific Words

Compare these paragraphs, noticing the words in color.

First Draft

Joe held the fishing line tightly and brought a small fish to the surface. The fish hit tiredly against the boat, its gray side shining in the sunlight. Joe put his hand into the water. With his wet hand he held the moving fish while he took the steel barb from its mouth. Then he put the fish back into the water.

Revised Draft

Joe held the fishing line tightly and pulled a small trout to the surface. The fish thumped tiredly against the boat, its silvery side gleaming in the sunlight. Joe dipped his hand into the current. With his moist hand he gripped the wriggling trout while he unhooked the steel barb from its mouth. Then he dropped the fish back into the stream.

Points to Observe

⊚ The words in color in the first draft have been changed to more specific words in the revised draft.

⊚ The revised draft creates clearer, more interesting word pictures.

For Practice

Write the sentences below, using the word in parentheses that is more specific.

1. The snake (crawled, slithered) through the grass.
2. The accident caused a (lot, flurry) of excitement.
3. What made the smokestack (topple, fall)?
4. The soldier lowered his (rifle, weapon).
5. The impatient child kept (moving, fidgeting).
6. The villain's expression was (bad, sinister).
7. The cheerleaders were (happy, jubilant) over the victory.
8. Leo strode (briskly, quickly) to the front of the room.

8. Proofreading Your Writing

Even though you may be a careful writer, what you write often contains mistakes, such as misspelled words. What should you do in order to get your writing ready for someone else to read?

The paragraph below is the writer's first draft. He has read it over carefully and made some corrections on his paper. This process is called proofreading. Read the paragraph to decide what to look for when you proofread your writing.

> Once when I was crossing a ~~neighbors~~ *neighbor's*
> yard, a dog jumped at me and tripped
> me. At first I thought I was in
> real trouble, then he ~~begain~~ *began* to lick my
> face, and I knew he *only* wanted to play.

Notice the kinds of corrections the writer made on his paper.

1. He crossed out misspelled words and wrote the correct spellings above them.

2. He corrected sentences to make them begin and end where they should.

3. He inserted a word left out of the first draft.

Where to Go for Help in Proofreading

In the pages to follow, you will find rules about how to use punctuation marks, capital letters, quotation marks, and apostrophes. Refer to these rules whenever they will help you in proofreading something you have written.

Rules for Using Capital Letters

- Capitalize each important word in a proper noun.

Topeka	the Lake of the Ozarks
Linden Avenue	the John Hancock Building

- Capitalize a title of respect when it is used in place of a name.

  Soon Mother will call us in to supper.

- Capitalize a title of respect or an abbreviation for a title of respect when it appears before a person's name.

Captain Simpson	Grandmother Hines
Capt. Simpson	Rev. Douglas

- Capitalize the first word in a sentence or a quotation.

  The road to town was muddy.

  Phyllis said, "It must have rained last night."

- Capitalize the names of days of the week and months of the year, but not the names of seasons.

Wednesday	September	autumn

For Practice

Write the following sentences, using capital letters wherever necessary. _____

1. One museum in london is called the british museum.
2. The college ken attends is city college of new york.
3. Alex said, "here is a letter from uncle george."
4. The governor of ohio was gov. worthington.
5. did mr. o'neill wear green on st. patrick's day?
6. Last summer dad's vacation began on monday, june 24.

A Rule for Writing Book Titles

- Underline the title of a book.

  <u>Huckleberry Finn</u>, by Mark Twain

For Practice

Write the following sentences, underlining the book titles.

1. Her favorite book was The Wind in the Willows.
2. For her report she read Heroes of Today, by Mary R. Parkman.
3. Both children and adults enjoy The Little Prince.

Rules for Using End Punctuation

⊙ Use a period at the end of a statement and at the end of a command or a polite request.

> The cat was hungry.   Please open the door.

⊙ Use a question mark at the end of a question.

> Did the doorbell ring?

⊙ Use an exclamation point at the end of a word or sentence that expresses strong feeling.

> Help! Let me out of here!

For Practice

Write the following sentences, adding end punctuation.

1. Did you see the sunset last night
2. Valerie's hometown is Denver, Colorado
3. Ouch That water is hot
4. Take the eight o'clock train to Chicago

Rules for Using Apostrophes

⊙ Use an apostrophe in a contraction to replace the letters that are omitted.

> I'm   he'd   they're   aren't

⊙ Use an apostrophe before the −s in the possessive form of a singular noun.

> Mr. Smith's house   a child's toy

347

- Use an apostrophe after the –s in the possessive form of a plural noun ending in –s.

    a girls' club   the boys' gymnasium

- Use an apostrophe before the –s in the possessive form of a plural noun not ending in –s.

    the men's sweaters   the children's books

For Practice

Write the following sentences, using apostrophes wherever necessary.

1. Theyll come as soon as theyre ready.
2. Youre going to miss your plane.
3. Its time to give the kitten its milk.
4. This isnt Carlas coat. Is it yours?
5. The boys belonged to a boys club.
6. The childrens librarian told a story.

Rules for Using Quotation Marks

- Use quotation marks to set off the speaker's exact words in a direct quotation.

    Angelo said, "Let's go to the zoo."
    "My home," remarked Rudolph, "is near yours."

- When quotation marks are used along with other punctuation marks in sentences like the following, put the other punctuation marks first.

    "Does anyone know," asked Marge, "what time it is?"
    "Shut the window!" shouted Dad.

For Practice

Write the following sentences, using quotation marks wherever necessary.

1. Norbert shouted, Look out for the train!
2. I believe, said Carrie, that it will rain before morning.

348

3. Is the elevator broken? asked Ron.

4. Please answer the telephone, said Anne.

Rules for Using Commas

⊙ Use a comma after an introductory expression.
   No, the bus hasn't come yet.

⊙ Use commas to set off interrupters.
   You know, of course, that Smith is a miser.

⊙ Use commas to set off nouns used in direct address.
   I hope, Esther, that you will write to me soon.

⊙ Use commas to separate items in a series.
   We had pancakes, sausage, and milk for breakfast.

⊙ Use commas in a date to set off the year.
   He moved on August 9, 1968, to Alaska.

⊙ Use commas to set off the state in naming a city and state.
   His home in Siloam Springs, Arkansas, was for sale.

⊙ Use a comma before the conjunction that joins the two parts of a compound sentence.
   The judge entered the courtroom, and everyone stood up.

⊙ Use a comma after the first part of a sentence that begins with a subordinator.
   Before we left for camp, we packed our bedrolls.

For Practice

Write the following sentences, using commas wherever necessary.

1. We cooked green beans tomatoes and squash.
2. This book I believe is worth reading.
3. On June 14 1968 the new shopping center opened.
4. Our trip to Miami Florida was over too soon.
5. Well I think you're right.
6. If we win this game we'll play for the championship.
7. May I see you Dr. Lindblom on Tuesday?
8. It was getting dark but we finished the game.

9. Preparing Public Writing

Suppose you have written a poem, a story, or a report. Your first, rough copy is good enough for your own use. Sometimes, however, you want to present your writing to someone else to read. Writing that will be read by someone besides the writer is public writing.

The poem below is the writer's first copy. Suppose he wanted to prepare a copy for a class poetry book.

T K
the king

The chicken is a noble bird,

So proud of strut, so strong of wing.

No wonder he appears at luncheon

Billed as chicken à la king.

Notice what changes the writer made on his rough copy.

1. He corrected a mistake in spelling.
2. He made changes in some word choices.
3. He capitalized the title and the first word in each line of the poem.

Now he is ready to make a neat copy for the class poetry book.

Where to Go for Written Models

On the next few pages are models of some different kinds of public writing. Turn to the models when you need to prepare a neat copy of something you have written.

A Model for Stories and Reports

Anita Dixon
October 27, 197–

Noises in the Attic

I was determined to find the source of the strange noises I heard. They came from upstairs, so I decided to explore the attic. At the door I peered in, straining to see. A single pale light bulb hung from the ceiling. Its dim light cast mysterious shadows on the walls.

Suddenly, in one corner something moved. It stood up, and I saw that it was a skeleton of some sort. It started to walk towards me. I was too frightened to move or scream. But as the skeleton came closer, I recognized it. It was my little brother dressed in his Halloween costume.

Points to Observe

- The writer's name and the date are in the upper right-hand corner.
- The title of the story is on the top line.
- There is an indention at the beginning of each new paragraph.
- There are margins on both sides of the page.

A Model for Poems

Poems are written in many different forms. Often a poem is punctuated like a paragraph, but some poems have no punctuation at all. Most poems have titles, but some, such as limericks and haiku, may not have. Notice the forms the writer followed in the poems below.

Nan Donahue
October 14, 197–

Lakeshore

Listen,
A quiet night.
Just one soft sound I hear,
Lake water slowly licking up
The sand.

There once was a boy named Bernard
Whose head was exceedingly hard.
He fell, this cute tyke,
Head-first from his bike,
And broke up the whole boulevard.

Points to Observe

◉ The poems are centered on the page, with margins on both sides.

◉ The lines are arranged to follow particular poetic forms, the cinquain and the limerick.

◉ The punctuation is similar to that of paragraphs.

◉ The first word of each line is capitalized.

A Model for Scripts

Jeff Joseph
October 4, 197—

An Accident

Scene. A school yard near the door of the school. A nearby window is broken. The teacher steps outside just as Johnny is about to disappear around the corner.

Teacher. Johnny, wait a minute! Come here, please.
(Johnny stops, turns around, and walks back slowly.)
Johnny. Yes, Ma'am?
Teacher. Johnny, do you know anything about this broken window?
Johnny. Well, sort of—
Teacher. Yes?
Johnny. All I was doing was cleaning my slingshot when it accidentally went off.

Points to Observe

- Everything except the dialogue itself is underlined, including names of characters, descriptions of the scene, and stage directions.
- Names of characters are indented and followed by a period.
- Stage directions within the dialogue are enclosed in parentheses

353

A Model for Friendly Letters

Heading

808 Delles Road
Wheaton, Illinois 60187
May 8, 197—

Greeting

Dear Dan,

Body

How are you spending your vacation in Virginia?

Last Saturday Dad and I drove to the lake before sunrise. We rented a boat and spent the morning fishing. I caught five fish and Dad caught eight. They were just bluegills, but they tasted pretty good when Mom fried them for supper.

Dad says I can invite you to go fishing with us when you get home.

Closing

Your friend,

Signature

Peter

Points to Observe

- The letter is centered on the page, with margins on both sides and at the top and bottom.
- The letter has five parts.

3.

A Model for Business Letters

In most respects, the form of a business letter is the same as that of a friendly letter. Notice two important differences. The business letter has an inside address, and a colon is used after the greeting.

---

12 West Allen Road
Bloomington, Indiana 47405
April 14, 197–

Heading

Superior Hobby Supply House
1234 Vine Street
New York, New York 10019

Dear Sirs:

Greeting

Please send me a copy of the booklet Raising Ants Is Fun, which you advertised in the Indiana Mail for $1.00, postpaid. I am enclosing a money order for $1.00.

Body

Yours truly,
Donald Belanger

Closing

Signature

Points to Observe

- The letter is centered on the page, with margins on both sides and at the top and bottom.

- The letter has six parts.

For Individual Needs

Usage

1. Using Subject Pronouns

> 1. **He** went to every game.
> 2. **I** went to every game. } ⇒ 3. **He and I** went to every game.

Points to Observe

⊙ Sentences *1* and *2* have subject pronouns.

⊙ Sentences *1* and *2* were combined to form sentence *3.*

⊙ Sentence *3* uses the same subject pronouns as sentences *1* and *2.*

For Practice

A. Practice reading these sentences aloud. Listen for the subject pronouns.

1. Where did *he* find the rabbit?
   Where did *she* find the rabbit?
   Where did *he and she* find the rabbit?

2. Should *they* rake the leaves?
   Should *I* rake the leaves?
   Should *they and I* rake the leaves?

3. Are *you* going fishing today?
   Are *they* going fishing today?
   Are *you and they* going fishing today?

4. Did *you* swim?
   Did *he* swim?
   Did *you and he* swim?

5. *You* should try some of this cake.
   She should try some of this cake.
   You and she should try some of this cake.

B. Write each sentence twice, completing it with a different subject pronoun each time.

1. Are you and — twins?
2. Have Martha and — practiced their song together?
3. Fred and — flew their kites in the park.

2. Using Object Pronouns after Verbs

> 1. Mary called **her.**
> 2. Mary called **me.** } ⇒ 3. Mary called **her and me.**

Points to Observe

⊙ Sentences *1* and *2* have object pronouns.

⊙ Sentences *1* and *2* were combined to form sentence *3*.

⊙ Sentence *3* uses the same object pronouns as sentences *1* and *2*.

For Practice

A. Practice reading these sentences aloud. Listen for the object pronouns.

1. The coach is calling *him.*
   The coach is calling *me.*
   The coach is calling *him and me.*

2. Theresa sent *her* some pictures.
   Theresa sent *me* some pictures.
   Theresa sent *her and me* some pictures.

3. I followed *him* into the classroom.
   I followed *her* into the classroom.
   I followed *him and her* into the classroom.

4. Will you write *them* some letters from camp?
   Will you write *us* some letters from camp?
   Will you write *them and us* some letters from camp?

5. The deer saw *him.*
   The deer saw *me.*
   The deer saw *him and me.*

B. Write each sentence twice, completing it with a different object pronoun each time.

1. The stranger questioned Father and —.
2. The dog frightened — and the lady.
3. Will you give Michael and — the key?

3. Using Object Pronouns after Prepositions

> 1. Tom wrote **to her.**
> 2. Tom wrote **to me.** } ⇒ 3. Tom wrote **to her and me.**

Points to Observe

⊙ Sentences *1* and *2* have object pronouns following a preposition.

⊙ Sentences *1* and *2* were combined to form sentence *3*.

⊙ Sentence *3* has the same object pronouns as sentences *1* and *2*.

For Practice

A. Practice reading these sentences aloud. Listen for the object pronouns following the prepositions.

1. Will you come to the game *with him?*
   Will you come to the game *with me?*
   Will you come to the game *with him and me?*

2. Here is a photograph *of her.*
   Here is a photograph *of me.*
   Here is a photograph *of her and me.*

3. Please pass the lemonade *to him.*
   Please pass the lemonade *to us.*
   Please pass the lemonade *to him and us.*

4. Some tickets came *for her.*
   Some tickets came *for them.*
   Some tickets came *for her and them.*

5. Do not leave *without them.*
   Do not leave *without us.*
   Do not leave *without them or us.*

B. Write each sentence twice. Complete it with a different object pronoun each time.

1. Will you come to the play with Linda and —?
2. A letter to Ronald and — was lying on the table.
3. The new boy stood near the teacher and —.

4. Choosing Between *We* and *Us* Before Nouns

1. **We** are ready.
2. **We boys** are ready.
3. The dog followed **us.**
4. The dog followed **us girls.**

Points to Observe

⊙ Sentence *1* has a subject pronoun. Sentence *3* has an object pronoun.

⊙ When a noun is added in sentence *2*, the same subject pronoun is used as in sentence *1*.

⊙ When a noun is added in sentence *4*, the same object pronoun is used as in sentence *3*.

For Practice

A. Practice reading these sentences aloud. Listen for the pronouns *we* and *us*.

1. We planned a picnic for the class.
   We *girls* planned a picnic for the class.

2. Did you bake the cookies for *us*?
   Did you bake the cookies for *us children*?

3. May *we* come in?
   May *we students* come in?

4. Good food and a lot of rest are important for *us*.
   Good food and a lot of rest are important for *us athletes*.

5. Should *we* wash the car?
   Should *we girls* wash the car?

B. Write each sentence, completing it with either *we* or *us*.

1. — swimmers earned our lifesaving badges.

2. Amanda discussed the movie with — girls.

3. Should — people be waiting in line?

4. The alarm clock woke — campers at five o'clock.

5. Soon — marchers will reach our destination.

5. Using *Himself, Ourselves,* and *Themselves*

> Dad bought **himself** a new car.
> The boys built **themselves** a tree house.
> We made **ourselves** some leather moccasins.

Points to Observe

⊙ *Him* may be combined with *–self*.

⊙ *Them* and *our* may be combined with *–selves*.

For Practice

A. Practice reading these sentences aloud. Listen for *himself, themselves,* and *ourselves.*

1. Can Andrew defend *himself?*
2. The children played by *themselves* in the sandbox.
3. Why did Joe write *himself* a letter?
4. We ate the entire watermelon *ourselves.*
5. The girls dressed *themselves* in their mother's clothes.
6. The baby can support *himself* on a chair.
7. The boys looked for *themselves* in the photograph.
8. George scowled at *himself* in the mirror.
9. They sometimes praise *themselves* too highly.
10. We prepared *ourselves* some popcorn.

B. Write each sentence, completing it with *himself, themselves,* or *ourselves.*

1. The mayor — took us around the city.
2. After the game we talked to the players —.
3. The girls made skirts for —.
4. He told — that his plan wouldn't work.
5. We wanted to break the good news —.

C. Write five sentences of your own, using *himself, ourselves,* or *themselves* in each sentence.

6. Choosing Between *Here is* and *Here are*

> Your glove **is here** on the dresser.
> **Here is** your glove on the dresser.
> Your gloves **are here** on the dresser.
> **Here are** your gloves on the dresser.

Points to Observe

⊙ *Here is* is used with singular nouns like *glove*.

⊙ *Here are* is used with plural nouns like *gloves*.

For Practice

A. Practice reading these sentences aloud. Notice when you say *here is* and when you say *here are*.

1. Some new books *are here*.
   Here are some new books.
2. The slipper you lost *is here*.
   Here is the slipper you lost.
3. Five baby rabbits *are here* under the porch.
   Here are five baby rabbits under the porch.
4. Your library card *is here*.
   Here is your library card.
5. Several letters *are here* on the table.
   Here are several letters on the table.

B. Write each sentence so it begins with *here is* or *here are*.

1. Two clowns are here to entertain the children.
2. Five kinds of fruit are here.
3. The package you've been waiting for is here.
4. Some people are here looking for you.
5. Your muffler is here on the chair.

C. Write five sentences of your own, beginning each sentence with *here is* or *here are*.

7. Choosing Between *There is* and *There are*

> A book **is** on the shelf.
> **There is** a book on the shelf.
>
> Some books **are** on the shelf.
> **There are** some books on the shelf.

Points to Observe

⊙ *There is* is used with singular nouns like *book*.

⊙ *There are* is used with plural nouns like *books*.

For Practice

A. Practice reading these sentences aloud. Notice when you say *there is* and when you say *there are*.

1. Four men *are* in the boat.
   There are four men in the boat.
2. A ghost *is* in the attic.
   There is a ghost in the attic.
3. Fifteen crows *are* on the telephone wire.
   There are fifteen crows on the telephone wire.
4. A candle *is* in the window.
   There is a candle in the window.
5. Twelve guests *are* at the party.
   There are twelve guests at the party.

B. Write each sentence so that it begins with *there is* or *there are*.

1. Some llamas are in the children's zoo.
2. A beetle is on that banana.
3. Several small planes are in the hangar.
4. A friend is waiting for you.

C. Write five sentences of your own, beginning each sentence with *there is* or *there are*.

364

8. Choosing Between *Don't* and *Doesn't*

> **Does** that seal perform?   **Do** those seals perform?
> No, it **does not.**   No, they **do not.**
> No, it **doesn't.**   No, they **don't.**

Points to Observe

⊙ *Doesn't* is a contraction of *does not* and is used with singular subjects like *he, she,* and *it.*

⊙ *Don't* is a contraction of *do not* and is used with plural subjects like *they.*

For Practice

A. Practice reading these sentences aloud. Listen for the contractions *don't* and *doesn't.*

1. *Do* those bees sting?
   No, they *don't* sting.
2. *Does* the weatherman predict bad weather?
   No, he *doesn't* think it will rain.
3. *Does* John know the answer to that riddle?
   No, he *doesn't* know the answer.
4. *Do* Harry and Luis plan to come for dinner?
   No, they *don't* have time to eat.
5. *Does* Minnie like mustard on her hot dogs?
   No, Minnie *doesn't* like mustard.

B. Rewrite each sentence as a statement.

1. Doesn't it make any difference when we come?
2. Don't those ships look handsome?
3. Doesn't that jacket keep you warm?
4. Don't the children want any supper?
5. Doesn't the teacher know the answer?

C. Write two sentences of your own using *don't,* and two sentences using *doesn't.*

9. Choosing Between *Sit* and *Set*

> **Sit** in that chair.   **Set** the pitcher down here.
> We **sat** on the grass.   Someone **set** it down before.
> I **have sat** here before.   They **have set** it down carefully.

Points to Observe

- *Sit* means "to rest."
- *Set* means "to place something" or "to put something."

For Practice

A. Practice reading these sentences aloud. Notice when you say *sit, sat,* and *set*.

Sit, sat

1. Who is *sitting* in the porch swing?
   Aunt Helen is *sitting* in the porch swing.
2. Who *sat* there yesterday?
   I *sat* there yesterday.
3. Mark *sat* and talked with me for an hour.
   We *have sat* and talked together many times.
4. Did Cinderella often *sit* in the chimney corner?
   Yes, she often *sat* there.

Set

1. Are you *setting* the vase on the piano?
   Yes, I'm *setting* it there.
2. Where did you *set* the can of blue paint?
   I *set* it right there on the bench.
3. Will you *set* the pan on the stove?
   I *have set* it there already.
4. *Set* the stool in its proper place.
   I'll help you in *setting* it down.

B. Write eight sentences, using each of the following words and word groups twice: *sat, set, has sat, had set*.

10. Choosing Between *Rise* and *Raise*

> Did the balloon **rise** high?   **Raise** your hand.
> We **rose** at dawn.   They **raised** their hands.
> The sun **has risen.**   We **have raised** the flag.

Points to Observe

◉ *Rise* means "to get up" or "to go up."

◉ *Raise* means "to lift something up."

For Practice

A. Practice reading these sentences aloud. Notice when you say *rise, rose, risen, raise,* and *raised.*

Rise, rose, risen

1. When did the sun *rise?*
   It *rose* at five-thirty.
2. Are the floodwaters still *rising?*
   Yes, they *have risen* two feet already.
3. Is the tide *rising* along the shore?
   Yes, the tide is *rising* along the shore.
4. Do you know if the moon *has risen* yet?
   Yes, it *rose* twenty minutes ago.

Raise, raised

1. Did Herman *raise* his hat as he walked by?
   Yes, he *raised* his hat.
2. Did anyone *raise* the question of dues?
   No one *has raised* that question yet.
3. Did the grocers *raise* their prices?
   Yes, they *raised* them last week.
4. Can you *raise* that picture higher on the wall?
   I *have raised* it as high as I can reach.

B. Write six sentences, using the following words and word groups: *raise, rise, raised, rose, have raised, has risen.*

11. Choosing Between Let and Leave

> **Let** me taste the pie.　　　　**Leave** me alone.
> Tom **let** me use his boat.　　Diana **left** her hat here.
> I **have let** the cat go.　　　　She **has left** for France.

Points to Observe

⊙ *Let* means "to allow" or "to permit."

⊙ *Leave* means "to depart" or "to go away from."

For Practice

A. Practice reading these sentences aloud. Notice when you say *let*, *leave*, and *left*.

Let

1. Will you *let* me see your new book?
   Yes, I'll *let* you see it.
2. Did you *let* Dennis do as he liked?
   Yes, we *let* him do as he liked.
3. Do your parents ever *let* you go camping?
   Yes, they *have let* me go often.
4. Did Sue *let* you borrow her mandolin?
   No, she wouldn't *let* me borrow it.

Leave, left

1. When did the Muellers *leave* home?
   They *left* yesterday.
2. Did you *leave* the key somewhere?
   Yes, I *left* it under the mat.
3. Did Steve *leave* his bike out in the rain?
   Yes, he *has left* it out all week.
4. Should we *have left* earlier?
   No, we *left* at the right time.

B. Write ten sentences, using each of the following words and word groups twice: *leave, left, have left, let, has let*.

12. Choosing Between *Lie* and *Lay*

> **Lie** here and rest.
> The baby is **lying** down.
>
> **Lay** the books on the table.
> The mason is **laying** the bricks.

Points to Observe

- *Lie* means "to rest" or "to recline."
- *Lay* means "to put something down."

For Practice

A. Practice reading these sentences aloud. Notice when you say *lie* and *lying*, and when you say *lay* and *laying*.

Lie, lying

1. The rake was *lying* in the garden.
2. How long did you *lie* in the sun?
3. The lost wagon was *lying* on its side in the weeds.
4. Somewhere on the island lost treasures *lie* buried.

Lay, laying

1. John is *laying* the tablecloth on the table.
2. Will you please *lay* a blanket over my feet?
3. When did the enemy soldiers *lay* down their arms?
4. Grandmother will *lay* her sewing aside and talk to us.

B. Write these sentences, completing each with *lie, lay, lying,* or *laying*.

1. Mark was — his fishing pole in the bottom of the boat.
2. A bear can — fast asleep for months.
3. Why don't you — your head on this cushion?
4. Railroad workers were — a new track for the train.
5. Let's — our sleeping bags near the fire.

C. Use each of these words in a written sentence of your own.

      lie   lying   lay   laying

13. Using Negative Words

> I have **no** time to waste.
> I do **not** have any time to waste.
> I **don't** have any time to waste.

Points to Observe

⊙ Words like *no, nothing,* and *not* are negative words.

⊙ Contractions made with *not* are also negative words.

⊙ Only one negative word is used in each sentence.

For Practice

A. Practice reading these sentences aloud. Listen for the words that give negative meanings to the sentences.

1. There was *no* one in the attic.
   There *wasn't* anyone in the attic.
2. The treasure has *never* been found.
   The treasure *hasn't* ever been found.
3. The train seemed to be going *nowhere.*
   The train *didn't* seem to be going anywhere.
4. We hunted for blueberries, but we found *none.*
   We hunted for blueberries, but we *didn't* find any.
5. The letters were *never* delivered.
   The letters *weren't* ever delivered.

B. For each sentence below, write a new sentence that expresses the negative meaning in a different way.

1. Harry's Halloween mask frightened no one.
2. Please ask me no more questions.
3. I have never seen a unicorn.
4. The children have no homework tonight.
5. I have no stamps for your collection.

C. Write five sentences of your own, using a negative word in each sentence.

14. Using Some Adjectives in Comparisons

tall	beautiful
taller	more beautiful
tallest	most beautiful

Points to Observe

- Most one-syllable adjectives use *-er* and *-est* in comparisons.
- Most adjectives of more than two syllables use *more* and *most* in comparisons.

For Practice

A. Practice reading these groups of adjectives aloud. Listen for *-er* and *-est* in one group, and *more* and *most* in the other.

One Syllable	More than Two Syllables
ripe	dependable
riper	more dependable
ripest	most dependable
low	delicious
lower	more delicious
lowest	most delicious
smart	ridiculous
smarter	more ridiculous
smartest	most ridiculous
weak	serious
weaker	more serious
weakest	most serious

B. Write nine sentences, using these words.

1. high	2. amusing	3. miserable
higher	more amusing	more miserable
highest	most amusing	most miserable

371

15. Using Two-syllable Adjectives in Comparisons

pretty	careful
prettier	more careful
prettiest	most careful

Points to Observe

- Some two-syllable adjectives use *–er* and *–est* in comparisons.
- Some two-syllable adjectives use *more* and *most* in comparisons.

For Practice

A. Practice reading these groups of adjectives aloud. Listen for *–er* and *–est* in one group, and *more* and *most* in the other.

–er, –est	More, most
friendly	fragile
friendlier	more fragile
friendliest	most fragile
gloomy	distant
gloomier	more distant
gloomiest	most distant
happy	careless
happier	more careless
happiest	most careless
silly	awkward
sillier	more awkward
silliest	most awkward

B. Write nine sentences, using these words.

1. dirty	**2.** graceful	**3.** skillful
dirtier	more graceful	more skillful
dirtiest	most graceful	most skillful

16. Comparing with *Good* and *Bad*

> That is a **good** pear.
> This pear is **better.**
> Here's the **best** pear of all.
>
> That is a **bad** pear.
> This pear is **worse.**
> Here's the **worst** pear of all.

Points to Observe

- *Better* and *worse* are the forms of *good* and *bad* used to compare two persons or things.

- *Best* and *worst* are the forms of *good* and *bad* used to compare more than two persons or things.

For Practice

A. Practice reading these sentences aloud. Notice when you say *better, best, worse,* and *worst.*

Better, best

1. That chocolate cake is *better* than this one.
   Mother baked the *best* cake in the contest.
2. Albert is a *better* badminton player than Carmen.
   He is the *best* player in the school.
3. That was a *better* story than the one we heard Monday.
   It was the *best* one I've heard in a long time.
4. The corn looked *better* than the squash.
   The carrots looked *best* of all.

Worse, worst

1. I can't remember a *worse* summer for swimming.
   Grandpa says it's the *worst* summer he's ever seen.
2. This storm was *worse* than the one we had last week.
   It was the *worst* storm I've ever been in.
3. This grade is *worse* than the one I got last month.
   It's the *worst* grade I've ever received in math.

B. Write six sentences using the following words.

good   better   best   bad   worse   worst

17. Using *Well* as an Adjective and as an Adverb

Adjective	Adverb
Janet feels **well** today.	Janet cooks **well**.
Do you feel **well**?	Do you cook **well**?

Points to Observe

- *Well* may be used as an adjective to describe someone's health.
- *Well* may also be used as an adverb describing how something is done.

For Practice

A. Practice reading these sentences aloud. Notice the two meanings of *well*.

Describing Health

1. Edna doesn't feel *well*.
2. I feel *well*.
3. Are your parents *well*?
4. Exercise keeps you *well*.
5. How *well* do you feel?

Telling How

1. Does Charlotte skate *well*?
2. How *well* can you swim?
3. She sings *well*.
4. Can you dance *well*?
5. He writes *well*.

B. Write an answer to each of these questions. Use *well* in each answer.

1. Would Marge know how to sew this torn pocket?
2. Does your brother's coat fit you?
3. How did the medicine make you feel?
4. Does Pete know how to play the saxophone?
5. How is your father feeling?
6. Did you learn how to speak Italian?
7. How did they perform in the play?
8. Are your grandparents in good health?
9. What do you think of that author's writing?
10. How are you?

18. Choosing Between Adjectives and Adverbs

> The owl looked **wise.**
> The owl looked **wisely** at us.

Points to Observe

⊙ Adjectives like *wise* are used to describe nouns.

⊙ Adverbs of manner like *wisely* tell how something was done.

⊙ Many adverbs of manner end in *–ly.*

For Practice

A. Practice reading these sentences aloud. Listen for the adjective and adverb in each pair of sentences.

1. Arnold gave the *correct* answer.
   He answered the question *correctly*.
2. Both the bull and the matador seemed *brave*.
   They struggled *bravely* throughout the bullfight.
3. Did the ship have a *safe* voyage?
   Yes, it moved *safely* through the stormy sea.
4. The crowd was *noisy*.
   People laughed and talked *noisily*.
5. We were caught in a *sudden* downpour.
   It came so *suddenly* that we were all drenched.

B. Add *–ly* to each adjective in italics below. Use each adverb in a written sentence.

1. Jane looked *thoughtful* as she listened to the song.
2. The acrobat performed at a *dangerous* height.
3. Mike did *careful* work when he painted the house.
4. The groundhog looked around with *sleepy* eyes.
5. The dog looked friendly, but he was *fierce*.

C. Write three pairs of sentences of your own. Use an adjective and an *–ly* adverb in each pair of sentences.

For Individual Needs

More Practice

Pages 18–19   Noun Phrases and Verb Phrases

A. Add a noun phrase before each verb phrase to form a sentence. Write each sentence.

1. — crawled across the floor.

2. — howled in the distance.

3. — won a silver trophy.

4. — found the gold.

5. — is near the river.

6. — suddenly stopped working.

7. — stepped on my toes.

8. — grows in the field.

B. Add a verb phrase after each noun phrase to form a sentence. Write each sentence.

1. The bus driver —.

2. A branch from the tree —.

3. Some hockey players —.

4. Photographers —.

5. The steep mountain trail —.

6. Some baby elephants —.

7. An angry passenger —.

8. The paper bag —.

Pages 20–21   Subjects and Predicates

A. Below is a list of noun phrases and verb phrases. Use each noun phrase as the subject in a sentence of your own. Use each verb phrase as the predicate in a sentence of your own. Write each sentence.

1. laughed at the clown

2. a magician

3. Barbara's skates

4. ate all the cheese

5. a lifeguard at the pool

6. escaped from the zoo

7. the delivery truck

8. is staring at us

B. Write each sentence below. Draw one line under the noun phrase that serves as the subject. Draw two lines under the verb phrase that serves as the predicate.

1. The old dolls were in the attic.

2. My sister's parrot is noisy.

3. Greg planted some parsley.

4. A lion is sleeping on the porch.

5. A thorn on that bush tore my coat.

6. Jennifer found a cave.

Change each pair of sentences into a single sentence by joining the noun phrases that are used as subjects. Try to use different connecting words in some of the sentences.

CONNECTING WORDS   and   or   both . . . and   either . . . or

1. The musicians practiced daily.
   The dancers practiced daily.

2. The streets were slippery.
   The sidewalks were slippery.

3. Rachel will fly the plane.
   Pete will fly the plane.

4. Eileen wrote this poem.
   Her father wrote this poem.

5. Muffins are in the oven.
   Apple pies are in the oven.

6. The boxes were empty.
   The crates were empty.

7. Harvey bought a pumpkin.
   My brother bought a pumpkin.

8. The thunder scared my puppy.
   The lightning scared my puppy.

9. The referee stopped the game.
   The timekeeper stopped the game.

10. A truck blocked the driveway.
    A car blocked the driveway.

Pages 24–25   Combining Verb Phrases in the Predicate

From each pair of sentences, make a new sentence by combining two verb phrases in the predicate. Try to use different connecting words in some of the sentences.

CONNECTING WORDS   and   but   either . . . or   neither . . . nor

1. A car drove through a puddle.
   A car splashed mud on me.

2. Ruth won the race.
   Ruth sprained her ankle.

3. We pitched the tents.
   We built a campfire.

4. People stood in line.
   People waited for tickets.

5. Jerry studied the results.
   Jerry wrote a report.

6. I bought peanuts.
   I fed the deer.

7. The collie broke its leash.
   The collie ran away.

8. Tom lost a quarter.
   Tom found a dollar.

9. The lion paced in its cage.
   The lion roared fiercely.

10. They listened outside the door.
    They heard nothing.

Pages 48–49   The Noun Phrase

Supply a suitable noun phrase made with a determiner and a noun to go with each verb phrase below. Write the sentences that you make.

1. — paddled the canoe.

2. — scampered under the fence.

3. — played soccer.

4. — are in the basement.

5. — ran from the barn.

6. — gave us a message.

7. — seems friendly.

8. — startled the audience.

9. — ate the flowers.

10. — whistled softly.

Pages 50–51   The Noun Phrase with Proper Nouns

Rewrite the sentences below. For each noun phrase in italics, substitute a noun phrase made with a proper noun.

1. *The mayor* is on television.

2. *That girl* caught a frog.

3. *A mountain* towered above us.

4. *The country* welcomes visitors.

5. *A man* is selling tractors.

6. *The city* is overcrowded.

7. *That month* finally came.

8. *This zoo* is near my home.

9. *The street* was repaired.

10. *My teacher* plays the guitar.

Pages 52–53   The Noun Phrase with Pronouns

A. Supply a suitable noun phrase made with a personal pronoun to go with each verb phrase below. Write the sentences that you make.

1. — shoveled snow.

2. — was on the top shelf.

3. — boarded the plane.

4. — planned the reunion.

5. — lost a tennis ball.

6. — spilled all the water.

7. — is near the bus station.

8. — will buy the tickets.

B. Supply a suitable noun phrase made with an indefinite pronoun to go with each verb phrase listed in exercise A. Write the sentences that you make.

Pages 56–57   Dictionaries and Meaning

Each word in italics in the following sentences has more than one meaning. Find the word in a dictionary. Write the definition that fits the word as it is used in the sentence.

1. The knight wore a coat of *mail*.
2. There's a *lock* in the canal.
3. I scratched a *leaf* of the table.
4. Where is the county *seat*?
5. He studied a *fault* in the earth.
6. The cabin was in a *hollow*.
7. We tried to climb a *sheer* cliff.
8. That's a *lame* excuse.
9. Here's a *branch* of the main bank.
10. Don't make a *rash* decision.

Pages 82–83   The Base Form and the s Form of the Verb

Write the following sentences. Complete each one with either the *s* form or the base form of the verb in parentheses.

1. Our dog — rabbits. (chase)
2. Icicles — on the roof. (form)
3. They — a toboggan. (own)
4. This key — the door. (open)
5. That train — freight. (carry)
6. Daisies — near the pond. (grow)
7. Passengers — seat belts. (wear)
8. The pet store — hamsters. (sell)
9. The bells — every hour. (chime)
10. A wall — the mansion. (surround)

Pages 84–85   The ed Form of the Verb

Rewrite each sentence below. Change the verb from an *s* form or a base form to an *ed* form.

1. Wendy draws funny cartoons.
2. The farmers plant soybeans.
3. Our cats hide in the closet.
4. Frost covers the windshield.
5. Inspectors examine all luggage.
6. We choose partners for the game.
7. Each contestant wins a prize.
8. The trucks carry lumber.
9. Scientists test the water.
10. Helen teaches swimming.

Pages 86–87   Tense

The verb in each sentence below is in italics. Write **present tense** or **past tense** to show the tense of the verb. Write **present time, past time, future time,** or **all times** to show what idea of time each tense form expresses.

1. The creek *flowed* into a river.

2. This milk *tastes* sour.

3. We *catch* fireflies every summer.

4. A boat *patrolled* the harbor.

5. The train always *stops* in Akron.

6. Tim *studied* rock formations.

7. Lou *takes* a driving test tomorrow.

8. A porpoise *swam* in the tank.

9. I *deliver* the papers next month.

10. Our puppy *wakes* me every morning.

Pages 88–89   The Special Verb <u>Be</u>

Write the following sentences. Complete each one with a present or past tense form of the special verb *be*.

1. The paint — wet yesterday.

2. I — treasurer of the club now.

3. Ellie — ready to skate now.

4. We — near Trenton yesterday.

5. You — the captain now.

6. Geese — on the lake yesterday.

7. Dan — home yesterday.

8. The fog — very dense now.

9. The leaves — colorful now.

10. The theater — empty now.

Pages 112–113   Two Kinds of Verb Phrases

A. Supply a suitable verb phrase containing a transitive verb to go with each subject below. Write each sentence that you make.

1. The acrobat —.

2. A dragon —.

3. A siren —.

4. The man —.

5. The football team —.

6. Mrs. Colby —.

7. A bright light —.

8. Two chipmunks —.

B. Make another sentence with each example from exercise A. This time add a verb phrase containing an intransitive verb.

Pages 114–115   Noun Phrases That Follow Transitive Verbs

A. Write the following sentences. In each sentence underline the noun phrase that is used as a direct object.

1. Marianne finally heard the alarm.

2. I will meet your plane.

3. The shark scared the small fish.

4. A sheep dog followed me.

5. No candidate opposed Mayor Jones.

6. We rented the new apartment.

7. Caroline repairs clocks.

8. The fire engine already passed you.

B. Write the following sentences. Complete each one with a noun phrase used as the direct object. Try to use some noun phrases of each different kind, including pronouns.

1. Kristin finally found —.

2. Dinosaurs ate —.

3. Arnie photographed —.

4. We welcomed —.

5. High winds ruined —.

6. The fence surrounded —.

7. Some children played —.

8. Joan memorized —.

Pages 116–117   Dictionaries and Pronunciation

Write answers to the following questions. Use a dictionary to find the pronunciation of any word that is new to you.

1. Does *waif* rhyme with "life" or "safe"?

2. Does *guile* rhyme with "fill" or "file"?

3. Does *lieu* rhyme with "tie" or "true"?

4. Does *carafe* rhyme with "staff" or "safe"?

5. Does *cache* have the same sounds as "cash" or "catch"?

6. How many syllables are there in *adobe*?

7. How many syllables are there in *anemone*?

8. How many syllables are there in *victual*?

9. Which syllable of *rattan* receives greater stress?

10. Which syllable of *feline* receives greater stress?

Pages 118–119 More about Dictionaries and Pronunciation

Each word in italics in the following sentences has more than one common pronunciation. Find each word in a dictionary. Write the respellings that show how different people pronounce the word. Then underline the respelling that shows how you pronounce the word.

1. The vase held a *bouquet* of yellow daisies.

2. There was *dew* on the grass.

3. Whose name is written on the *envelope?*

4. Jed carefully examined the horse's *hoof.*

5. I prefer butter to *margarine.*

6. What is the *ratio* between licensed drivers and automobiles?

7. There are many *juvenile* books in the public library.

8. The baseball *diamond* was wet and muddy.

9. We helped the *refugee* find a home.

10. A camera is not a *luxury* for a photographer.

Pages 144–145 Clipped Words

Write the following sentences. Complete each one with a clipped word made by shortening the word in parentheses.

1. Janice works in a chemical —. (laboratory)

2. We had only a gallon of — left in the tank. (gasoline)

3. A — hovered over the expressway. (helicopter)

4. Tonya showed me a — of her grandparents. (photograph)

5. We finished the — problems early. (mathematics)

6. Theresa answered the — in the paper. (advertisement)

7. I had a long — in French today. (examination)

8. Each employee received a — from the manager. (memorandum)

9. The basketball players ran into the —. (gymnasium)

10. The moving — was packed with furniture. (caravan)

383

Pages 146–147   Blends

A. Write the following sentences. Complete each one with a blend made by combining parts of the two words in parentheses.

1. The — was heavy near the river. (smoke + fog)

2. Don't — paint on your clothes. (splash + spatter)

3. My family stayed at a — near Atlanta. (motor + hotel)

4. Rosa showed me how to — the baton. (twist + whirl)

5. The restaurant served — all morning. (breakfast + lunch)

B. Use each blend that you made in exercise A in a sentence of your own. Write each sentence, and underline the blend.

Pages 148–149   <u>Be</u> Plus a Noun Phrase

Complete each sentence below. Add a verb phrase made with a form of the verb *be* plus a noun phrase completer.

1. Jill's favorite sport —.

2. We —.

3. That building —.

4. Those birds —.

5. Mario —.

6. The people in the car —.

7. The new animal at the zoo —.

8. Vicki and Carmen —.

9. I —.

10. The author —.

Pages 150–151   <u>Be</u> Plus an Adjective

Complete each sentence below. Add a verb phrase made with a form of the verb *be* plus an adjective completer.

1. Our geese —.

2. Isaac's painting —.

3. The salesclerks —.

4. This nail —.

5. The sunset —.

6. The sounds of the forest —.

7. My chocolate sundae —.

8. Your shoes —.

9. This box of popcorn —.

10. Laura's story —.

Pages 152–153   Be Plus an Adverb

Complete each sentence below. Add a verb phrase made with a form of the verb *be* plus an adverb completer.

1. Jesse and Greg —.
2. Our furnace —.
3. I —.
4. The empty bottles —.
5. Our picnic basket —.

6. The kangaroos —.
7. Your telescope —.
8. A taxi —.
9. Old newspapers —.
10. Aunt Eleanor —.

Pages 154–155   Be Plus a Prepositional Phrase

Complete each sentence below. Add a verb phrase made with a form of the verb *be* plus a prepositional phrase completer.

1. I —.
2. Your helmet —.
3. The onions —.
4. Several pigeons —.
5. A rhinestone collar —.

6. The candles —.
7. Broken glass —.
8. Rosa Garcia —.
9. Some logs —.
10. The butterfly —.

Pages 180–181   The Auxiliary Have

A. Write each of the following sentences. Use a present tense form of the auxiliary *have* with the *en* form of the verb in parentheses.

1. A branch (fall) from the tree.
2. Birds (steal) all the berries.
3. We (break) the secret code.
4. The witness (speak) to no one.

5. The curtain (rise) early.
6. Gail and Joy (forget) the rules.
7. I (hide) the vanilla wafers.
8. We (take) the dogs for a walk.

B. Write each of the sentences in exercise A. Use a past tense form of the auxiliary *have* with the *en* form of the verb in parentheses.

385

Pages 182–183   More about the en Form

Write each of the following sentences, using the *en* form of the verb in parentheses.

1. Faye has (paint) the ceiling.
2. The leaves have (began) to fall.
3. We have (sell) our boat.
4. None of the plants had (grow).
5. The bear has (catch) a fish.
6. The men had (hear) noises outside.
7. Roland has (sing) with the band.
8. Our puppy had (fight) with a cat.
9. I have (cook) the meat loaf.
10. Rita had (leave) work early.

Pages 184–185   The Auxiliary Be

A. Write each of the following sentences. Use a present tense form of the auxiliary *be* with the *ing* form of the verb in parentheses.

1. That boat (sail) to the island.
2. I (teach) a ceramics class.
3. Connie (plant) a fir tree.
4. Rocks (slide) down the cliff.
5. The Smiths (arrive) by train.
6. Your dog (chew) my shoe.

B. Write each of the following sentences. Use a past tense form of the auxiliary *be* with the *ing* form of the verb in parentheses.

1. Naomi (read) the want ads.
2. We (wait) for the ski lift.
3. Kevin (fix) the leaky pipe.
4. People (laugh) at the clown.
5. A guard (raise) the barricade.
6. The miners (hope) to find gold.

Pages 186–187   Verb Phrases with Have and Be

A. Make sentences from the following word groups by using forms of the words in parentheses. Make your sentences in the present tense.

1. Freda (have) (be) (pack) boxes.
2. The sun (have) (be) (shine).
3. I (have) (be) (chop) wood.
4. Roberto (have) (be) (lose) weight.
5. We (have) (be) (walk) in the rain.
6. The horses (have) (be) (race).

B. Make sentences from the following word groups by using forms of the words in parentheses. Make your sentences in the past tense.

1. The dogs (have) (be) (bark).

2. I (have) (be) (weave) a rug.

3. We (have) (be) (play) cards.

4. Shops (have) (be) (close) early.

5. Milt (have) (be) (sleep) all day.

6. Sandra (have) (be) (wash) the car.

Pages 188–189   Writing Direct Quotations

Each sentence below contains a direct quotation. Write each sentence, using quotation marks, capital letters, and punctuation marks where they are needed.

1. Rosalind said I'll have a piece of strawberry pie

2. Where are the rackets asked Joel we want to play tennis

3. Mr. Martinez warned the water in the pool is cold

4. This is the last stop announced the bus driver

5. My bicycle said Melinda has a flat tire

6. That barge on the river is loaded with coal said Stanley

7. Ryoko announced I have three kittens to give away

8. This castle said the guide is four hundred years old

9. Where's the road map asked Jesse I think we're lost

10. My soup is cold said the angry customer

Pages 190–191   Writing Dialogue

Rewrite the fable "The Gnat and the Lion." Use as many direct quotations as you can. Begin a new paragraph each time there is a different speaker.

The Gnat and the Lion

One day a tiny gnat boasted to a huge lion that he was not afraid of the lion. The lion warned that she was stronger than the gnat and said that the gnat should be afraid of her. The gnat just laughed and said that lions could only bite and scratch. The gnat insisted that he was more powerful than any lion and then challenged the lion to a fight. *(Continued.)*   387

The gnat began the fight by stinging the lion on the nose. When the lion tried to crush the gnat with her paw, the gnat dodged away and the lion scratched herself instead. The fight continued in this manner until the gnat said that he was clearly more powerful than the lion.

However, just as the triumphant gnat prepared to leave, he flew directly into a spider's web. He cried out for help and struggled in vain to free himself. The boastful gnat had beaten the largest of beasts only to become the victim of a little spider.

Pages 210–211   Bases, Prefixes, and Suffixes

Add a prefix or a suffix to each base in parentheses to make a word that will complete the sentence. Choose the prefixes and suffixes from the list at the right. Write each sentence.

1. Diana was — about losing her money. (happy)	dis–
2. The caterpillar crawled — across the porch. (slow)	un–
3. A flock of geese flew —. (head)	re–
4. Cheating on tests is —. (honest)	over–
5. The waves are high on — days. (wind)	–ment
6. Do you have a — solution to our problem? (reason)	–y
7. I need to — these curtains. (length)	–ly
8. The — man broke an expensive vase. (care)	–less
9. We will — the damaged statue. (build)	–able
10. Paul bought an — of chocolate candy. (assort)	–en

Pages 212–213   Free Bases and Bound Bases

A. Both words in each pair below contain the same free base. Write the words on your paper, and underline the free bases.

1. displace, placement

2. preview, interview

3. heroism, heroic

4. discharge, rechargeable

5. kindness, unkindly

6. unbreakable, breakage

388

B. Both words in each pair below contain the same bound base. Write the words on your paper, and underline the bound bases.

1. distract, attract

2. inscribe, subscribe

3. spectacle, inspection

4. mission, missile

5. fraction, fracture

6. dictate, diction

Pages 214–215 Combining Sentences with Conjunctions

Combine each pair of sentences below to make a compound sentence. Remember to use a comma before the conjunction in writing each compound sentence.

1. The front door opened.
   A terrier bolted into the yard.

2. The gate was locked.
   Norman crawled under it.

3. I looked for the book upstairs.
   Heidi looked in the basement.

4. Come to school early tomorrow.
   You will miss the meeting.

5. The fire went out.
   We searched for more wood.

6. Ann was nominated for president.
   She lost the election.

7. Broil the hamburgers carefully.
   They will burn.

8. The sky darkened.
   Thunder rumbled in the distance.

9. Homer lost his wallet yesterday.
   He found it in the garage.

10. Gwen wanted to paint the ceiling.
    She couldn't find a ladder.

Pages 216–217 Combining Sentences with Subordinators

Combine each pair of sentences below with a suitable subordinator. Write each sentence that you make.

1. Shoppers complained.
   The store was closing early.

2. We sat on the beach.
   We looked for seashells.

3. The game was exciting.
   Our team lost by one point.

4. I'll play my guitar.
   You'll sing a ballad.

5. Lionel's shoes were muddy.
   He took a shortcut to school.

6. People raced out of the factory.
   The whistle blew.

7. No one could visit us.
   Our street was flooded.

8. I won't play badminton with you.
   You know all the rules.

9. Angela rowed faster.
   The boat sprung a leak.

10. Skip waited.
    Amy ran home to get her coat.

Pages 218–219   Using Conjunctions and Subordinators

A. Combine each pair of sentences with a conjunction or a subordinator. Use commas wherever they are needed.

1. My sunglasses broke.
   I dropped them on the floor.

2. One astronaut showed us a film.
   Another described the moon.

3. Gilbert ran around the track.
   I timed him on a stopwatch.

4. We will visit the planetarium.
   The museum is closed.

5. We ate hot dogs at the fair.
   We were still hungry.

6. Vivian learned Spanish.
   She spent the summer in Mexico.

7. Kay has a mandolin.
   She doesn't know how to play it.

8. I'll hold the ladder.
   You climb up to wash the window.

9. The rabbit scampered away.
   Ed tried to catch it.

10. The scouts built a birdhouse.
    They found some plywood.

B. Read the sentences that you wrote for exercise A. Put a check before each one that contains a subordinator. Then rearrange each checked sentence so that it begins with a subordinator.

Pages 220–221   Using Commas

Write the following sentences. Use commas where they are needed. (Every sentence needs at least one comma.)

1. Cal does this train go through Salina Kansas?

2. This building I believe has twenty-six floors.

3. Two lions a tiger and a leopard were in one building at the zoo.

4. A famous battle was fought at Gettysburg Pennsylvania in July 1863.

5. On January 3 1959 Alaska became our forty-ninth state.

6. Katie bought goldfish sunfish snails and seaweed for her aquarium.

7. No the cake isn't frosted yet.

8. This anchor I hope will keep the boat from drifting.

9. I know Brad that this is the wrong address.

390   10. High winds uprooted trees knocked down signs and damaged many homes.

Pages 222–223 More about Using Commas

Write the following sentences. Use commas where they are needed. (Not every sentence needs a comma.)

1. While I searched for a saw, Rinaldo measured the board.

2. The taxi was delayed by the snow, and we almost missed our plane.

3. Whenever he saw a snake, Bart panicked and ran.

4. Andrea found a jack and changed the flat tire.

5. When it started raining, the officials postponed the game.

6. Becky is excited because she's a finalist in the diving contest.

7. I wanted to walk across the pond but the ice was too thin.

8. If that box is empty, my frog has escaped.

9. Rose ordered an omelet, and I ordered two hard-boiled eggs.

10. Before the piano was tuned Doug refused to practice his lessons.

Pages 244–245 Noun-forming Suffixes

Complete each sentence below by adding a noun-forming suffix to the word in parentheses. Write each sentence.

1. I don't have an — on my pencil. (erase)

2. The bickering partners finally reached an —. (agree)

3. How much — is there between the truck and the building? (clear)

4. Delores found some — on whales in the encyclopedia. (inform)

5. Is the country suffering from a — of water? (short)

6. Our class held a — on space travel. (discuss)

7. These broken dishes are the result of your —. (careless)

8. Margery, do you know the — of this word? (define)

9. Guarding the gate is a big — for Raymond. (responsible)

10. I missed my — with Dr. Collins. (appoint)

Pages 246–247 Verb-forming Suffixes

Complete each sentence below by adding a verb-forming suffix to the word in parentheses. Write each sentence.

1. Can Todd — the bolt with this pliers? (loose)

2. I — for missing your birthday party. (apology)

3. I will — the fabric before ironing it. (damp)

4. The shopping center will — a variety of stores. (central)

5. Our group will — this short story. (drama)

6. The crew must — the load before the boat sinks. (light)

7. We will — ourselves with the volleyball rules. (familiar)

8. The workers had to — the hole for our new well. (deep)

9. You should never — information on your driver's license. (false)

10. The judge will — the prisoner's sentence. (less)

Pages 248–249 Combining Sentences with Relative Clauses

A. Combine each pair of sentences below. Make the first sentence a relative clause inside the second one. Begin each relative clause with *who*.

1. The lady owns a circus.
   The lady trained this lion.

2. My cousin lives in Colorado.
   My cousin likes to ski.

3. The mechanic owns this garage.
   The mechanic repaired our truck.

4. The senator spoke at our meeting.
   The senator was reelected.

5. The girl is in my class.
   The girl won the bicycle race.

6. The florist sold me these roses.
   The florist owns a shop downtown.

7. The people wanted movie tickets.
   The people were waiting in line.

8. The woman is playing the oboe.
   The woman is a famous musician.

9. The reporter investigated the fire.
   The reporter wrote this article.

10. The girls were canoeing.
    The girls saw a moose.

B. Combine each pair of sentences in exercise A in another way. This time make the second sentence a relative clause inside the first one. Begin each relative clause with *who*.

Pages 250–251   Relative Clauses Beginning with <u>Who</u> and <u>Which</u>

Combine each pair of sentences below. Make the first sentence a relative clause inside the second one. Begin each relative clause with *who* or *which*.

1. The groceries were in that bag.
   The groceries are mine.

2. The moat surrounds the castle.
   The moat is filled with water.

3. The sculptor made this statue.
   The sculptor lives in New York.

4. A boat ran out of gas.
   A boat was towed into the bay.

5. The tree is in our front yard.
   The tree is a weeping willow.

6. The golfer won the tournament.
   The golfer received a trophy.

7. The insects destroyed our plants.
   The insects were locusts.

8. The guide led our tour group.
   The guide is a college student.

9. The road is blocked by guards.
   The road leads to the palace.

10. That woman appeared at the trial.
    That woman is a lawyer.

Pages 252–253   Relative Clauses Beginning with <u>That</u>

A. Combine each pair of sentences below. Make the first sentence a relative clause inside the second sentence. Begin each relative clause with *who* or *which*.

1. The hamster belongs to Sid.
   The hamster is lost.

2. Some people saw a bobcat.
   Some people called the sheriff.

3. The baby cried through the show.
   The baby is my brother.

4. The wires led to the alarm.
   The wires were cut.

5. The plane needed refueling.
   The plane landed safely.

6. The player had the flu.
   The player missed the game.

7. The door led to the library.
   The door was locked.

8. The car started last.
   The car won the race.

9. A girl is my neighbor.
   A girl found this fossil.

10. The architect designed our house.
    The architect is famous.

B. Combine each pair of sentences in exercise A in another way. This time begin each relative clause with *that*.

Pages 254–255   Using Apostrophes in Contractions

Rewrite the following sentences. Use contractions wherever you can.

1. They are good friends.
2. Who would want this old shirt?
3. She had waited for two hours.
4. Martha had not received the note.
5. The game would not last long.

6. It is a nice day for baseball.
7. I have interviewed for a job.
8. You are late for work again.
9. We are camping near the lake.
10. Who is that man on television?

Pages 256–257   Using Apostrophes in Possessive Nouns

Rewrite each group of words below, placing an apostrophe in the possessive nouns.

1. those girls lunches
2. an elephants trunk
3. the mens speeches
4. the canaries cages
5. the familys new home

6. the announcers voice
7. those countries rulers
8. Leroys model car
9. some womens jobs
10. those babies toys

Pages 276–277   Adjective-forming Suffixes

Complete each sentence below by adding an adjective-forming suffix to the word in parentheses. Write each sentence.

1. The marshmallow candy was soft and —. (stick)
2. This is the most — chair in our house. (comfort)
3. The space flight was —. (success)
4. Brad's story was more — than Kevin's. (believe)
5. Jeannette is a talented and — ballet dancer. (grace)
6. I cleaned the floor until it was —. (spot)
7. My sister arrived in her — new car. (shine)

394

8. The — man walked around the ladder. (superstition)

9. All the model's clothes were —. (style)

10. Running around the track made me —. (breath)

Pages 278–279   Adverb-forming Suffixes

Complete each sentence below by adding an adverb-forming suffix to the word in parentheses. Write each sentence.

1. Gerard — left the auditorium. (quiet)

2. Irene tapped — on the window. (light)

3. Move the dresser — through the door. (side)

4. The wagon train began to move —. (on)

5. The contestant — accepted the third-place trophy. (cheerful)

6. Everyone cheered as the bus turned —. (home)

7. Lay the sticks — on the fire. (cross)

8. The citizens marched — to the city hall. (peaceful)

Pages 280–281   Adjectives in the Noun Phrase

Combine each pair of sentences by making an adjective a part of a noun phrase. Write each sentence that you make.

1. The kitten drank all the milk.
   The kitten was thirsty.

2. The pavement burned my feet.
   The pavement was hot.

3. The girls climbed up the cliff.
   The girls were adventurous.

4. The snake crawled along the road.
   The snake was harmless.

5. A wind uprooted the tree.
   A wind was powerful.

6. The forest surrounds our cabin.
   The forest is dense.

7. The flowers grow near the creek.
   The flowers are delicate.

8. The riddle made me laugh.
   The riddle was silly.

9. The mule refused to move.
   The mule was stubborn.

10. The waves splash against the pier.
    The waves are gentle.

Combine each pair of sentences by making a verb a part of a noun phrase. Write each sentence that you make.

1. The river damaged our boat.
The river was raging.

2. The monkey swung by its tail.
The monkey was chattering.

3. Joe's report is very long.
Joe's report is written.

4. A watchdog guards the house.
A watchdog is snarling.

5. The luggage was in the airport.
The luggage was missing.

6. The bear wore a funny hat.
The bear was dancing.

7. This door connects the two rooms.
This door is hidden.

8. The child annoyed the babysitter.
The child was shrieking.

9. The light guided us to the shore.
The light was blinking.

10. The envelope contained money.
The envelope was stolen.

A. Combine each pair of sentences by making an adverb a part of a noun phrase. Write each sentence that you make.

1. The chairs have canvas seats.
The chairs are outdoors.

2. A rancher raises sheep.
A rancher is nearby.

3. The plants need water.
The plants are inside.

4. The toys belong to my brother.
The toys are upstairs.

5. The apartment was for rent.
The apartment was above.

6. The streets are icy.
The streets are there.

B. Combine each pair of sentences by making a prepositional phrase a part of a noun phrase. Write each sentence that you make.

1. The hay has disappeared.
The hay was near the barn.

2. The statue attracts tourists.
The statue is in the park.

3. A store sells giant yo-yos.
A store is around the corner.

4. The plaster crumbled.
The plaster was on the ceiling.

5. The sign directed us to Hammond.
The sign was above the bridge.

6. That restaurant serves good soup.
That restaurant is by the hotel.

Pages 286–287   **Using Capital Letters in Proper Nouns**

Write each of the following sentences. Use capital letters wherever they are needed.

1. When did mayor lupke visit fall creek?

2. Does inez live on harlem boulevard?

3. Is n. a. miller and company located on third street?

4. My home is in albany near the hudson river.

5. The amazon river is in south america.

6. Will greta attend st. joseph's college next year?

7. The new york public library has a book about senator boggs.

8. Have you ever seen the rock of gibraltar?

9. The department of labor contacted judge marie dobson.

10. Meet me near rattlesnake lake on tuesday morning.

Pages 288–289   **More about Capital Letters**

Write each of the following sentences. Use capital letters wherever they are needed.

1. That building is the john hancock building.

2. Yesterday aunt mabel and my aunt from detroit visited us.

3. Is lombard street a famous street in san francisco?

4. We saw two other governors with governor reagan.

5. The mackenzie river is a canadian river.

6. Is baylor university near any other university in texas?

7. How long has lieutenant jackson been a lieutenant?

8. One park with a fountain is grant park in chicago.

9. The catskill mountains are the only mountains I've seen.

10. Is greenville county bigger than this county?

Pages 310–311   Rules for Adding Suffixes

Follow the spelling patterns as you join each word and suffix below. Write the new words you make on your own paper.

> employ + –er → employer

1. joy + –ous → —
2. repay + –ment → —
3. play + –ful → —
4. pay + –able → —
5. stray + –ing → —

> like + –ness → likeness

11. peace + –ful → —
12. amuse + –ment → —
13. forgive + –ness → —
14. entire + –ly → —
15. use + –less → —

> merry + –ment → merriment

6. heavy + –er → —
7. greedy + –ness → —
8. plenty + –ful → —
9. comedy + –an → —
10. cheery + –ness → —

> fame + –ous → famous

16. advise + –er → —
17. approve + –al → —
18. store + –age → —
19. type + –ist → —
20. oppose + –ing → —

Pages 312–313   More about Adding Suffixes

Follow the spelling patterns as you join each word and suffix below. Write the new words you make on your own paper.

> ship + –er → shipper

1. brag + –ing → —
2. sad + –en → —
3. wit + –y → —
4. red + –ish → —
5. trap + –er → —

> admít + –ed → admitted

6. transmit + –er → —
7. control + –ing → —
8. forget + –ing → —
9. admit + –ance → —
10. occur + –ed → —

Combine each pair of sentences below by using a conjunction to connect noun phrases, verb phrases, adjectives, or prepositional phrases. Write each new sentence that you make.

1. I led the pony out of the barn.
   I led the pony into the field.

2. Juanita campaigned a lot.
   Juanita won the election.

3. An opossum is under our porch.
   A raccoon is under our porch.

4. The kitten swatted at the ball.
   The kitten hit me instead.

5. Owen slid down the hill.
   Owen slid into the creek.

6. The cave was cold.
   The cave was damp.

7. The cake is filled with custard.
   The cake is filled with jelly.

8. The truck was coming here.
   The truck stopped in Salem first.

9. The coach gave me the ball.
   The coach gave me a catcher's mitt.

10. Mrs. Mason drove into the city.
    Stacy drove into the city.

11. Mr. Stokes loaded the truck.
    Some neighbors loaded the truck.

12. The eels were long.
    The eels were slippery.

Pages 317–319   Some More Language Choices

Make two different sentences by combining each pair of sentences with two different connecting words.

1. It started raining.
   Peggy turned off the sprinkler.

2. The arrow hits the target.
   A bell rings.

3. Ramon likes broccoli.
   He prefers cauliflower.

4. Eva wraps the package.
   You can mail it.

5. We waited impatiently.
   The skating rink was opened.

6. You buy the yarn.
   I'll crochet a sweater.

7. The stagecoach stopped suddenly.
   The passengers lurched forward.

8. The village had to be evacuated.
   The volcano erupted.

9. Wilbur was hungry.
   He refused to eat the oyster stew.

10. The senators complained.
    The bill was vetoed.

11. Aladdin rubbed the lamp.
    A genie appeared.

12. The gate was closed.
    The sheep could not run away.

Index

(ACKNOWLEDGMENTS continued from page 4.)

of Harper & Row, Publishers./ "Trees" by Nelda Dishman: From MIRACLES: POEMS BY CHILDREN OF THE ENGLISH-SPEAKING WORLD by Richard Lewis. Copyright © 1966, by Richard Lewis. Reprinted by permission of Simon and Schuster, Inc./ Excerpt from GREAT AMERICAN HEROINES by Arnold Dolin: By permission of Lion Press./ "John Henry" from THE CHILD'S BOOK OF FOLKLORE edited by Marion Vallat Emrich and George Korson: New York: The Dial Press, Inc., 1947./ "A scientist living at Staines" by R. J. P. Hewison: Punch, London./ "My Father's Onions" from "A Dozen Methods for Stimulating Creative Writing" by Edward N. Hook: Reprinted from ELEMENTARY ENGLISH, February 1961. Copyright 1961 by the National Council of Teachers of English. Reprinted with permission of the publisher./ "Dreams" by Langston Hughes: Copyright 1932 by Alfred A. Knopf, Inc., and renewed 1960 by Langston Hughes. Reprinted from THE DREAM KEEPER, by Langston Hughes, by permission of Alfred A. Knopf, Inc./ "Water-Front Streets" by Langston Hughes: Copyright 1926 by Alfred A. Knopf, Inc., and renewed 1954 by Langston Hughes. Reprinted from SELECTED POEMS, by Langston Hughes, by permission of Alfred A. Knopf, Inc./ "A Cat Called Blackie" by Richard Iron: From JOURNEYS: PROSE BY CHILDREN OF THE ENGLISH-SPEAKING WORLD by Richard Lewis. Copyright © 1969, by Richard Lewis. Reprinted by permission of Simon and Schuster, Inc./ "The Garden Hose" by Beatrice Janosco: By permission of the author./ Cover from JENNIFER, HECATE, WILLIAM McKINLEY, AND ME, ELIZABETH by E. L. Konigsburg: Copyright © 1967 by E. L. Konigsburg. Used by permission of Atheneum Publishers./ Cover from . . .AND NOW MIGUEL, text by Joseph Krumgold; illustrations by Jean Charlot. Copyright 1953 by Joseph Krumgold. Thomas Y. Crowell Company, publishers./ Excerpts from THE MOST WONDERFUL ANIMALS THAT NEVER WERE by Joseph Wood Krutch: Copyright © 1969 by Houghton, Mifflin Company. By permission of the publisher./ "The tight string broke" by Kubonta: From CRICKET SONGS: JAPANESE HAIKU, translated and © 1964 by Harry Behn. Reprinted by permission of Harcourt Brace Jovanovich, Inc./ Excerpt from BEN AND ME by Robert Lawson: By permission of Little, Brown and Co. Copyright 1939 by Robert Lawson./ "Iceberg," "Mosquitoes," "They Just Go Round" from THE RAINBOW BOOK OF FOLK TALES AND LEGENDS by Maria Leach: Copyright © 1958 by Maria Leach. Reprinted by permission of The World Publishing Company./ "Why Chicken Lives with Man" from HOW THE PEOPLE SANG THE MOUNTAINS UP by Maria Leach: Copyright © 1967 by Maria Leach. All rights reserved. Reprinted by permission of The Viking Press, Inc./ "An Indian Summer Day on the Prairie" by Vachel Lindsay: From COLLECTED POEMS by Elizabeth G. Lindsay. By permission of The Macmillan Company./ "Crows" by David McCord: From FAR AND FEW by David McCord, by permission of Little, Brown and Co. Copyright 1952, by David McCord./ Excerpt from "OUGH" by David McCord: From ALL DAY LONG by David McCord, by permission of Little, Brown and Co. Copyright © 1965, 1966 by David McCord./ "book review" by Don Marquis: From THE LIVES AND TIMES OF ARCHY AND MEHITABEL by Don Marquis. Copyright 1933 by Doubleday & Company, Inc. Reprinted by permission of the publisher./ "April" by Marcia Masters: By permission of the author./ "A Commercial for Spring" by Eve Merriam: Copyright © 1964 by Eve Merriam. From IT DOESN'T ALWAYS HAVE TO RHYME. Used by permission of Atheneum Publishers./ "Catalogue" by Rosalie Moore: Reprinted by permission; Copyright © 1940, 1968 The New Yorker Magazine, Inc./ "When spring comes" by Michael Patrick: From MIRACLES: POEMS BY CHILDREN OF THE ENGLISH-SPEAKING WORLD by Richard Lewis. Copyright © 1966, by Richard Lewis. Reprinted by permission of Simon and Schuster, Inc./ Excerpt from BEOWULF THE WARRIOR retold by Ian Serraillier: Reprinted by permission of Henry Z. Walck, Inc., publishers./ "Seal" by William Jay Smith: Reprinted by permission of William Jay Smith. Copyright © 1957 by William Jay Smith./ "A little white mouse" by Mona Thomas: From MIRACLES: POEMS BY CHILDREN OF THE ENGLISH-SPEAKING WORLD by Richard Lewis. Copyright © 1966, by Richard Lewis. Reprinted by permission of Simon and Schuster, Inc./ Excerpt from THE ADVENTURES OF TOM SAWYER by Mark Twain (Harper & Row)./ Excerpt from PAUL BUNYAN AND HIS GREAT BLUE OX by Wallace Wadsworth. Copyright 1926 by George H. Doran Company. Reprinted by permission of Doubleday & Company, Inc./ Excerpt from ALL ABOUT MOUNTAINS AND MOUNTAINEERING by Anne Terry White: By permission of Random House, Inc. Copyright © 1962 by Anne Terry White./ Cover by Garth Williams from CHARLOTTE'S WEB by E. B. White: Copyright, 1952, by E. B. White. Reprinted by permission of Harper & Row, Publishers./ "Slave of the Moon" by Mary Yarmon: From MIRACLES: POEMS BY CHILDREN OF THE ENGLISH-SPEAKING WORLD by Richard Lewis. Copyright © 1966, by Richard Lewis. Reprinted by permission of Simon and Schuster, Inc.

408